Henry Whalley Nicholson

From Sword to Share

A Fortune in Five Years at Hawaii

Henry Whalley Nicholson

From Sword to Share
A Fortune in Five Years at Hawaii

ISBN/EAN: 9783337715960

Printed in Europe, USA, Canada, Australia, Japan

Cover: Foto ©Suzi / pixelio.de

More available books at **www.hansebooks.com**

FROM SWORD TO SHARE;

OR

A FORTUNE IN FIVE YEARS AT HAWAII.

BY

CAPT. H. WHALLEY NICHOLSON.

WITH MAP AND ILLUSTRATIONS.

SECOND EDITION.

LONDON :

W. H. ALLEN & CO., 13 WATERLOO PLACE, S.W.
PUBLISHERS TO THE INDIA OFFICE.

1889.

LONDON:

W. H. ALLEN AND CO., 13, WATERLOO PLACE, S.W.

To Lady Brassey.

My dear Lady Brassey,

Retransmission from the Hawaiian Islands of a reciprocal tithe of the substantial sentiments you were so good as to entrust to my presentation there, proves more than earnest desire avails, or ordinary libraries could contain; for, familiar as that country is to the sun's direct rays, the too brief sojourn of the "*Sunbeam*" on its waters will be ever held in tender memory by all in that sun-caressed kingdom.

Nor are such impressions confined to the Pacific; for whatever the threshold crossed—be it in Great Britain, "Greater Britain," or other realms— there, a treasured copy of *A Voyage in the Sunbeam* will be found shedding its welcome and instructive lustres.

Owing to your thoughtful kindness, the remi-

a *

niscences from which I have, at request, compiled *From Sword to Share*, are very pleasant also; and, notwithstanding any defects, may I venture to solicit permission to dedicate these experiences to you, in humble tribute of respect, esteem, and regard; and to add an expression of sincere wishes for long continued health and happiness to you and yours on seas and shores.

        Remaining

           Yours very truly,

94 *Piccadilly*,
   September 1881.

PREFACE.

"O ke poo o ke kanaka palaualelo ka hale paahanaia
no ka diabolo."*

These pages pertain but to the smallest constitutional kingdom on the globe, yet upon which
much political, commercial, and social interest
centres, and about which recent and reliable
information is sought.

It is a matter of history that prior to the advent
of Liholiho (Kamehameha II.) and his Queen
Consort Kamamalu in England—where they and
attendants landed at Portsmouth from the whaleship *L'Aigle*, May 22nd, 1824—nine-tenths of
the world were ignorant of its existence.

* "The head of a lazy man is the devil's workshop."

On the demise of Kamamalu, July 8th, followed by that of Liholiho on the 13th of the same month and year, in London, their remains were borne back to Hawaii in the English frigate *Blonde*, under the charge of General Boki ; and in the interim, till the visit of the Dowager Queen Emma, accompanied by the Hon. Mrs. Bishop, some fifteen years since (1866–67), the marine and mundane position of this country would seem to have possessed but few claims on general notice.

Numerous as have been the publications bearing upon the subject, none seem to reflect this Archipelago and its resources in other garb than that witnessed by the all too-susceptible tourist.

The object of this volume is to supply an expressed demand, and to independently present, amid everyday life, undisguised facts and figures ; and the Author begs to tender to official and other reliable sources of published information (nine thousand miles distant) very grateful acknowledgments.

The season for its publication would appear opportune, during the *tour du monde* now under accomplishment by H.M. King David Kalakaua, in view to the recuperation of the Hawaiian race, the improvement of its moral condition, and the development of the resources of his kingdom.

Entering so largely upon universal interest as the sugar industry does, and the strenuous efforts made by producers for the abolition of sugar bounties affecting England, France, Holland, and Belguim, it is a matter of importance that every source of supply should be fully known and expanded, together with other enterprises congenial with the Sandwich Islands.

Nothing is so powerless, so trying to the temper, nor so subversive of dignity and dangerous to principle as poverty ; and look where one will, in in these times of compulsory retirements and other matters that have of late

"O'er pale Britannia passed,"

one finds English *gentlemen*, by every sentiment and kindred tie, eager to earn their daily bread by labour, were it only procurable.

Hawaii apparently offers a fortuitous field, as there, in the most perfect climate in the world, can they handle the share and shovel, more profitably than they may have done the sword or style, and should the within experiences serve the rank and file of those still "waiting for something to turn up," much will have been effected, and if availing themselves of the opportunities afforded for time, energy, and small capital in the Sandwich Islands, the author tenders them an earnest

ALOHA!

CONTENTS.

CHAPTER VIII.

KINGS AND THEIR COUNSELLORS.

CHAPTER IX.

RECIPROCITY.

CHAPTER X.

CONSTITUTION.

CHAPTER XI.

INSTITUTIONS.

CHAPTER XII.

SOCIETY.

CHAPTER XIII.

EXCHEQUER.

CHAPTER XIV.

INVESTMENTS UNDER HAWAIIAN LAWS.

CHAPTER XV.

VERNERY.

CHAPTER XVI.

AMUSEMENTS.

CHAPTER XVII.

PULPIT AND PRESS.

CHAPTER XVIII.

NATIONAL FORCES.

CHAPTER XIX.

SOURCES OF REVENUE

CHAPTER XX.

COFFEE.

CHAPTER XXI.

RICE.

CHAPTER XXII.

CANE.

CHAPTER XXIII.

OAHU.

CHAPTER XXIV.

INTER-ISLAND TRANSIT.

CHAPTER XXV.

MAUI.

CHAPTER XXVI.

MOLOKAI, LANAI, KAHOOLAWE, AND HAWAII.

CHAPTER XXVII.

MADAME PELE AT HOME.

CHAPTER XXXI.

HOW IT 'S DONE!

CHAPTER XXXII.

PRACTICAL PLANTING.

CHAPTER XXXIII.

MAUNA LOA'S LATEST ISSUES.

CHAPTER XXXIV.

A WAY-UP TIME.

APPENDIX.

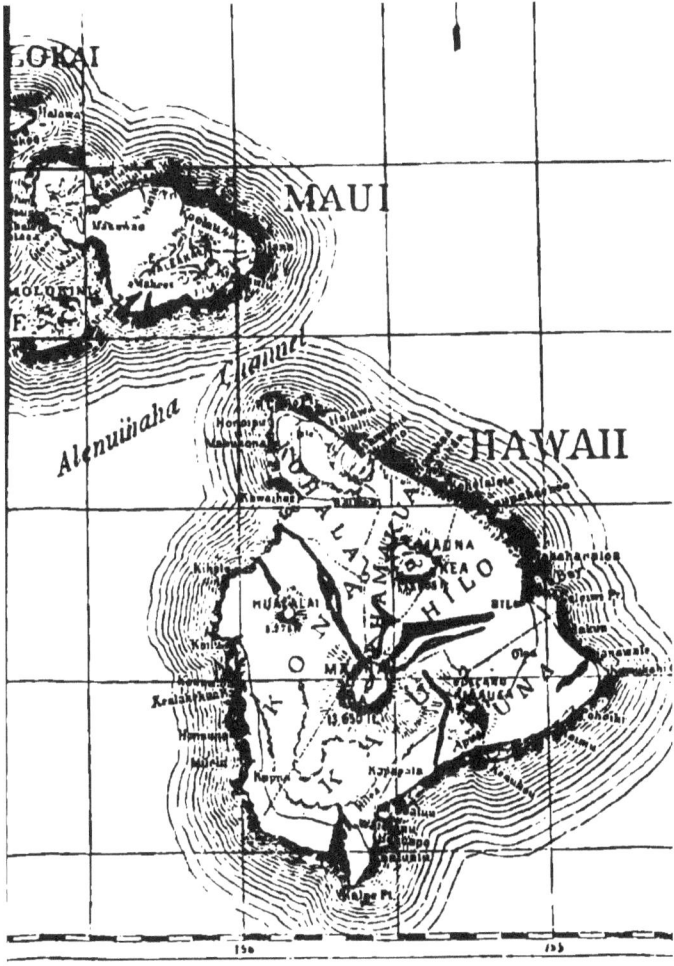

FROM
SWORD TO SHARE.

CHAPTER I.

WAYS AND MEANS.

" I've heard my Grandmother say that Heaven gives almonds
to those who have no teeth. That's nuts to crack.
I've teeth to spare, but where shall I find almonds?"

WITHIN the ordinary period allotted to the oldest
inhabitants of Mayfair generally, and to the vene-
rable Hall Porter of the Broad Arrow Club in
particular, some three or four ex-army men were
discussing brandies-and-soda with that never-to-be-
exhausted topic of "ways and means," in the
luxurious smoking-room of the aforesaid palatial
bachelor's home.

Though of different grades in rank, all were
within the same decade, as regards age, and had
erstwhile borne the colours of their regiments in

1

various climes; and served our Queen and country
with more or less personal distinction, as circumstances arose and opportunity offered, though with
but scant benefit to themselves; for one and all
had been affected by that very questionable policy
of abolition of purchase in 1871, commonly called
" the Cardwell scare."

One had essayed poultry-farming; some the
milk business—with rather less than more success.
Another had been attracted by the profits of the
wine trade, on the strength of his fictitious extensive connection and ability to " place " any
amount of strong " military ditto." While others
took to companies, in order to be taken in. A
dashing ex-A.D.C. had entered into partnership
with a gentleman in the City, whose experience
was accepted as an equivalent for the investment
of a commission commutation, until, as our friend
observed, " the man of experience got all the
commutation, and I found myself without means
or experience."

There was not a county in the kingdom that
had not been inundated with unsuccessful appli-
cations—supported by yards of printed testimony of
efficiency—for Chief of Constabulary, by each and

everyone present; and notwithstanding the diver-
gence of experience and opinions among these
veterans of the Beggarly Gentility Brigade, it was
unanimously agreed that a man must live, and
something must be done—though how—did not
transpire at this sitting.

While an ex-brother-in-arms was descanting
volubly on the various merits of ostrich-farming
in Africa, cattle-raising in the " loan ? " far west,
and colonial enterprises generally; together with
the " Claimant's " perspicuity on the due appor-
tionment of brains and money, a page-boy brought
in a bundle of letters.

In the casual glance accorded their superscrip-
tions I observed some unfamiliar stamps, franking
the well-known writing of an old chum, who had
served in the same regiment as myself in past
years, and with whom I had maintained a gossiping
correspondence from time to time.

" Old man gone at last ? " asked Vernon.

" Fourteenth application, I expect," drawled out
Colville of " Ours."

" *Un petit souper* with Clarice," suggested Max-
well, after a refresher from the beaker of soda-
and-b., to which he affectionately clung.

" No!—all wrong ; it's from old Con ; but what the postmark may be, goodness knows ! Somewhat longitudinally west of Greenwich, I take it."

This interruption caused an ultimate dissolution of the *colérie* towards its individual mode of killing time till dinner, and afforded an opportunity to peruse Con's missive, which ran thus :

*   *   *   *

My dear Pro,

      Are you inclined to make a fortune in five years, on a capital of five hundred, in a perfect climate ? If so, write home, where I am sending particulars by this mail.

Yours ever,

To Captain Pro,   N. Statu-Con.

      Broad Arrow Club,

          London.

" What in the name of wonder can be up now ? " was my ejaculation, for his last communications gave one to understand that my friend's fortune was, to all intents and purposes, permanently assured, in the full enjoyment of an easy, influential, though not over-lucrative, colonial appointment.

Conjecture would not help matters, further than towards the fundamental source of every masculine action,—woman ! ; and as these hopeful anticipations seemed to justify a further contribution towards the Imperial revenue, to the extent of a penny postage-stamp, a solicitation was at once fired off in the direction suggested, for more specific information anent this *in embryo* Bonanza. More especially as my friend's earnestness of purpose had passed the test of a quarter of a century's friendship.

In the course of a post or two the mystery was solved, in so far, that my friend's attention had been directed to the production of sugar in the Sandwich Islands as a fair and lucrative investment for time. energy, and money.

CHAPTER II.

WESTWARD HO !

" Ever drifting, drifting, drifting
  On the shifting currents of the main
Till in sheltered coves and reaches
    Of sandy beaches
  All have found repose again."

" SANDWICH ISLANDS ! where 's that ? " questioned
everyone, only to be saluted with its proverbial
re-echo ; for beyond a very expensive public school
education, and a subsequent course of transport
over many thousand miles, at her Majesty's expense as well as my own, I had not gone. However,
by dint of much hunting up of latitudes and longi-
tudes ; the perusal of works by sundry æsthetic
tourists ; and writing here, there, and everywhere

but to the right place ; one gathered a meagre report that it was a locality where the rowdy and hoodlem element had to succumb to hard work and sobriety.

Letters were perused with avidity from friends' friends residing on, or who had visited, the islands ; hinting that money was to be made and well-salaried appointments and situations were to be had for the asking,—enough, at all events, to clinch a pre-conceived resolve to go and see for oneself.

Having come to this conclusion, and got together what money was get-at-able, we crossed to New York, did the Falls, and pushed on to San Fran-cisco with as little delay as possible ; thence, after a further seven days' enjoyable trip, we sighted (at 100 miles distance) the group of islands forming the Hawaiian Archipelago, whose appearance, as seen towards sunset, gives one the impression of small, but dense and well-defined, rain-clouds.

In proceeding from Europe, any one of the numerous lines of steamers from Liverpool, London, Glasgow, Havre, and Bremen will convey one to New York, Boston, Halifax, Quebec, or Montreal, with speed and comfort ; distance from 3,000 to 3,500 miles from port to port.

Thence by either of the railway routes converging on Omaha, *via* Chicago—the Burlington and Quincy cars being preferable—and from there by the Central Pacific Railway to San Francisco. The rate of transit by express trains is about 500 miles in the twenty-four hours. The distance from New York to San Francisco is about 3,300 miles, and occupies six days. The rates of passage from New York to San Francisco are : first class, $138 ; second class, $105. There is also an emigrant class, at the rate of $65.

This class is attached to the fast trains, and conveyed therewith to and from Omaha, and points eastward ; but between Omaha and all points westward, emigrant cars are thence attached to the freight trains, which occupy a considerable time longer, and should not be adopted except under the emergency of impecuniosity—at all events, when bound from east to west.

Dining-cars are attached to all fast trains between the Eastern Coast and Omaha, where breakfast, dinner, and supper can be obtained in the greatest comfort, at 75 cents (3s.) a meal ; but from Omaha and westward the train stops for refection of passengers and railway employés at

certain intervals and stations, the average charge
being $1 (4s.) per meal.

One or more Pullman sleeping-cars are attached
to each fast train, and to which those bearing first-
class tickets only are admitted, at an extra charge
of $22 for the through route.

The second-class cars being almost identical
with the first-class accommodation, a little management will procure needful rest and sleep, provided
the perpetual call of the conductors to produce
" Tickets " will permit such intermittent oblivion.

The emigrant cars are comfortably fitted up, and
accommodate forty-eight persons in each car.
Special rates are made for Colonists or immigrants
going through in large parties together. Information respecting this may be obtained from any
of the Government Immigration Agents in the
United States of America, or in Canada, and it is
always well to provide oneself with a hamper or
basket of provisions, as thus the expenses in transit
are lessened, and the voyager made more independent.

250 lbs. of luggage is allowed for through first-
class passengers, and 100 lbs. for second and
emigrant classes ; and it should be impressed upon

all travellers to disencumber themselves of all parcels, for there are no porters available on change of carriages, &c. ; and further, to despatch all heavy baggage by freight trains, or, better still, by sailing vessel.   Each one pound of baggage in excess of the amounts above mentioned are respectively charged 35 cents (say 1s. 6d.) per lb. from New York to San Francisco.

The chief places of interest *en route* are Niagara Falls, the sublime grandeur of which is awe inspiring in its never-ceasing emotional action on mind and matter.

Chicago is worthy more than a cursory glance, especially the numerous porcine establishments, at which one sees the animals driven in at one end of a tubular arrangement to make a *début* at the other in the form of a sausage, ham, or side of bacon, according to the requirements of the market.

Omaha has little but commerce to interest the traveller ; and Cheyenne, some 500 miles westward, is notable only as a depôt for the branch lines southward.   Ogden, at the foot of the Rocky Mountains, claims interest from its proximity to Salt Lake City and Mormon proclivities ; and if it

be convenient to lay over a train or two at Reno
or Truckee, the adjacent mines will repay one for
the time allotted to such visit

As we neared San Francisco, anxiety was rife
anent hotel accommodation. The merits of "The
Palace," that monster hive of the Far West, were
variously commented upon. One travelled American
gentleman expatiated more freely than others on
its capacity, and informed us, among other things,
that the roof served as a race-track, half-a-mile
in circumference, its attractions of an afternoon
being analogous with those of "The Row."

"But how about the ascent of the carriages?"
queried a sceptical Britisher.

"Oh! they go up in the elevator," readily
replied our Yankee friend.

It was unanimously agreed to put this enterprise
of an English baronet's papa-in-law to the test.

Amongst numerous drawbacks towards comfort,
in the largest but one in the world, of hotels, the
watchmen at this establishment have a limited
notion of the chain of responsibility, or a strict
attention to duty.

The janitor on guard in my corridor omitted to
call me, as previously directed ; and on reporting

the circumstance to the manager, regret was
expressed, and remedial measures promised.

Having an appointment early the next day, I
again left instructions at the office, of the hour I
desired to be aroused. The watchman again failed
in his duty.

Being much exercised (upon waking) to find the
hour of my engagement passed, I summoned this
negro watchman to my room, and, in expos-
tulation, told him that this was the second occasion
his negligence had caused me serious incon-
venience.

"Yes, I know," replied he. "Rather rough on
you, ain't it?"

Emancipation has a philanthropic ring about
it, when pronounced, and an ingenious guise in
print; but if the above be a sample of its
practical results; acting equipose to the yoke, shed
by a black Adonis—nearly related to our friend
Uncle Sam—is just a trifle "too thin" for even a
Britisher.

Actual comfort in these colossal communities is
unknown; so, to all intending sojourners in San
Francisco, let the "Occidental" and "Baldwin"
be tried, as first-class hotels; and the "Russ

House " hotel, in that of the second degree ; and the " Imperial," in the third.

The Pacific Mail Company's steamers meet the mails from Europe once a month ; the dates of their departure from San Francisco may be ascertained from the principal London and Liverpool shipping agents. The inclusive passage rate to Honolulu from England is : first class, £75 ; second class, £60.

A cheaper route by sailing vessel round Cape Horn—time occupied being from 11G to 130 days —is and can be adopted.

Mr. Manley Hopkins is His Hawaiian Majesty's representative in London ; and Mr. R. C. Janion, of Messrs. Janion & Co., Liverpool, the Hawaiian Consul at that port, will afford all necessary information as to their sailings.

Vessels also leave Glasgow and Bremen for Honolulu, *via* Cape Horn direct, about once every three months ; freight charges for iron being about 30s. per ton, other goods 40s. to 50s. per ton.

NOTE ON SIGNALS.

Right arm of the Telegraph, seaward ; left arm inland.

NOTE.—To find the number of any Signal indicated; multiply the number—which number is shown in the key—of lower arm by seven, and add the upper arm—if there is any up.

Any vessel coming in sight of the outer station is announced by raising a blue flag which means "sail ho." The arms are raised as soon as the rig can be distinguished. A vessel showing her national colours at the main, indicating a mail on board, is announced by raising a large blue flag with the letter M in addition to the "sail ho" signal.

For a war steamer two small flags are raised.

MARINE SIGNALS—EXPLANATION.

1 Fore and aft schooner from Maui.

2 Fore and aft schooner coming past Coco Head.

3 Fore and aft schooner coming from leeward of Lanai.

4 Topsail schooner coming from Maui.

5 Topsail schooner coming past Coco Head.

6 Topsail schooner leeward of Lanai.

7 Brig coming from Maui.

8 Brig coming past Coco Head.

9 Brig from leeward of Lanai.

10 Bark coming from Maui.

11 Bark coming past Coco Head.

12 Barkentine from windward.

13 Ship coming from Maui.

14 Ship coming past Coco Head.

15 Ship from leeward of Lanai.

16 Whaleship coming from Maui.

17 Whaleship coming past Coco Head.

18 Whaleship coming from leeward of Lanai.

19 Vessel in distress.

20 Ship-of-war past Coco Head.

21 Steamer from southward.
22 Steamer from Maui.
23 Steamer coming past Coco Head.
24 Vessel from southward.
25 Schooner
26 Schooner Prince.
27 Schooner Mary Ellen.
28 Clipper ship.
29 Schooner Kinau.
30 Schooner Iolani.
31 Schooner from west.
32 Signal for Pilot.
33 Schooner Fairy Queen.
34 Schooner Waiola.
35 Schooner Luka.
36 Schooner Ka Moi.
37 Schooner Jenny.
38 Steamer Kilauea.
39 Schooner Pauahi.
40 Schooner Manuokawai.
41 Schooner Pueokahi.
42 Schooner Kulamanu.
43 Schooner Annie.
44 Schooner Kamaile.
45 Schooner
46 Schooner Marion.
47 Schooner Uilama.
48 Schooner Nettie Merrill.

CHAPTER III.

TROPICAL GLIMMERINGS.

" No more the thirsty entrance of this soil
    Shall daub her lips with her own children's blood."

RETROSPECTIVE digression has brought us under
the scintillations of Hesper, and though two bells
has just rung out, all thought of past lagging time
on board ship is banished by the exciting influences
around us ; for as the steamer skirted one island,
and traversed the narrow channels between others,
the shore seemed but a stone's-throw from the deck,
whereon all the passengers congregated.

The general idea was that of steaming up a
tropical Windermere when the ship's rocket was
fired, and by 11 P.M. we turned the point of
Diamond Head, near which, on Coco Point, the

MARINE SIGNALS FOR THE PORT OF HONOLULU.

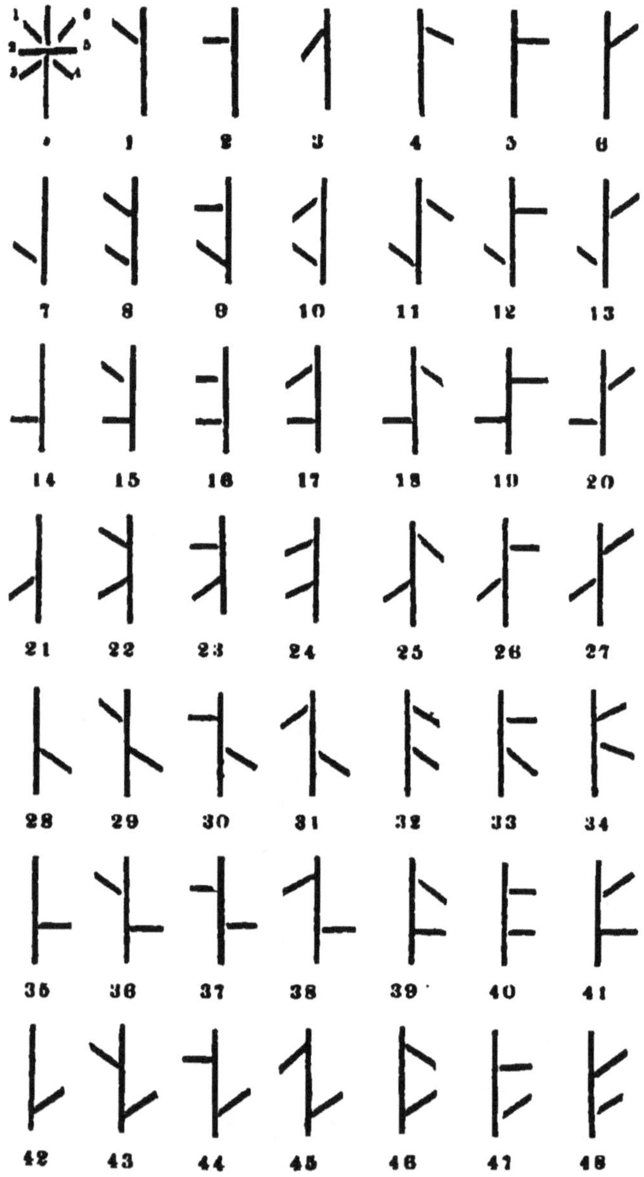

signal and telegraph station is situated, and whence the lights of Honolulu were almost in view.

As the port of Honolulu is difficult to make, in even fair weather, the following directions should be strictly observed.

Make the outer anchorage, or Bell Buoy, with staff or ball painted white—lat. 21° 16′ 56″, long. 157° 48′ 51″—moored in twelve fathoms of water. From this buoy, steer down and make the Spar buoy, or sail on till the lighthouse on the reef (white) and the light-house on the shore (green) are in a line.

Haul up about N. by E. and keep them in one till within about 150 feet of the lighthouse; then haul over and make towards the end of the long wooden wharf, at the end of the esplanade, till round the light-house; then steer up N.W., along the esplanade to the anchorage of from thirteen to eighteen fathoms of water.

The passage in, at night, ought never to be attempted except with a fair wind, or in tow, and a pilot on board; but on the occasions of the periodical visits by the mail steamers, lights are affixed to the innumerable buoys in, and surrounding the harbour and channel, and as we steamed slowly through them, memory of past pleasures in other climes was emotionally awakened by this extemporised nocturnal Venetian welcome.

But agitation, engendered by this pretty effect, was all too speedily disturbed as we drew nearer to the diminutive wooden light-house, from our olfactory senses being saluted with the most objectionable effluvia ever experienced westward of Barking Reach.

Whether the gas pipes had burst, or the aborigines were intent upon high farming, matters not, except that we had to endure it during a very tedious approach to, and settlement of the steamer alongside, the Lilliputian steamer wharf at 1 A.M.

This wharf was a scene in itself—swarming with humanity in every hue, type, race, and habiliment.

Those who appeared to be more or less in authority, and they were very numerous, were armed with flaming torches.

One of the first to pass the gangway was my old friend Con, and our greetings over, it was a source of mutual gratification, that time seemed to have dealt lightly with us since the stirring episodes of more youthful days.

Notwithstanding the before-mentioned exceptional odour, and the emphatic assurance of my friend that the sheets had been airing for the past three months, I elected to remain on board until daylight, when compensation was fully realised for such quiescence.

As the sun rose from the sea in all its Oriental splendour, the light fell fully upon the high and rugged mountains and their sparsely verdant covering, such intense relief from the constant view of cerulean and ultramarine blue.

But the most refreshing of all was the advance towards civilisation on the part of this quondam cannibal kingdom, evidenced in a Brobdingnagian hoarding, announcing, through three feet type, the diploma of a " Tonsorial Artist, and Court Chiropodist to His Majesty, &c. &c.," and having come so far it was comforting at least to learn that royalty, &c. &c., indulged in the curtailment of extremities to just and modest proportions.

●

CHAPTER IV.

HONOLULU.

" But first the landlord will I trace :
  Grave in his aspect and attire,
  A man of ancient pedigree,
  A justice of the peace was he,
    Known in all Sudbury as ' The Squire.' "

As we gaze from the deck once more, the scenery
is certainly most picturesque and attractive. The
high mountains in the background, and the town
(pardon !) city of Honolulu enveloped in tropical
foliage, presents an inviting appearance.

Leaving our baggage to the custody of a voluble
kanaka with his hand-cart, we resist the impor-
tunities of a brigade of buggy-owners, and walk to
the Hawaiian Hotel. The wharves and surrounding ground are lumbered with every sort of mer-

chandise ; timber and bags of sugar predominating ; the former lately imported from, and the latter awaiting shipment to, San Francisco. One is astonished to find so much shipping, principally of small tonnage, at, and in connection with, this port ; but signs of commercial civilisation are more numerous as we proceed up the unpaved principal street.

With the exception of the Custom House and some half-dozen public stores and buildings of coral stone, all the houses are of wooden structure, and the roads of crushed coral, black lava, and sand. These latter, especially where the traffic is greatest towards the wharf, are in an execrable condition.

The fact of having to pay $2 for the privilege of landing must not be omitted, and a nearer view of the commercial centre of the town is not entrancing.

The streets are narrow, dusty, and uncared for, and the whole impresses one mournfully from its cramped and general blowsy appearance.

As we pass the only bank (Bishop & Co.) on our way to the post-office, its prosperous aspect and cleanly concrete condition cheers one up a little. The Post-office, too, has some pretensions to architecture, substantiality, and organisation. But

" go slow ! " for here it would seem that the whole
population had been gathered together, and our
thoughts speed back to St. Martin's-le-Grand on
Lord Mayor's Show Day.

" What is all this crowd doing here ? " we ask
of our friendly cicerone.

" Waiting for the distribution of the mail," he
replies.

" Don't they deliver letters, then, in these
parts ? "

" No ; you have to fetch them yourself."

Well, in any other similar space it would be
difficult, if not a costly process, to collect the
representatives of so many races and nationalities.

Here were natives, Australians, Chinese, English,
French, Germans, Portuguese, Poles, Swedes,
Swiss, South Sea Islanders, Spaniards, Tahitians,
Venezuelans, Westphalians, Yankees, New and Old
Zealanders—half, three-quarter, and every other
caste—all vociferating, smoking, and expectorating
round the principal opening.

Here we found the Postmaster-General, in the
ubiquitous shirt-sleeves and cigar in mouth, calling
out names in alphabetical rotation, though the cigar
employment did not seem to be conducive towards

clearness of pronunciation of the various nomen-
clatures.

The more fortunate owners or renters of letter-
boxes were diving into their receptacles and rushing
off to their respective places of business.

After considerable delay the postmaster politely
sought our letters, when our route to the hotel was
thence resumed; and although the distance is
within a furlong, the safety of limb, if not of life,
was frequently endangered through the indiscriminate perambulations of the buggies, or "ex-
presses," as they are here styled.

In our query relative to the police regulations on
this subject, our friend directed attention to a
member of the local force, who, habited in white
trousers, blue yachting-coat with plaque on breast,
and a white German foraging-cap on his head, was
calmly seated on a three-legged stool at the junction
of four streets, and placidly contemplating the
scene while eating bananas.

As Paris is to France, so is the Royal Hawaiian
Hotel to Honolulu, and Honolulu to Hawaii; so
that the principal feature in this archipelagian
kingdom is its hotel, the only habitable hostelry.
Its proportions are good, and concrete stone con-

struction with spacious verandahs offer an inviting
appearance. The premises cover about an acre of
ground, which is well shaded with trees; but there
was an air of lethargy pervading it, rather ener-
vating than otherwise to those not having yet
broken their fast. A closer intimacy with it, its
kind host and charming hostess, gives one sincere
and pleasurable reminiscences of the comfort and
geniality there provided.

Honolulu has a truly tropical condition and
aspect. Being situated on the southern side of the
island of Oahu it is very hot in the day-time,
especially from June to September ; but the refreshing trade breezes, or those from the mountain
gorges, make the evenings and nights most enjoyable and re-invigorating.

A bath and breakfast, with a smoke in the
well-shaded verandah, brought us round to the
time when the presentation of letters would be
acceptable to those to whom we were accredited.

This effected, let us settle down to a practical
rather than poetical observation of the manners,
customs, and capabilities of this most climatically
favoured small country.

CHAPTER V.

LANDMARKS OF TIME.

" The warrior showed,
Sea-crafty man,
The landmarks."

THE true longitude of Honolulu is a matter of importance, on account of its bearing on the safety of navigation in an ocean so full of small islands and reefs.

It is laid down on the chart of Wilde's exploring expedition at 157° 52′ 30″. Professor C. S. Lyman, of New Haven; Fleurriais, a French astronomer, sent here about 1867; and Captain Daniel Smith, resident of Honolulu, all calculated the longitude and settled it at 157° 48′ 45″. Captain Tupman, R.M.A., of H.M.S. *Scout*, who commanded the Transit of Venus expedition to these Islands in 1874, gave his first determination very similarly. After his return to England and completion of the calculations (dependent on observations taken on the spot) he fixed the longitude at 157° 51' 48", *i.e.* of the Transit of Venus observatory, a difference of three miles from that previously assigned it—which may be accounted for by Captain Tupman's calculations being made on the basis of the *actual* place of the moon rather than its place as predicted by the Nautical Almanac.

This also accounts for the previous agreement between four erroneous determinations. The difference of time, therefore, between the steamer-wharf Honolulu, and Greenwich, is 10 hours, 31 minutes, 28 seconds, which has been universally adopted, and is in all probability perfectly correct.

Previous to the arrival of the ship *Resolution* (Commander Cook), and the discovery of these islands in 1778, little is known of its past history, and what has been gathered, through tradition, respecting ancient events, is conflicting and unsatisfactory; but the following tabulation in connection with Hawaiian history may be accepted as being as near to the truth as it is possible to get at it.

A.D. 1716. Keaulumoku (known in after years as Haku Mele, or Poet), born at Naohaku, Kohala, Hawaii.

A.D. 1740. Paleioholani, King of Oahu, on passage to Molokai, sees a ship.

A.D. 1752. Kalaniopuu, King of Western Hawaii.

A.D. 1753. Kamehameha I. born, at Kokoiki, Kohala, Hawaii.

A.D. 1773. Kaahumanu, born at Kauiki, East Maui, of Keeaumoku and Namahana, his wife, ex-Queen of Maui.

A.D. 1778. Discovery of Oahu and Kauai, by Captain Cook, in the *Resolution* and *Discovery*, while *en route* to the north-west coast, anchoring off Waimea, Kauai, January 18th.

On the return from the north-west coast, Maui was discovered, November 26th, and Hawaii on December 1st.

A.D. 1779. January 17th, Captain Cook anchored in Kealakekua Bay, Hawaii.

February 14th, Captain Cook was slain at Kaawaloa, Kealakekua Bay, Hawaii.

February 23rd, sailing of *Resolution* and *Discovery* under Captain Clarke.

Without inflicting on the reader an unnecessary chronological detail of wars and struggles between the chiefs and their followers, suffice it to remark that Cook's estimate of the population in 1779 was 400,000. This is considered too high an estimate, but from the evidence of numerous fish-ponds, enclosures, water-courses, taro patches, temples, &c. these islands must, in former times, have been very thickly peopled.

The islands forming the kingdom of Hawaii are thirteen in number, eight of which only are inhabited, viz. :

	Area in statute square miles.	Acres.	Height in feet.
Hawaii	4,210	2,500,000	13,805
Maui	760	400,000	10,032
Oahu	600	360,000	4,060
Kaui	590	350,000	4,800
Molokai	270	200,000	2,800
Lanai	150	100,000	2,000
Niihau	97	70,000	800
Kahoolawe	63	30,000	400
Total	6,740	4,010,000	

Population of the Hawaiian Islands, according to the latest Census—December 1878.

Hawaii.

Hilo	4,231	
Puna . .	1,043	
Kau . . .	2,210	
North Kona . .	1,967	
South Kona . .	1,761	
North Kohala .	3,299	
South Kohala .	718	
Hamakua . .	1,805	
	———	17,034

Maui.

Lahaina . .	2,448	
Wailuku . .	4,186	
Hana . . .	2,067	
Makawao . .	3,408	
	———	12,109

Oahu.

Honolulu . .	14,114	
Ewa and Waianae .	1,699	
Waialua . .	639	
Koolauloa . .	1,082	
Koolaupoko .	2,402	
	———	20,236

Kauai.

Waimea	.	.	. 1,197
Koloa .	.	.	. 1,008
Puna .	.	.	. 1,832
Koolau, Kilauea, and			
Hanalei	.	.	. 1,597

	5,634
Molokai	2,581
Lanai	214
Niihau	177
Kahoolawe . . .	unknown.
Total .	57,985

By Nationality.

Natives	.	.	.	. 44,088
Half-castes		.	.	. 3,420
Chinese	.	.	.	. 5,916
Americans .		.	.	. 1,276
Hawaiian, born of foreign				
parents .		.	.	. 947
Britons	.	.	.	. 883
Portuguese		.	.	. 436
Germans	.	.	.	. 272
French	.	.	.	. 81
Other foreigners .			.	. 666
	Total	.		57,985

Width of Channels from Point to Point.

	Miles.
Oahu and Molokai	23
Diamond Head to S.W. of Molokai .	30
Molokai and Lanai	7
Molokai and Maui	9
Maui and Lanai	9
Maui and Kahoolawe . . .	6
Hawaii and Maui	25
Kauai and Oahu	61
Niihau and Kanai	15

Steamer Distances from Port of Honolulu to Principal Landings.

Honolulu to—

	Miles.
Hilo, on Hawaii, direct . .	192
Kahului, on Maui, direct . .	90
Nawiliwili, on Kauai, direct .	98
Niihau, direct	144
Kaulapapa, on Molokai, direct .	50

Occupying from ten to fifty hours in transit.

Ocean Distances from Honolulu to—

	Miles.	Days in transit. Steam.	Sailing.
San Francisco . .	2,200	7	16
Portland . . .	2,460	—	16
Panama . . .	4,620	—	18
Tahiti . . .	2,380	—	25

	Miles.	Days in transit.	
		Steam.	Sailing.
Auckland . . .	3,810	14	40
Sydney . . .	4,484	17	45
Hong Kong . .	4,893	18	50
Yokohama . .	3,440	12	35

1

CHAPTER VI.

TRAFFYC IN YE OLDEN TYME.

" To rob the public two contractors come :
  One cheats in *corn*, the other cheats in *rum*—
  Which is the greater, if you can explain,
  A rogue in *spirit*, or a rogue in *grain* ? "

TRADING was inaugurated in 1786, by Captains
Portlock and Dixon, in the *King George* and *Queen
Charlotte*, and the first steamer in Hawaiian waters
was H.M.S. *Cormorant*, Sir G. W. Gordon commander, arriving from Callao 22nd May 1846—
that attracted considerable attention from natives
and members of the mission bands alike.

It will be in remembrance that Queen Emma,
widow of Kamehameha IV., visited Europe and the
United States of America 1866–67, resulting in the

inauguration of a monthly steam service between the Islands and California from January 27, 1866.

A propos of the commercial attributes of this nation, a story is told illustrative of the manners and customs of the olden times under Kamehameha I.

In the early days of foreign intercourse with these islands (about the end of the eighteenth century) it was the custom that all trading with vessels should first be personally performed by the king ; then the chiefs according to their rank, down to the vassals and serfs, in their turn.

At the time of Captain Barber's visit to Honolulu in the brig *Arthur*, with a cargo of furs, this custom prevailed.

The merits of the Captain's rum having been fully tested, and freely and favourably commented on by foreigners, Kamehameha visited him with a view to trade. Negotiations were quickly completed, and the purchase was to be delivered the following day.

However, before leaving the ship, the King asked for a couple of bottles of the rum, which were readily given him, under the presumption they would soon be consumed at an orgie on nightfall.

Early next day the King came on board, accompanied by his staff and retainers, to superintend the transfer of his purchase. As seated in his chair on deck, he noticed a difference in the colour of the liquor now under transhipment to that shown him previously.

He sent an attendant for one of the bottles procured the day before, and calling for two glasses, he filled one with the contents of the open cask, and the other from that of the bottle.

These he held and placed side by side, held them up to the light, smelled and tasted them with the air of a connoisseur; then, with a searching look at the Captain, said:

"Barber, here no all the same."

Barber, perceiving he had been detected in dilutation, endeavoured to explain to the King that it was some mistake, and that he would have a cask of the better kind brought up.

This was of no avail, for the King ordered all the rum to be returned to the casks, telling the chiefs that they might trade if they liked; he had obtained all he wanted. But no trade whatever was done with this vessel.

When the brig *Arthur* was subsequently lost on

3 *

the south-west point of Oahu, now called Barber's Point, Captain Barber found the natives stealing not only whatever drifted ashore, but appropriating for their own uses whatever they fancied from the stores, stock-in-trade, and portions of the vessel itself.

In this dilemma he sought counsel of John Young, who eventually accompanied him to the island of Hawaii, where the King then was, superintending the building of his fleet of canoes. After a tedious passage they arrived to find the King dispensing rum all round to the workmen, as was said to be his custom. In this distribution he included Young. Barber, hot and thirsty from his voyage and journey, asked the King for a drink also, when he was met with the well-merited rebuke from His Majesty, " Oh, Barber, you no like rum ; you like water."

The King, however, passed him the bottle, and on learning the object of their visit, with the particulars, quietly told Barber to go back.

Barber appealed to Young, saying, " Are we to get no help, and all this journey for nothing ? "

Young told him that there was nothing left for them to do but to obey. They returned to Kailua

and their boat, which they found ready provisioned
for the return voyage. On shoving off, a native,
bearing a small white bundle, sprang into the boat,
where he sat without speaking or sleeping during
the trip.

On arrival at Honolulu this man was the first to
leap ashore, when he was lost sight of.

The next afternoon Barber's things were all
brought in, and placed side by side at Pakaka, or
Robinson's wharf, even to pieces of rope, bolts,
nails, &c.   The silent voyager had been one of the
King's spittoon-bearers, sent with the royal command to deliver up all belonging to the wreck of
the *Arthur*.   Thus, in all his intercourse with
foreigners, Kamehameha ever showed himself to be
their friend.

In regard to the creation of this ocean-washed
kingdom, tradition associates all volcanic phenomena, in Hawaiian legendary lore, with the
goddess Pele; and the circumstance is singular that
to this celebrated mythological personage is also
attributed a great flood that occurred in ancient
times.

The legends of this flood vary, but are mainly
connected with Pele, and her actions and influences

in this part of the Pacific Ocean. The story goes
to this effect :—

Pele was the daughter of Kanehoalani by his
wife Kahinalii, Kamohoahi and Kahuilaokalani
being her two brothers.

Pele is said to have been born in a far distant
land on the horizon towards the south-west. There
she lived with her parents until her marriage with
Wahieloa, a daughter named Laka and son Mene-
hune being the result of the union; but after a
time Pele's husband, Wahieloa, was enticed from
her by Pelekumulani.

The deserted Pele, being of a marital tempera-
ment, started on her travels in search of her
husband, and came in the direction of the Hawaiian
Islands.

At the time of these reported wanderings these
islands were a vast waste, there being neither sea
nor fresh water.

When Pele departed on her journey, her parents
gave her the sea to go with her and bear her
canoes onward.

So she sailed forward, flood-borne by the sea,
until she reached the land of Pakuela—and thence
onward to the land of Kanaloa. From her eyes

salt tears streamed forth as she went, and her
brothers composed the celebrated ancient mele :—

> " Oh, the sea, the great sea !
> Forth bursts the sea,
> Behold it bursts on Kanaloa," &c.

But the sea continued to rise until only the highest
peaks of the great mountains Haleakala (on Maui),
Maunakea and Maunaloa (on Hawaii), were visible,
all else being covered.

In course of time the sea receded, until reaching
its present level.

This event is called Kai-a-Kahinalii (sea of
Kahinalii), because it was from Kahinalii, her
mother, that Pele received the gift of the sea, thus
brought to Hawaii.

From that time, Pele forsook her native land
Hapakuela, and has dwelt in this country of her
adoption, Hawaii Nei, ever since ; her family subsequently following her example.

On Pele's first arrival at Hawaii Nei, she dwelt
on the island of Kauai. Thence she went to
Kalaupapa * (Molokai), and lived in the crater of
Kauha-Ko, at that place.

* Now the Leper Establishment.

Subsequently she departed for Puulaina, * near
Lahainaluna (on the Island of Maui), and excavated
that crater.   This accomplished, she moved to
Haleakala, also on Maui, where she remained until
she had hollowed out that immense aperture ;   and
finally, she settled at Kilauea (Hawaii), where she
has ever since remained.   The progress of Madame
Pele, as stated in the tradition, coincides with the
later geological observation, in positioning the
earliest volcanic action, in this group, on the
island of Kauai, and the latest on that of Hawaii,
where it is still in incessant activity—and with
which allusion will be met in the course of our
inspection of the kingdom.

     * The hill visible from Lahaina on Maui.

CHAPTER VII.

CLIMATIC.

" It is so like the gentle air of spring,
  As, from the morning's dewy flowers, it comes
  Full of their fragrance, that it is a joy
  To have it round us——"

THE climate is simply and uniquely perfect, as experienced in no other locality of commerce or pleasure.

The peculiarity consists in the extreme uniformity in averaged temperature, together with the very moderate warmth. Full tropical heat is almost unknown in these islands—a cool place, if there be shade and a slight breeze, can almost always be found. European cloth clothing can be worn the year through, and pith helmets are a luxury rather

than a necessity; puggarees are unseen even on
straw hats, and it appears to be the only cane-
growing country within the tropics, where the
white man, of any nationality, can easily labour all
day long, even in the hottest season (usually from
June to September), under the rays of the sun.

The attributed cause of this agreeable moderation
and uniformity of the Hawaiian climate is the
expanse of water surrounding this Archipelago,
which is always of an uniform temperature, and
over which the hot air currents from the continents
must pass for several days ere reaching Hawaii;
and the sea determining the temperature of the
air, Hawaii is thus fenced from Arctic blasts and
torrid siroccos alike, and rendered salubrious,
balmy, and dry—so different to the Indies (East
and West), Fiji, and Polynesia generally.

It is, moreover, exempted from cyclones,
encountered at Fiji, Samoa, and other islands
between it and Australia and New Zealand, and
the ocean hereabouts is not only nominally, but
practically, Pacific, and the air and water seldom
far from 70° Fahr.

The revelation of the real cause seems to be due
to Dr. Carpenter, in his discoveries of the deep-sea

explorations of the *Challenger*, to which we would refer the reader, as being full of interest ; but the effect of such a climate upon the well-being of mankind, and the recuperation of those with a tendency to phthysis, calls for full consideration and estimation on the part of doctors and patients. But the Meteorological Table for Honolulu, for the years 1873–1877 inclusive, with rainfall up to and for December 1880, given in the next page, will furnish support to such views as have herein been advanced.

Average Monthly Meteorological Table.

Honolulu 1873 to 1877 inclusive, with Rainfall to 1881.

—	1873.			1874.			1875.			1876.			1877.			1878.	1879.	1880.
	Bar.	Ther.	Rain.	Bar.	Ther.	Rain.	Bar.	Ther.	Rain.	Bar.	Ther.	Rain.	Bar.	Ther.	Rain.	Rain.	Rain.	Rain.
January .	30·08	74½	1·98	29·93	73	9·02	29·96	72	4·45	30·00	75	3·73	30·02	71½	3·24	0·26	13·09	4·01
February .	30·07	73½	5·15	29·88	73	9·75	29·91	73	2·92	30·09	76	4·73	30·08	72¼	2·90	1·01	3·15	7·05
March .	30·09	74½	8·89	29·97	75	4·40	30·02	75	3·86	29·86	75½	6·43	30·05	72¾	0·94	0·29	0·49	4·72
April .	30·08	76	1·25	30·02	74	3·24	30·02	74	4·22	30·11	75	3·58	30½	73¾	3·41	3·08	4·13	3·82
May . .	30·05	79½	0·27	30·04	77	1·75	30·04	78	4·16	30·20	77	5·87	30·09	74¼	7·27	0·96	3·59	0·75
June . .	30·05	80	1·27	29·96	78	1·60	29·97	78½	2·44	30·13	78	1·07	30·13	76¼	1·14	3·00	1·80	2·03
July . .	30·05	80½	0·58	29·95	80	1·25	29·96	80	0·95	30·17	79	1·42	30·13	76½	2·27	2·13	2·89	7·39
August .	30·06	81	0·07	29·95	80½	0·30	29·95	81	1·09	30·08	76½	2·58	30·11	76¼	1·19	4·76	3·17	1·97
September	30·00	81	0·05	30·01	79	1·02	29·94	79	3·11	30·03	78½	0·51	30·10	76	2·64	1·71	1·46	2·55
October .	30·03	78	0·33	30·00	77	2·50	29·97	77	0·95	30·05	78	0·37	30·09	76¼	1·63	2·62	2·46	1·98
November .	30·04	76	6·05	29·91	67	5·84	29·95	79	4·45	30·01	77	3·35	30·11	76¾	2·24	1·80	4·98	8·62
December .	30·01	75	11·96	30·00	62	5·75	30·00	74	4·46	30·06	75½	2·92	30·08	74	3·43	2·35	10·71	9·82

CHAPTER VIII.

KINGS AND THEIR COUNSELLORS.

"Le Roi est mort, Vive le Roi!"

UNTIL its consolidation kings in the Sandwich Islands were as numerous as craters until, in 1782, Kamèhameha the Conqueror brought his *confrères* under subjection, and volcanic irascibility centred itself within the confines of Kilauea on Hawaii.

The following table shows the Hawaiian dynasty from such consolidation to the present time.

THE KINGS OF HAWAII—THEIR BIRTH, ACCESSION, LENGTH OF REIGN AND AGE.

Name.	Born.	Began to Reign.	Died.	Age.	Length of Reign.
Kamehameha I. .	1753	1782	May 3, 1819	66 years.	37 yrs.
Kamehameha II.	1797	May 8, 1819	July 13, 1824	27 „	5 „ 3 mos.
Kamehameha III.	Mar. 17, 1814	March, 1833	Dec. 15, 1854	40 „ 9 mos.	21 „ 9 „
Kamehameha IV.	Feb. 9, 1834	Dec. 15, 1854	Nov. 30, 1863	29 „ 9 mos.	8 „ 11½ „
Kamehameha V.	Dec. 11, 1830	Nov. 30, 1863	Dec. 11, 1872	43 „	9 „ 11 days.
Lunalilo	Jan. 31, 1835	Jan. 9, 1873	Feb. 3, 1874	39 „	1 „ 25 „
KALAKAUA . . .	Nov. 16, 1836	Feb. 13, 1874	Now Reigning		

The name of Kamehameha conveys all that is patrician, but among these insular celebrities that of John Young is constantly occurring.

This *protégé* of Kamehameha I. arrived in Honolulu A.D. 1789, in the first American ship (*Eleanor*, Captain Metcalf) visiting these islands, and to which ship he was boatswain.

John Young was detained from rejoining his ship, March 17th, 1790, by Kamehameha I., after the Metcalf massacre off Oloalu, Maui, and he and Isaac Davis (the sole survivor of that massacre) became attached to Kamehameha.

An anecdote is related of John Young, showing how he accidentally obtained power and influence over the natives.

The close friendship which the king maintained for him naturally created much jealousy and ill-feeling on the side of the king's party, principally the priesthood, who on several occasions threatened his life.

At one time Kamehameha told him that a certain kahuna (medicine man) was going to kill him, and to accomplish this purpose had already started for the woods to build his prayer-hut to pray him to death. On hearing this John Young said that he

would go too, and, ascertaining the whereabouts of
this kahuna, built himself a small round thee-leaf
hut, just as his enemy had done, and ran his
prayer store right opposite, giving out that he was
going to pray the kahuna to death.

This fact so worked upon the superstitious fears
of the kahuna, that a short time sufficed to effect the
issue desired to be accomplished upon Young, and
so terminated the chief's interest in mundane affairs.

From superstitions so powerful and prevalent in
those days, it may be presumed that this turning
the table on his enemy had a great effect, and that
no one tried their power of prayer upon him
thereafter.

On the death of Lunalilo, February 3rd, 1874,
without issue, or his nomination of a successor,
Queen Emma, great grand-daughter of John Young
and relict of Kamehameha IV., was a rival candidate with David Kalakaua (Day of Battle) an
Hawaiian chief, son of Kapaakea and Keahokalole,
for the throne, and whose claims may be said to
have been almost identical.

The members of the Legislative Assembly being
summoned to an extraordinary session, the question
whether the representatives of 1872 or those of

1874 were qualified to elect a sovereign arose. This was settled amicably, if not legally, by the oaths being administered to each member. The explanation of the new representatives attending the session instead of the old, whose term of office was as yet unexpired, may be given in the clever and energetic arrangements of the cabinet, with Kalakauan proclivities, who despatched the summons and the little steamers (the only inter-island conveyances), of which the members of the ministry were owners and managers, to fetch them. Thus the adherents of Kalakaua were brought to the capital, and the election of Kalakaua was secured by a vote of thirty-nine as against six for Queen Emma at the scrutiny of the ballot.

Queen Emma being the popular candidate, the announcement of this result was received with anything but public favour.

The mob, inflamed by the utterances of heated orators, wrecked the carriage in which the committee were about to wait upon the newly-elected king, and severely maltreated the occupants with the debris—in fact, one of the committee probably owes his life to the prompt interference of the British Commissioner, Major Wodehouse.

Then ensued a scene of siege and rapine upon the Court House,* and representatives therein sheltered, never to be obliterated. The mob, maddened by individual and general tumult, besieged the Court House with impromptu rams, and gained entrance to, and command of, the building, where they destroyed public and private property with impartial discrimination, and mutilated representatives and documents alike. Some foreigners endeavoured to protect the former, when the marines from H.M.S. *Tenedos*, and the United States war-ships *Tuscarora* and *Portsmouth* arrived, and whose appearance, accompanied by a Gatling gun, had a desirable and pacific effect. The mob being dispersed; all the public buildings were guarded, and the town virtually and practically under the protection of Great Britain and the United States of America, by whom order was restored.

The next day King Kalakaua was privately installed, and took the oaths, in the Hawaiian and English languages, binding himself to support the Constitution.

---

* Now the offices of Messrs. Hackfield & Co.

The subsequent proclamation of this succession seemed to cause as much satisfaction then as resentment previously.

The Hawaiian race is most amiable and even courtly in manner, and easily pleased. The women are comely rather than good-looking, with well-formed hands and feet. Their dress is the " Holuku," a kind of shapeless morning wrapper, with a yoke. These are of every hue and pattern (chiefly gaudy), and the popular head-gear consists of straw hats or bonnets *à la mode* in Paris, London, or New York some three years previous to their arrival in Honolulu.

Both sexes are indolent, sensual, and lascivious, the women being entirely innocent of any attention to domestic duties or appliances, while the men, if working at all, perform their vocations in a most dilatory and slipshod manner.

Their element is the saddle and the sea, wherein all shine. The women ride straddle, and one and all appear part and parcel of the steeds so bestrode, which is the general mode of locomotion, and they will do anything and go anywhere to obtain the prohibited means of intoxication.

Though simple and child-like in their attributes,

assimilation to the customs of more known civilised countries seems easy—if the portentous length of the police reports latterly published serve for guidance.

Their chief diet is poi, also raw fish, sea-weed, beef, and roast pig, of which they eat enormous quantities, and when gorged to repletion, they have recourse to "Lomi lomi," a system of rubbing— or of being rubbed—adopted by the attendants at our Turkish bath establishments, which furthers digestion, and re-animates the partially or wholly exhausted sybarite towards further gastronomic feats.

Water and the juice from the cocoa-nut form their chief beverages; and a distillation from the thee-plant, with other fermented drinks whensoever procurable, is eagerly imbibed.

The, as yet, most politic event of King Kala-kaua's reign is the existing Reciprocity Treaty with the United States of America, giving advantageous terms to these islands, especially in its sugar in-dustry, and its importance warrants the devotion of the next chapter to a verbatim recapitulation.

CHAPTER IX.

RECIPROCITY.

" Thou, too, sail on, O Ship of State,
    Sail on, O UNION, strong and great."

Text of the Treaty of Reciprocity between the United States of America and the Hawaiian Islands.

WHEREAS, by the advice and approval of the Legislature of our Kingdom, we did enter into a convention with the United States of America on the subject of Commercial Reciprocity, which said Convention was concluded and signed by our Plenipotentiaries and the Plenipotentiary of the United States of America, at the city of Washington, on the 30th day of January 1875, and as amended by the Contracting Parties, is word for word as follows :

The United States of America and His Majesty the King of the Hawaiian Islands, equally animated by the desire to strengthen and perpetuate the friendly relations which have heretofore uniformly existed between them, and to consolidate their commercial intercourse, have resolved to enter into a Convention for Commercial Reciprocity. For this purpose the President of the United States has conferred full powers on Hamilton Fish, Secretary of State, and His Majesty the King of the Hawaiian Islands has conferred like powers on Honourable Elisha H. Allen, Chief Justice of the Supreme Court, Chancellor of the Kingdom, Member of the Privy Council of State, His Majesty's Envoy Extraordinary and Minister Plenipotentiary to the United States of America, and Honourable Henry A. P. Carter, Member of the Privy Council of State, His Majesty's Special Commissioner to the United States of America. And the said Plenipotentiaries, after having exchanged their full powers, which were found to be in due form, have agreed to the following articles.

ARTICLE I.

For and in consideration of the rights and
privileges granted by His Majesty the King of the
Hawaiian Islands in the next succeeding article
of this Convention, and as an equivalent therefor,
the United States of America hereby agree to
admit all the articles named in the following
Schedule, the same being the growth and manufacture or produce of the Hawaiian Islands, into
all the ports of the United States, free of duty.

Schedule.

Arrowroot, bananas, castor-oil, nuts, hides and
skins undressed.

Pulu.

Rice.

Seeds, plants, shrubs, or trees.

Muscovado, brown, and all other unrefined sugar,
meaning hereby the grades of sugar heretofore
commonly imported from the Hawaiian Islands,
and now known in the markets of San Francisco
and Portland as "Sandwich Island sugar," syrups
of sugar-cane, melado, and molasses.

Tallow.

Vegetables, dried and undried, preserved and unpreserved.

ARTICLE II.

For and in consideration of the rights and privileges granted by the United States of America in the preceding Article of this Convention, and as an equivalent therefor, His Majesty the King of the Hawaiian Islands hereby agrees to admit all the articles named in the following Schedule, the same being the growth, manufacture, or produce of the United States of America, into all the ports of the Hawaiian Islands, free of duty.

Schedule.

Agricultural implements, animals, beef, bacon, pork, ham, and all fresh, smoked, or preserved meats ; boots and shoes ; bricks, lime, and cement ; butter, cheese, lard, tallow ; bullion ; coal ; cordage ; naval stores, including tar, pitch, resin, turpentine, raw and rectified.

Copper and composition sheathing, nails and bolts ; cotton and manufactures of cotton, bleached and unbleached, and whether or not coloured, stained, painted, or printed.

Doors, sashes, and blinds.

Eggs.

Fish and oysters, and all other creatures living in the water, and the products thereof; fruits and nuts, and vegetables, green, dried, or undried, preserved or unpreserved ; grain, flour, meal, and bran, bread and bread-stuffs of all kinds.

Hardware; harness, and all other manufactures of leather.

Hides, furs, skins, and pelts dressed or undressed.

Hoop-iron and rivets, nails, spikes, and bolts, tacks, brads, or sprigs.

Ice ; iron and steel, and manufactures thereof; leather ; lumber and timber of all kinds, round and hewed, sawed and unmanufactured, in whole or in part.

Machinery of all kinds, engines and parts thereof; oats and hay.

Paper, stationery, and books, and all manufactures of paper or of paper and wood.

Petroleum and all oils for lubricating or illuminating purposes.

Plants, shrubs, trees, and seeds.

Rice.

Sugar, refined or unrefined; salt, soap, starch; shooks, staves, and headings.

Tobacco, whether in leaf or manufactured.

Textile manufactures, made of a combination of wool, cotton, silk, or linen, or of any two or more of them other than when ready-made clothing.

Wool, and manufactures of wool, other than ready-made clothing.

Wagons and carts for the purposes of agriculture or drayage.

Wood, and manufactures of wood, or of wood and metal, except furniture, either upholstered or carved, and carriages.

ARTICLE III.

The evidence that articles proposed to be admitted into the ports of the United States of America, or the ports of the Hawaiian Islands, free of duty, under the first and second articles of this Convention, are the growth, manufacture, or produce of the United States of America or of the Hawaiian Islands respectively, shall be established under such rule and regulations and conditions for the protection of the revenue, as the two Governments may, from time to time, respectively prescribe.

ARTICLE IV.

No export duty or charges shall be imposed in the Hawaiian Islands, or in the United States, upon any of the articles proposed to be admitted into the ports of the United States, or the ports of the Hawaiian Islands, free of duty under the first and second articles of this Convention. It is agreed on the part of His Hawaiian Majesty that, so long as this treaty shall remain in force, he will not lease or otherwise dispose of, or create any lien upon any port, harbour, or other territory in his dominions, or grant any special privilege or rights of use therein to any Power, State, or Government, nor make any treaty by which any other nation shall obtain the same privileges, relative to the admission of any article free of duty, hereby secured to the United States.

ARTICLE V.

The present Convention shall take effect as soon as it shall have been approved and proclaimed by His Majesty the King of the Hawaiian Islands, and shall have been ratified and duly proclaimed on the part of the Government of the United States, but not until a law to carry it into operation shall have been passed by the Congress of the United States of America. Such assent having been given, and the ratifications of the Convention having been exchanged, as provided in Article IV., the Convention shall remain in force for seven years from the date at which it may come into operation ; and further, until the expiration of twelve months after either of the contracting parties shall give notice to the other of its wish to terminate the same ; each of the high contracting parties being at liberty to give such notice to the other at the end of the said term of seven years, or at any time thereafter.

ARTICLE VI.

The present Convention shall he duly ratified, and the ratifications exchanged at Washington City, within eighteen months from the date hereof, or earlier if possible.

In faith of which the respective Plenipotentiaries of the high contracting parties have signed this present Convention, and have affixed thereto their respective seals.

Done in duplicate, at Washington, the thirtieth day of January, in the year of our Lord one thousand eight hundred and seventy-five.

[Seal.]   HAMILTON FISH.
[Seal.]   ELISHA H. ALLEN.
[Seal.]   HENRY A. P. CARTER.

And whereas the said Convention, as amended, was ratified by ourselves on the 17th April 1875, and by His Excellency the President of the United States of America, on the 31st May 1875, and the said ratifications were exchanged at the City of Washington, June 3rd, 1875:

Now, therefore, we do proclaim and make public the same, to the end that it, and every clause and article thereof, may be observed and fulfilled with good faith by every person within our kingdom. And the said Convention shall go into effect as soon as intelligence is received that the Government of the United States has made the necessary provisions for carrying it into operation.

In witness whereof, we have hereunto set our

hand, and caused the seal of our kingdom to be affixed, this 17th day of June, A.D. 1876.

KALAKAUA R.

By the King,
    W. L. Green, Minister of Foreign Affairs.

N.B.—Import duties are levied on goods not included in the above schedules, to the extent of twenty-five per cent, *ad valorem*; and luxuries, especially fermented drinks, are very heavily tariffed.

CHAPTER X.

CONSTITUTION.

" Lead the most noble to the vacant chair ;
'T will brace the Constitution if he 's there."

At the period of our arrival at Honolulu, H.B.M.'s Commissioner was absent on a tour of inspection amongst the islands, in view to personal inquiry into the condition of the various types of labourers on the sugar-cane plantations, and to make a report to his Government thereon.

The labour question, like others, has been a vexed one for Hawaii for the past fifteen years, and remains so ; and until the planters and others interested will co-operate to obtain constant, cheap, and organised supplies, with a large proportion of the female sex, towards the recuperation of the

country and its decreasing native population, so it
will remain.

The advisers of His Majesty King Kalakaua
seem quite incapable, or unwilling, to deal
with the subject in a consistent and statesman-
like way; and to the suggestion of trying East
Indian coolie immigration, which is considered to
be an effective mode of meeting the difficulty, they
are apparently and practically averse, notwithstanding the countenance of the King, that a trial
should be made, and the expressed willingness of
H.B.M.'s Commissioner to favourably represent
the subject, as he previously did in 1878, to his
Government in England, and where facilities
towards a convention were then accorded the
Hawaiian Commissioner.

That the stipulations required by the British
Government would necessitate deviation from the
Hawaiian Constitution—difficulties that are more
conjectural than actually apparent—and the impecuniosity of the Board of Immigration, are the
arguments urged in its disfavour—at least, as
advanced by the Hawaiian Cabinets.

The real motive in opposition seems to be
the fear of an extension of British influence,

as against that of the American element, at present preponderating, where a latent hope for the ultimate annexation of these islands to the United States seemingly exists.

This alternative would benefit neither the great nor the little country, and gratify no one except a few egotistical place-hungerers.

What the kingdom really requires is a Government with a policy, and an Opposition to keep it in check; greater attention evinced on the part of the British Government in its geographical position and capabilities; and support from Downing Street of the increasing interests of British subjects resident in this Archipelago, with accorded facilities towards East Indian coolie immigration.

In this the natives of Hawaii and our great Indian Peninsula would alike be benefited, in the relief of one over-populated country, to the ultimate re-population of that with more limited soil—that is so essentially rich, in all but its cultivation, from residential and enfranchised sources.

The City of Honolulu has a population of 14,115 souls, as ascertained by the Census of December 1878, comprising the British, American, and other foreign settlers.

Population of Honolulu.

Natives	...	...	9,272
Half castes	...	...	1,311
Chinese	...	...	1,300
Americans	...	...	597
British	...	...	478
Germans	..	...	139
French	...	...	39
Portuguese	...	...	256
Other Foreigners	...	...	723
	Total	...	14,115

Since that date the population has greatly increased, more especially as regards the Chinese portion, of which the actual approximate number in Honolulu, and under quarantine regulations awaiting transport to the various plantations, may be estimated at 4,000, the proportion of sexes in that class being 200 males to one female. *Verb sap!*

The Capital, as well as the kingdom generally, is under the direct watch, ward, and control of the King and his advisers, a list of whom, together with a register and directory of the court, cabinet, judiciary, and principal Government officers, will be found in the Appendix.

5

The existing form of government is a Constitutional Monarchy with Liberal proclivities.

His Majesty King Kalakaua is keenly sensible of the requirements and interests of his people and kingdom, and is, moreover, an educated gentleman, fully alive to the advantages of travel and personal experience through observation, and is at present (1881) absent from Hawaii on a tour round the world *viâ* Japan, China, India, and Europe, purposing to visit England about the month of July.

The Legislature is composed of twenty nobles, appointed for life by the King, and twenty-eight representatives elected biennally by the people.

The ordinary session is of about eighty days duration, once in two years, when these nobles and representatives assemble, and, sitting together, form one legislative body, on whose acts the King has a veto.

The Aliiolani Hale, or Government Buildings, is situated on King Street, nearly opposite the New Palace. It was erected in 1872–73, and contains the Hall of the Legislative Assembly, and is the head-quarters of all the Government officials, including the cabinet ministers, judges, governors;

and the Bureaux of Public Instruction, Marshal of
Police, the Registrars and Public Record Office,
Public Library and Museum are thereto gathered ;
and for which it is admirably adapted in structure
and accommodation in accordance with the present
requirements of the population and resources of the
country.

The Hall of Assembly is used, out of session, as
the Court of Equity and Common Pleas.

Nearly facing this handsome stone-built edifice
are the Palace grounds, wherein the new Palace,
nearly completed, is under construction. In the
meanwhile His Majesty resides within the walled
enclosure, in a small but comfortable wooden bunga-
low. Each entrance to the grounds is guarded by
a sentry, who, for want of an opportunity to " show
how fields were won," shoulders his rifle in a fairly
soldier-like way.

His Majesty is readily accessible to those who
may be presented through the proper channels, or
who are accredited.

His chief hours are passed in the reception of
various officials, and study—principally directed to
military tactics and political history !

He derives recreation from aquatics, the instruction of his small army (some sixty souls) in military evolutions, and an occasional flutter on the race-course at Kapiolani Park, so named after his consort. Queen Kapiolani is rarely seen except on paper in the photographers' windows. During His Majesty's absence his elder sister, H.R.H. the Princess Lydia Kamakaeha (Mrs. Dominis), heiress apparent, acts as Regent. H.R.H. Princess Miriam Likelike (Mrs. Cleghorn) resides at Waikiki, about four miles out of Honolulu towards Diamond Head, who, with her husband, is the most hospitable and genial of hosts.

Their little daughter, the Princess Victoria, is heiress presumptive to the throne. She delights in styling herself a little English girl, and with some justifiable pretensions from her parentage, sympathies, and drawning accomplishments under the guidance of an English lady, as Resident Governess.

Her Majesty Queen Dowager Emma, relict of Kamehameha IV., resides in a commodious residence at the corner of Hotel and Nuuanu Streets. She is a gracious and accomplished lady, and with the Princess Ruth and Mrs. Bishop (wife of the Banker) the last of the Kamehameha line, and is in receipt of a permanent grant from the Treasury of £5,200 per annum.

The Princess Ruth, sister of their late Majesties Kamehameha IV. and V., is the richest, as is she the most charitable, lady of this kingdom. Her new palace on Emma Street rivals, if it does not surpass, that under construction for the King.

CHAPTER XI.

INSTITUTIONS.

" Well fare you gentlemen ! Give me your hand."

THE chief public institutions are the Insane Asylum at Kapalaina, two miles north of Honolulu, where provision is made for temporary and permanent cases of insanity.

It derives its principal support from Government aid : the management is fair, and receives Hawaiians and foreigners.

The gaol is situated at Leleo, north, and not far from, the Post Office in Merchant Street.   Most of the criminals from the other islands are sent here ; and its inmates are those chiefly under sentence of hard labour, and are employed on the roads and in other Government convict work.

It appears to answer generally the purposes of such institutions, so far as a tropical temperature permits.

On the same road, about one mile from the Post Office, is the Reformatory School for juvenile delinquents, who receive, under the supervision of the Board of Education, instruction in the elementary branches and manual labour.

The schools are a great feature of this country, mainly supported by Government.

Every district is provided with schools, presided over principally by natives, where all, who choose, can receive elementary instruction; and it is a noteworthy and pleasing fact that an Hawaiian who cannot, at all events, read and write, is as rare as a black swan. On page 72 is a comparative table of the school population for 1880, from Board of Education report to the Legislature.

The number of schools of all denominations in the kingdom on the 1st January 1880 was 210, with an attendance of 7,164 pupils.

The number of pupils reported in 1878 was 6,991, showing an increase of 173 during the past two years.

The tables showed an excess of 932 boys over

Island.	In Schools January 1st, 1880.		
	Boys.	Girls.	Total.
Hawaii	1,281	990	2,221
Maui	925	659	1,584
Molokai	152	107	259
Lauai	2	4	6
Oahu	1,874	1,157	2,531
Kauai	844	188	532
Niihau	20	11	31
Totals . . .	4,048	8,116	7,164

girls, or 57 per cent. of boys and 43 per cent. of girls in the whole school population. There has been a slight decrease in the excess of boys since 1878.

In nationality the percentage of pupils is approximately thus :—

Hawaiians 79 per cent. : half-caste Hawaiians 13 per cent. : all other nationalities 8 per cent.

The enumeration of children of legal school age, by the census of 1878, indicates 1,494 children, or nearly 18 per cent. of the census school population not represented in any of the schools of the kingdom.

After making liberal deductions for the foreign

HAWAIIAN NATIONAL ANTHEM.

THE last eight bars of the Hawaiian National Anthem (spoken of in p. 75 opposite), as far as memory serves me, run somewhat as follows :—

children, whose parents prefer to educate them at home, and the children living in sparsely settled districts where there are no schools, and those from bodily infirmity unable to attend school, there still remains about ten per cent. of the census school population who are absentees.

A large portion of this deficiency in the school-going population is doubtless among the children of the Chinese, included in the census, and Hawaiian children between the ages of twelve and fifteen ; these being the classes often drawn off to the industrial pursuits of the kingdom.

In addition to the public institutions there are numerous seminaries and schools where the vernacular and English are taught; others of more pretension are springing up ; but there is a great dearth of higher class schools for girls and boys, at which those of the citizens of Honolulu, and residents on the islands generally, could attend for classes.

Mixed schools have hitherto been in vogue ; but the indiscriminate attendance of boys and girls under the same source and course of instruction, has a detractive, if not demoralising effect, especially upon dawning womanhood.

Of all institutions connected with Honolulu, the one most to be commended is the Queen's Hospital, at the foot of Punch-bowl Hill. This stone building was erected in 1860, chiefly through the efforts of King Kamehameha IV., and named after his consort Queen Emma.

It is a well-found institution, with pleasant grounds for the exercise of the convalescents. Dr. Robert McKibbin is its supervisor, and it is open to Hawaiians and foreigners alike, who receive the greatest comfort and attention free.

Kapiolani Park at Waikiki, four miles from Honolulu, bids fair to afford the inhabitants of the city many pleasant hours in the future.

The new race-course is in good condition, and the bathing facilities are attractive.

The members of the Royal Family and several of the richer citizens have already erected summer residences in this part, and an enterprising livery-stable-keeper runs an omnibus or wagonette, at certain hours, out and back to Honolulu.

The pleasurable resource of this sun-streamed city is the Royal Hawaiian Band, consisting of some forty native performers, under the instruction and direction of Mr. (or, as he is called, Professor)

Berger, the composer of the Hawaiian national anthem, that reminds one of a combination of the "Watch on the Rhine" and "God save the Queen," the latter preponderating.

The Hawaiian nation proper may be categorised as a thoroughly musical one; and as music is typical of character and nationality, the native melodies are sweet and flowing, and the harmonies most grateful and soothing to the ear, with a solidity of tone.

Their ear for music is very acute and correct, and the training of this really excellent band does the utmost credit to their "maestro," for they render the works from the old and new masters as consistently as it is possible for those never having enjoyed the opportunities afforded to European or American executants.

A curious feature in their reading music is, that unless the flat or sharp be actually marked in every instance the note occurs, the Hawaiian will assuredly play a natural; for all the assiduity of Mr. Berger has failed to initiate them into the mysteries of the keys and cadences, other than that of C natural, so that each piece has to be thus carefully scored before issue to the performers, thereby considerably augmenting the bandmaster's manifold duties.

The band performs regularly every Saturday from 4 P.M. to 6 P.M., in the small enclosure, Emma Square, which is set out with tropical plants. From the newly-instituted Saturday half-holiday these promenade concerts are well attended by pedestrians, equestrians, and owners of every kind of wheeled conveyance. The best-appointed chariot is that of the Princess Ruth, with attendants in yellow-feathered capes.

Moonlight concerts are frequently given by the band, either at Emma Square, or still more enjoyably in the grounds of the hotel, whence all social and pleasant influences seem to emanate.

As previously remarked, the residents of Honolulu, of all nationalities, are intensely hospitable, but the sets and cliques are as numerous as hairs in a horse's tail; the upper ten—or officialdom—being the most exclusive.

Visits are usually paid in the evening after dinner, the general hour for which is 6 P.M.; and look in wherever one may, music, singing, dancing, or some such recreation, is sure to be in progress. But a surprise dance or what-not at the residence of a certain hospitable lady at Waikiki is, of all others, the most enjoyable. This amiable lady and her husband not only entertain constantly, but are thoroughly *au fait* at this self-imposed task.

Leading out of the dining and drawing rooms is a spacious " lanai," or highly-polished platform, on the sand. This is covered in to exclude the rays of the sun, the sides being open and partially shaded by well-foliaged trees. The platform extends to the wooden palisade, up to which the Pacific Ocean comes calmly lapping, if not actually knocking at the garden gate. Situated as this residence is (amid a grove of gigantic cocoa-nut palms), the scene, when illuminated by strongly reflecting lamps, is truly picturesque, refined, and enjoyable in all its accessories.

•

CHAPTER XII.

SOCIETY.

"Manners maketh man."

LIKE most centres of civilisation, Honolulu possesses an excess of marriageable females over the
presentable members of the sterner sex ; and a
new arrival meets a warm welcome from *les de-
moiselles* (especially if a good dancer), and by
mamas if an eligible " parti."

Their fashions are certainly of anterior date to
that of Paris, but the costumes are fairly well
chosen and put on, especially those imported from
San Francisco. But the hues are decidedly more
than attracting in their density and height of
colour.

If there be cliques, there are occasions when

clique meets clique, and notably at a "Maile Ball" given occasionally by the bachelorhood of Honolulu, in reciprocation of past hospitalities.

At these réunions, in the large dining-hall of the Hawaiian Hotel, everyone (who is anyone) meets in accordance with a previous week's invitation ; and, on arriving about 9 p.m., one observes gentlemen in every species of toilet, from the shooting-coat to the claw-hammer-opera-hat-armed guise, similarity only being encountered in the regulation white tie and white-gloved accoutrement —the last, on close inspection, revealing very varied texture in cotton, silk, or kidded goods. After conversing with acquaintances for a considerable period, the *tempus* appears to *fugit* most languidly.

Not a vestige of a petticoat is visible, and one is led to suppose a partner must be selected from the motley groups of curiously-cut continuations that listlessly meander the corridors.

Being only an Englishman, one forbears to be inquisitive or to seek the ladies' hiding-places; so abiding the issue, with what equanimity one may, one returns to the ever-engrossing sole topic of conversation, " sugar."

In these parts one seems to eat, drink, and
inhale nothing but sugar, wholesale and retail;
which becomes slightly monotonous to one only
conversant with the detail as an article of daily
and universal consumption. The utmost simulated
anxiety on the subject being all but exhausted, a
martial strain from the ball-room salutes the ear.
There is a general scare and scatter amongst the
men, who rush about like an army of railway
porters at the announcement of the incoming
Flying Scotsman, and, left to one's own resources,
one sees that the British Commissioner has
attached himself to a comely matron of the upper
ten, others following suit in their several social
degrees, who march steadily through the corridor
to the ball-room.

On the first occasion of my assistance at these
gatherings, I was suddenly rushed at by an out-of-
breath-frock-coated-cotton-gloved steward, whose
insignia of office was commensurate with the
magnitude of his egotism, and who placed me,
nolens volens, without form or ceremony, under
the wing of an ample-skirted American matron.

Falling into the ranks, we entered the ball-room,
proceeded in routine past the dais at the further

end, and made our obeisance to the King, who accorded a dignified yet cordial acknowledgment.

Each couple having performed this duty the march ceased, a quadrille was formed, and the ball formally opened.

My companion seemed a pleasant but (to English notions) peculiar person, who took especial care never to omit the appendix " sir " to all remarks or replies to my interrogations. At request she presented me to one of her charges, a plump Californian belle, who favoured me with her co-operation in a set of the quadrille now formed.

Dame Nature's evident first intentions were to make P. C. B. good-looking, albeit disguised in a costume pertaining to a semi-promenade and nocturne arrangement, of A.D goodness knows what?

We accomplished the first figure creditably enough, and while the sides were finishing what we had commenced upon, I inquired if she did not prefer round dances.

" How ? " she interrogated.

On repetition of the question in another form, she replied:

" Yes, sir ; some ! "

P. C. B. then volunteered the information of her
return that day from one of the islands.

When I expressed a hope that the visit had
been an enjoyable one,—

" Oh, yes, I guess so, sir ; a way up time," was
her response.

Conjecturing as to what in the name of wonder
we had here, she inquired—if I was in sugar ?
and I could only reply that I hoped to be, when we
were called upon for fresh exertions. At these my
partner seemed perfectly *au fait*. But the intricacy
of the manœuvres was too much for a simple
English education in the terpsichorean art. Pushed
here, pulled there, toes stamped upon ; a very
palpable (if not tender) squeeze of the hand from
my *vis-à-vis* at every opportunity afforded for such
process, was distraction enough, when " Ladies in
the centre ! " was shouted by the self-constituted
M.C. of our set. There I was.—" Grand round,"
appealed he.—My partner was describing a circular
pas seul. " Ladies to the right, gents left ! " I
certainly was not in it, and rejoiced greatly on
coming up at the finish to a grand crash from the
band.

At the suggestion of refreshment my partner

"guessed she'd go for a cream ice," and to the discussion of it and my awkwardness, let us leave her, to the attentions of a swarthy youth, who runs a good business in hides and cigars.

Thence the tribute of personal respect was transferred to the King, with whom I conversed on general topics for some minutes, previous to a general survey of the decorations, that were simple yet tasteful, in flowering and foliaged festoons, the walls being draped with Hawaiian, English, and American flags.

This was the first opportunity afforded me of scrutinising the Hawaiian national emblem. The history of the present flag of these islands seems lost in oblivion, so far as the time and parties interested in its adoption are concerned; but the general belief among the old residents is that the present Hawaiian flag was made by the late Captain Alexander Adams, before his voyage to China in the brig *Kaahumana*, in 1817, and was first flown by him, not only in Chinese waters, but on the coast of California. There is also an impression that a flag was brought from China by him, but corroborative testimony is wanting as to who was authorised, in Chinese waters, to design a flag for

6 *

this little kingdom, though the description of a
St. George and St. Andrew's cross in the corner,
filled in with blue, with field consisting of red and
white stripes, almost virtually shows the East
Indian flag.

Reference to Captain Adams' journal gives the
following:—"April 1816.—The King of these
Islands having a strong passion to purchase the
brig (*Forrester*, of London), and expressing the
same, myself and Captain Ebbetts *was* accordingly
deputed to treat with him ; but he would not
purchase her without I would enter his service as
her commander. I resultingly acquiesced, the brig
being given up to him at Kealakekua, and called
by him *Kaahumanu*. . . . I was accordingly
honoured, in taking command, with the flag of
His Majesty and a salute of eleven guns."

This certainly refutes the general belief that the
flag was made by Captain Adams, as his own
narrative shows a flag to have been in existence
here before his time ; but whether the present or
some other one is uncertain.

It is evident, however, there have been more
than one. In another portion of Captain Adams'
journal, allusion, without description, is made to a

flag, when at Waimea, island of Kauai, at which port he touched for supplies on his way to China. He notes, March 12th, 1817 : "Gave the King our ensign to hoist in lieu of the Russian, who said it was on account of his having no other."

The king here mentioned is that of Kauai, and not Kamehameha ; for Kauai was under its own king until 1821, and his possession of a Russian flag, while the principal town was occupied by a Russian colony, was coincidental.

Vancouver, in his last visit to these islands (1793), gave King Kamehameha an English flag, with the assurance of England's friendship and protection. Reference is further made by Archibald Campbell, in his *Voyage Round the World*, 1806–1812, to the fact of his finding, on arrival at these islands, December 1808, that the English colours were used, "the King's residence being built close to the shore, and surrounded by a palisade upon the land side, and distinguished by the British colours."

In describing the period of 1816, Jarvis states the flag to be somewhat similar to that in present use, viz. "English Union, with seven alternated red, white, and blue stripes."

This is not corroborated by Byron in his *Voyage of the Blonde*, in 1825, in which he thus describes the flag :—" On all days of ceremony the Sandwich flag is hoisted on the forts ; it has seven white and red stripes, with a Union Jack in the corner."

Thus are the accounts conflicting.

The present flag has eight stripes, representing the islands of the group : white, red, and blue, with Union Jack in the corner.

To Captain Hunt of the " Basilisk " is ascribed the design of the present standard in 1845, when he is said to have changed the position of the stripes, by placing the white on the top instead of the bottom.

Whatever be the actual origin of the Hawaiian flag, it is an artistically designed union of the national emblems of the three Great Powers evincing substantial interest in this country's welfare, viz. England, France, and America, and who only are diplomatically represented.

While we have thus digressed, the dances on the programme, as well as the physical energies of the guests; have been more than half exhausted, and ample justice is being done to a capital refection ; and after claiming a waltz from a blonde acquaintance, whose paces were pefection amidst a crowd of good steppers, Morpheus claims one as his own for retirement and rest.

The latter is more easily sought than gained in Honolulu, owing to the incessant cock-crowing.

If it be actually necessary for these peripatetic roosters thus to relieve their feelings, it would be an undisguised alleviation could they manage to do so simultaneously at appropriate hours, or convey their sentiments to each other by wire. Here they commence operations at 11 P.M. and keep it up till daylight, and are an insufferable nuisance, especially as their vociferations are accompanied by the ubiquitous buzz of that tropical social pest the voracious mosquito, who is armed here *cap à pie*, knapsack and all.

CHAPTER XIII.

EXCHEQUER.

" Money, they say, is evil's root,
　But I most justly doubt it ;
Can we expect good thriving fruit
　From any stock without it ? "

THE rate of living at the Royal Hawaiian Hotel is
$3 per diem, or $17.50 per week, or about 10s. a
day, inclusive of bedroom, breakfast, luncheon, and
dinner, with attendance, such as the last named is.
The most comfortable as well as economical mode
for a bachelor is to procure a bedroom in the town
somewhere, and arrange with the proprietor of the
hotel for board, say $3 per week for a furnished
apartment and $8 for board.

The restaurants (pronounced here orthographi-

cally) are of the meanest order, analogous to the
commonest European and American eating-houses ;
the charge per meal varying from 25 cents to 50
cents, according to the class of hostelry, though at
these also arrangements may be made by the week.
Nowhere on the face of the globe does one obtain
so little for one's money as in Honolulu.

The stores and shops provide in a measure for
almost every necessary and many luxuries of life,
but at enormously advanced rates. The freight
between San Francisco and Honolulu is from $3 to
$4 per ton, and as previously referred to in the
Treaty of Reciprocity with America, most articles
come in free of export and import duties ; yet prices
at Honolulu range from 50 to 200 per cent., in
advance of the first-named Liverpool of the West ;
moreover, unpaid accounts of three months standing
are charged against the vendee at the rate of 12
per cent., which is further compounded at the same
rate every quarter. For list of free imports from
the United States of America see Appendix.

There is one bank only, viz. that of Bishop & Co.
before quoted. The rate of exchange with them is
$2\frac{1}{2}$ per cent., more than double a rate that would
yield them large profits.

Rents vary from $300 to $1,000 per annum. Suitable lots for house-building purposes can be purchased on fairly easy terms. And with provisions: meat in Honolulu is 10 cents per lb.; potatoes 3 to 5 cents; rice 6 to 10 cents; butter 40 to 60 cents; milk 10 cents per quart; eggs 60 to_ 75 cents per dozen. Fruit is dear, and vegetables are rare except in tins. Building materials are from $40 to $50 per thousand feet of lumber.

Mechanics' wages run from $2 to $5 a day; the price of a native saddle-horse ranges from $30 to $100; mules run from $100 to $150; milch cows about $20; draught oxen about $50, and, compared with other countries, the only moderation may be quoted in the tariffs of taxation.

COMPARATIVE TABLE OF RECEIPTS AND EXPENDITURES.

Hawaiian Islands, 1876–78, 1878–80, and 1880–82.

Revenue.	1876–78. $	1878–80. $	[Estimated. 1880–82. $
Custom House	361,371	582,846	548,400
Internal commerce . . .	85,807	122,946	98,950
Internal taxes	331,163	465,252	414,000
Fines, fees, perquisites, &c. .	132,600	190,265	122,850
Government realisations . .	153,572	318,527	257,000
Government stocks . . .	87,200	23,900	—
Cash in Treasury, April 1, 1880	—	—	338,880
	1,151,713	1,703,736	1,780,080

Expenditure.	1876–78.	1878–80.	1880–82.
	$	$	$
Civil List	76,000	65,500	104,000
Permanent settlements	14,025	15,075	19,600
Legislature and Privy Council	22,080	16,523	20,300
Judiciary Department	71,743	79,667	96,587
Department of War	54,642	67,993	{ Merged in Fgn. Affairs
,, Foreign Affairs	32,036	36,830	133,100
,, Interior	370,220	656,810	1,233,920
,, Finance	244,387	260,057	333,279
,, Attorney Genrl.	95,861	123,664	166,200
Bureau of Public Instruction	71,721	79,605	89,020
Miscellaneous	46,757	93,973	—
	1,110,472	1,495,697	2,196,006

THE PUBLIC DEBT.

(From Report of Minister of Finance to Legislative Assembly, 1880.)

	$
The debt on the 1st April 1878, was	444,800
Amount paid during past fiscal period	79,800
Balance of debt of 1878	365,000
Borrowed by authority of Act of September, 1876	23,900
Present debt April 1st, 1880	388,900

The interest charges on the above are:

Twelve per cent. per annum on	41,000
Nine ,, ,,	304,200
Seven ,, ,,	43,000
Bearing no interest. Bond due not called for	100
Debt as shown above	388,900
Of this there will be due and payable during the current fiscal period	89,600

	$	c.
Total imports, from Custom House tables 1879	8,742,978	89
Total exports, from Custom House tables 1879 . . , . . .	8,781,717	97

The legal rate of interest is 9 per cent. per annum, and on collateral tangible securities varies from 10 per cent. upwards.

Wages are proportionately very high, £1 per week being paid to a Chinese cook-man who acts as general servant, and generally objects to do the family washing.   There is a keen demand for female domestics, and a very good opening will be found for that class of labour, that is at present all but unknown.   The passage-money, in many instances, would be advanced toward procuring such competent help.

Skilled labour also finds ready employment, but for clerks and others without capital there seems to be no opening whatever, the market being already overstocked.   Large or small capitalists, however, will find remunerative results in every branch, whether professionally, commercially, mechanically, or agriculturally exercised; and all coins, except those issued from the Eternal City, are current in these islands.

CHAPTER XIV.

INVESTMENTS UNDER THE HAWAIIAN LAWS.

" He used to say, and never tired of saying,
The world itself was built upon the law."

RESPECTING investments, nothing as yet is more profitable than the produce and manufacture of sugar, except it be the advance of money on the security of growing crops, as performed by the agents and brokers of the various plantations. Land titles originate in the King; many lands are held under incompleted titles called "Land Commission Awards," issued by the Government, which require confirmation by Royal Patent, involving additional expenses, such as settlement of boundaries, and in some cases payment of additional consideration, amounting to one-fourth or even one-third of the original value, together with office fees for issue of Royal Patents. These titles by award are good, as far as they go, and pass by sale, mortgage, lease, &c. ; but the element of uncertainty and incompleteness attending them, renders such undesirable as collateral security.

Legal interest is 9 per cent. per annum. Interest, however, may be contracted for as high as $2\frac{1}{2}$ per cent. per month. Compound interest cannot be recovered in the courts.

Mortgages are foreclosed by bill in equity, in which case the decree provides for attachment of the mortgagor's other property in case the mortgaged property is insufficient for the debt and costs.

Where the mortgage deed contains power of sale, it may be foreclosed by three weeks' public advertisement in the Hawaiian and English languages by the holder thereof of his intention to foreclose, and afterwards by sale at public auction, and registry within thirty days of his affidavit of conformity with the statute.

Mortgages of both real and personal property, duly registered before bankruptcy or insolvency of mortgagor, are preferred claims against such bankrupt or insolvent estates.

Acts of bankruptcy are—failure to pay just demands for ten days after maturity and demand; attempt to leave the kingdom to escape creditors; attempt to avoid creditors or service of process for collection of debts; making conveyances in fraud of creditors; and secret removal of property to defraud or delay creditors.

Executions and attachments against property after the owner has committed an act of bankruptcy are void. Also transfers of property after act of bankruptcy, except to bonà fide purchasers, without notice.

Claims against deceaseds' estates must be presented within six months after administrators' or executors' notice, and sued within two months after rejection.

Taxes have to be paid on all investments. Borrowers, and persons indebted, pay taxes upon the full value of their real estate, regardless of encumbrances, and upon the balance of their personal estate over and above debts unsecured collaterally. This makes double taxation as to mortgaged lands; that is to say, the mortgagor is taxed on the full

value of the land, and the mortgagee upon the
amount of his investment.   Shares in corpora
are not taxed, the whole corporation property b
assessed to the officers of the company.

Mortgages are stamped one dollar for each
thousand dollars of the amount borrowed.   D
conveying real or personal property are stan
one dollar for each five hundred dollars of
consideration.

Bills of exchange and promissory notes
stamped twenty-five cents for the first five hun-
dollars, and for each five hundred dollars a
Acknowledgment of signature costs one dollar, and
every document should have each and every signature duly attested before an officer appointed by
Government to take acknowledgments.

Registration fees are fifty cents for one hundred
words.   The mortgagor pays for draft of mortgage,
stamps, and acknowledgments, and the mortgagee
the registry fees, unless there is an agreement to
the contrary.

Conveyancer's fee is ten dollars and upwards.

Intestate property goes to lineal descendants *per
stirpes* ; if none, one half to widow or widower,
and the rest to parents; if none, to brothers and

sisters and descendants; next to uncles, aunts, and descendants.

Wife has dower in all real estate of husband, one-third for life, and one-third of all personal estate by way of dower, absolute interest.

Husband must join wife in all legal acts.

Debts under two hundred dollars may be collected in police and district courts ; costs of court being four dollars, more or less.

Larger debts must be sued for in the circuit or supreme courts; jury costs, twenty to forty dollars.

Commissions allowed as attorney's fees to the successful party, in assumpsit, of 10 per cent. on the first hundred dollars of the judgment or amount sued for, and 2½ per cent. upon the balance.

7

CHAPTER XV.

VERNERY.

> " Here will we rest us, under these
> O'erhanging branches of the trees."

As previously remarked, the commercial portion of Honolulu is cramped, hot, dusty, dirty, and disagreeable. That affected by the Chinese, in and about Nuuanu Street, being actually offensive. The city is fairly well and permanently supplied with water, and darkness made visible by a few wretched oil-lamps ; but all sanitary arrangements are inefficient in the extreme, the soil teeming with undisturbed pollution.

With every change of ministry there is much talk, but scant action on this, as on many other necessary improvements.

Away from the actual business centre, however, where the residences of foreigners and natives extend by many routes, one's attention cannot fail to be arrested by these picturesque spots, each with commodious verandahs, and in distinct enclosures that vary in extent from the strip of garden to the five-acre lot. In most instances they are too thickly curtained with foliaged, flowering, and fruit trees for correct consideration of hygiene; yet one is deeply impressed how charmingly artistic and peacefully refined is the general aspect of these tropical homes. Few of their shade-affording clusters are indigenous, excepting the cocoa-nut palm, the screw-palm, bread-fruit tree, ohia (or native apple), the koa, the hau, and the kukui (or candle-nut tree). Most of the handsomest have been introduced from foreign countries, and these have within the last twenty years assumed considerable stature. Among them are the mango, tamarind. China orange, sweet orange, lime, citron, alligator pear, custard apple, rose apple, fig, coffee, banana, papaia, date-palm, magnolia, algaroba, acacia, eucalyptus, Norfolk and Caledonia pine, the royal and fan palm, Indian banyan, bamboo, Chinese plum, pepper, cinamon, spice trees; and

7 *

as may be said in the case of humanity, so the
flora of nearly every country under the sun is
represented in these beautiful isles of the sea.   It
is, however, sad to observe the decadence of Hawaiian vernery proper, apart from Honolulu.

As one roams through the forests, clothing the
sides and fringing even the summits of the highest
mountain-peaks of these islands, trees of varied
foliage will be found densely crowded together, and
sheltering an almost endless variety of ferns and
shrubs.

For a list of ferns, see Appendix.

With all this partial luxury of growth, on most
of the islands there is mingled an aspect of decay
that, in its isolated mode of attack, does not appear to be the natural effect from superabundant
growth.

The koa is all but exhausted, yet where a group
of this beautiful veined timber is found, a solitary
specimen may be observed withered and lifeless,
while its adjacent confrères yield forth a growth of
sound young timber.   In most instances an entire
grove of this tree will alone be lifeless, while all
around are vigorous trees of other kinds of equal
growth and age.

This peculiarity is particularly noticeable from a distance, and the effect cannot be produced through cattle, as in many parts their peregrinations are unknown; neither is it apparently caused through diminution, at first instance, of moisture. For trees and plants requiring such sustenance in a far greater degree than the koa, are seen thriving where the koa is dead or dying.

This effect can be attributable only to the exhaustion of the properties of the soil necessary for due development, and the change of site, so necessary to trees, as scene and association are, at times, to mankind.

The ohia, a native apple, is worthy consideration as a forest tree on these islands; its wood is close-grained, and fibre elastic and tough, and used for binding purposes.

It grows to greater perfection in situations difficult of access; but great quantities are readily obtainable, and the fruit, though tasteless, is most refreshing. There is no apparent natural agency destroying these trees, but, whenever and wherever approached by cattle, they disappear.

The native palm, found on the slopes of Mauna Loa (island of Hawaii), is now being attacked by a species of worm, like the borer, with speedy and destructive effect.

The "kou," most handsome of woods for cabinet work, is now almost unknown ; and, owing to the want of care evinced for the young saplings, they decrease in number each year.

The sandal-wood has been found, in single instances on the slopes of Mauna Kea (also on the island of Hawaii).

The Lauhala, or screw-palm, has few ornamental superiors, if we except the kukui—or candle-nut tree. These seem to grow well anywhere below an elevation of 2,000 feet, whereas all forest and fruit-trees, indigenous to the temperate zones, thrive well above that line, and up to that of the frosts.

Sicilian chestnuts, oak, and all the conifers, will attain perfection on the slopes of the mountains, on or near the line of winter frosts.

If only proper attention were paid to forest culture, these islands would be free from the possibility of drought, and rival, if not excel, many spots on the face of the globe in their luxuriance and variety of trees and plants.

CHAPTER XVI.

AMUSEMENTS.

"I have thought some of nature's journeymen had made
    men, and not made them well, they imitated
    humanity so abominably."

"I hope we have reformed that indifferently with us,
    Sir."

THE residents of Honolulu have, from all time, been
greatly dependent upon each other for intellectual
and recreative amusement, and it may be justly
remarked that the various elements of this small
community are essentially agreeable.

Natives and foreigners are the most enthusiastic
votaries of Terpsichore, and dance to perfection.
Occasional picnics and moonlight rides, together
with "surprise-parties," of which, on the *lucus a
non lucendo* principle, the host is always forewarned,

break the monotony of existence in a land free
from telegraphic, or even postal intelligence,
between the monthly mails. Until lately, base-
ball has been the sole athletic diversion of youth,
but its interests seem jeopardised by the Cricket
Club started in 1880. The brief sojourn of a ship-
of-war is more welcome than the arrival of the
mail steamers, when all seem to wake up and vie
with each other to render the reminiscences of
Honolulu as agreeable as possible.

During the stay of H.M.S. *Gannet,* we introduced
polo and lawn tennis ; but, somehow, these games
have met with very moderate patronage.

Previous to the year 1847 there had never been
a regular theatre here, the nearest approach to a
public entertainment being the occasional performance by a wandering conjuror.

Such an one was given in 1846, supplemented
by the doings of a "strong man," impersonated
by a sailor of an American whaling-vessel then in
port, who performed the feat of having an "adobie"
broken on his breast with a sledge-hammer. But
in the summer of 1847, a Yankee schoolmaster,
nicknamed "Mnemonics," from his attempt to
teach, what Dr. Stokes has since systematised,

arrived also in a whaler, and, having a few copies of the *British Drama* in his kit, organised a Dramatic Society from amongst the mechanics, in view to individual amusement and improvement.

Thirty years ago society in Honolulu was far more scanty and exclusive than at present, but this would-be professor of elocution and histrionic art was soon surpassed by his pupils.

The employer of many of these youths—a house-builder—took considerable interest in the matter, and eventually erected the "Thespian," a fair-sized wooden structure, having stage, boxes, and pit—which was opened to a crowded house, 11th September 1847, with "The Adopted Child," and "Fortune's Frolic," a printer on the staff of the *Polynesian* composing and delivering an address on the occasion.

The prices of admission were : boxes, $1 ; pit, 50 cents ; the two front rows being reserved for the ladies. The boxes held seventy-five, and the pit 200 persons, a private box being fitted up for the King (Kamehameha III.), who attended with his Premier, John Young, and other members of his ministry.

They were received with great cheering ; while

the orchestra, consisting of " Black George " with his clarionet, and " Indian Oliver " on a trombone, performed " God Save the King "—as may be conjectured—with considerable effect.

Theatrical interests grew so strong that a committee was formed to erect a theatre capable of accommodating 500 people, and, up to 1848, the " Thespian " did good business, when it was no more heard of.

The stock for a new Royal Hawaiian Theatre was soon taken up, the building commenced, and opened to a good audience in June 1848. Owing to the discovery of gold in California at this time, representations became intermittent; for the gold-fever raged as high in Honolulu as elsewhere, and diminished this sparse population to a great extent. But owing to the fact of so many as 150 whaling vessels being simultaneously in port, the theatre was opened again in 1849.

In the summer of 1853 a new shell of a theatre called the " Varieties " was built, and opened by a circus proprietor named Foley.

A Mr. Brown, while playing here, met with an accident—the slip of a dagger occasioning him a severe and self-inflicted wound.

Waller, the tragedian, and his wife, fulfilled an engagement here in 1854. But the history of this house was brought to a close by fire on the 6th July 1855, origin unaccounted for.

" Buffum's Hall " was the next histrionic enterprise, started by the late Walter Montgomery, in 1870, but never succeeded as a place of public resort. There have been several visitations also from circuses, and Wilson's Menagerie Show.

Among other professional celebrities visiting Honolulu are included the names of S. C. Massett, Kate Hayes, Lola Montez, Edwin Booth, Professor Anderson, Madame A. Bishop, Charles Backus, Joe Murphy, Charles Mathews, Madame Ristori, Signor and Madam Bianchi, Madame A. States, the Carandinis', Professor Hazelmeyer and Madame Cora, Madame Ilma di Murska, Herr Bandemann, Miss A. Montague, and Charles Turner.

Besides these, a profusion of minstrel troupes and almost every other species of exhibition or entertainment, from the barrel-organ upwards, have from time to time catered for patronage; so that Honolulu has not been without opportunity, of seeing some of the best professional talent or, to practise the art of criticism.

From its position as a port of call for the mail steamers between San Francisco and the Antipodes, many stars and lesser luminaries have now an opportunity to break the monotony of the voyage advantageously. The want of a hall for concerts, theatricals, public meetings, and the like, has been severely felt for many years, the Congregational churches having hitherto done duty therefor. The adaptable Chinaman erected a wooden theatre on the esplanade in the summer of 1879, and with a company from California performed to crowded houses of Celestials, and " outside barbarians." But from " the information received " by the police that its resources included an opium-smoking den, a raid was made, and the theatre closed by order of the authorities, October 1880.

The new music-hall, opened January 1881 with a company from San Francisco, is situate almost opposite the palace grounds and adjoining the Government buildings.

This edifice is brick-built, 120 feet by 60 feet, with walls 40 feet high and 20 inches thick at the base and 12 inches at the eaves.

The vestibule is 16 feet by 27 feet, with a ticket-office on the right-hand, and stairs leading to the family circle on the left, where 154 persons can be comfortably seated. Beyond this is the dress circle having 214 seats, and thence on a gradual descent is the parquette, 120 seats, fitted like those in the dress circle, with opera chairs. The entrance to the gallery (183 seats) is on the north side of the building. The distance between the seats is 3 feet 6 inches, so that the house comfortably holds 671 persons. Large exits are made on the lower floor against the possibility of fire, and the ventilation has been specially provided for. Two private boxes on the proscenium are reserved for the King and royal family, and there are retiring-rooms on each side of the dress circle.

The stage is 40 feet deep, and is provided with necessary scenery, traps, &c.

The scenic artist is Mr. T. W. Porter, an American, and the stage-fittings are entrusted to Mr. S. Gulliver and his forty years' experience.

The parquette in connection with the stage, can be turned into a ball-room 80 feet deep, and the green-room below the stage, 32 feet by 42 feet, into a supper-room; on each side of this are dressing-rooms, and the whole is well-lighted with gaseline.

Just as the perpetual *Pinafore* was about to be

produced, the Government closed the hall as a precautionary measure, owing to the outbreak of small-pox, introduced by the Chinese immigrants, who arrived in considerable numbers the middle of February 1881.

———————

CHAPTER XVII.

PULPIT AND PRESS.

" The world's a printing-house, our words are thoughts ;
Our deeds are characters of all sizes ;
Compositors are people of whose faults
The parsons are correctors—heaven revises."

OUR dogs bay the moon, children cry for it, and a
matron of the bovine family has been credited with
the performance of certain athletic exercises in that
district ; but to a resident of this sea-girt group has
been ordained the privilege of snaring the sun—
the legend of which runs somewhat that Huia, the
mother of Maui, was inconvenienced by the "going
down of the same" in her drying operations, and
steam laundries being then, as now, unknown in
these islands, she was obliged to gather up her

goods ("kapas") at sunset, still unfreed from moisture.

Maui's sympathy being aroused, he determined to make the sun go slower, and thus afford his mother a chance of conducting her industrial pursuit with a more satisfactory result.

From observations he found the sun rose towards Hana, and climbing the mountain of Haleakala (House of the Sun), found its course directed straight over him. On returning home he made a strong cord from the fibre of cocoa-nut husks previously gathered.

The cord being completed, he returned to the mountain, and as the sun rose above the spot where he had taken up his post, he, with a noose, snared one of the larger rays of the sun and broke it off, repeating the process until all the strong rays of the sun had been snared and snapped.

Then he shouted exultingly, "Thou art my captive, and now I will kill thee for thy going so swiftly." On which the sun appealed: "Let me live, and thou shalt see me go more slowly hereafter. Behold! hast thou not broken off all my strong legs, and left me only the weak ones?"

A compromise was thereupon effected, the sun pursuing his course more slowly, and Maui his, to report the exploit to mother.

Thus it is that, in these islands—at all events—the days are longer at one season of the year than at another, through the forethought of Maui snaring the sun. However that may be, Sunday is welcomed throughout the islands and reverently kept. A list of the places of worship will be found in the directory included in the Appendix. The Cathedral or Episcopal Church, in Emma Square, and the Congregational Church on Fort Street, are the most fashionable ; though the Roman Catholic Church, also on Fort Street, is running them very closely as regards devotees. Attending the temporary cathedral, it was not without emotion we recognised in the Bishop an old friend, Dr. Willis, ex-vicar in the district of New Brompton, Chatham, England.

As might be expected, the service is nicely conducted, but it is a most depressing ordeal.

The wooden structure, on a most admirable site, is very hot and badly ventilated. The service is partly choral, with some good voices in the surpliced choir of mingled whites and blacks,

8

augmented by many of the resident ladies, who sit apart in the south aisle.

The talents of the organist are worthy a better instrument than the church possesses ; and not-withstanding his every effort to elevate them to *vive* and sentiment in the chanting, the choristers persist in their flat and monotonous drawl. The Bishop and his *aides* are making strenuous efforts for funds to build a permanent stone edifice to meet the requirements of the population.

Turning into the British Club, that might be made the nucleus of an influential cotérie if properly organised, we found most of the English papers by the last incoming mail, also the various issues from the press of Honolulu, which principally consist of advertisement and correspondence columns—the latter teeming with vulgar invective and purposeless personality anent some public functionary or private individual.

Nothing denotes the characteristics and proclivities of a country more than its Press, and in the short period of its consolidated existence the kingdom of Hawaii has done much in the "Art Preservative," since its first introduction some fifty years ago.

An interesting account might be rendered of press work in the Hawaiian language; but in this instance a brief historical sketch of the newspapers and periodicals that from time to time have appeared in the English language (which will eventually be adopted as that of Hawaii) will suffice.

On the 7th January 1822, the first printing on these islands was executed at the establishment of the American Mission, in an edition of the *Primary Spelling Book*, in Hawaiian text, the King, Kamehameha II., pulling the first sheet.

The first newspaper, called the *Lama Hawaii* (" Light of Hawaii "), appeared at Lahainaluna (Maui) on the 14th February 1834, also in the Hawaiian language.

The van of progress in the English language was led by the *Sandwich Island Gazette*, printed at Honolulu 1836–1839, and appeared in troublous times, when a second attempt (the first occurred in 1827) was made to establish a Roman Catholic mission on these islands.

The *Gazette* was violently opposed to the Government of the day, and abused without stint the American Mission; collapsing, for want of sup-

8 *

port, in 1839. Its last issue appeared during the week that the French frigate *L'Artemise* (Captain Laplace) left Honolulu with £4,000, as a deposit and guarantee from the King of his future good-conduct towards France.

The *Hawaiian Spectator*, a quarterly of some thirty octavo pages, conducted by " an association of gentlemen," and printed at the American Mission, appeared from January 1838 to October 1839. Said to have been ably edited, and contain m
of interest respecting the islands.

The *Sandwich Island Mirror* appeared also, for a few numbers only, in monthly issues during 1839.

On the 6th June 1840 appeared the first number of the *Polynesian*, a weekly of independent views, first edited by James Jackson Jarvis, of Boston, Mass., who subsequently wrote a history of the islands. Its publication continued till February 1864, and among the twenty-four bound volumes reposing at the Government Library, much interesting matter respecting Hawaiian history may be gathered.

The *Friend*, still edited by its founder, the Rev. Dr. Damon, justly claims seniority in the Pacific newspaper world, and was first issued in January 1843, and is chiefly interesting in its monthly drafts of the past rise and fall of the whale fishery, and editorial impressions during a lately prosecuted tour in Europe.

In 1844 the *Cascade* and the *Monitor* appeared, and the *Oahu Fountain*, a temperance paper, had short existence between 1846–47.

The *Sandwich Island News* was issued as persistent oppositionist to the Government, from 1847 to 1849. The editor having an attack of the gold fever, it gave way to the *Honolulu Times*, which was followed, on the death of the editor, by the *Weekly Argus*. This paper had to be suspended in 1853, on account of the small-pox epidemic, during which one-tenth of the population perished. The *Argus* was resumed, but discontinued altogether in 1855.

The *Pacific Commercial Advertiser* made its first weekly appearance July 1st, 1855, and still continues, and may be said to support the King's party. It has also a semi-weekly edition in the Hawaiian language.

Since 1855, numerous small monthlies and weeklies have appeared for short periods ; the only one still in existence first saw daylight 21st January

1865. It is an eight-page weekly, published on Wednesdays under the auspices of the Government, but affects independence under a proprietorship and its title of *Hawaiian Gazette.* The *Saturday Press* is the latest weekly—there are no daily issues—appearing first in September 1880, in support of the commercial interests of Honolulu.

Honolulu journalism, with its increased facilities to that of former days, has not made the advancement anticipated. This is attributable to the limited means of receiving or imparting intelligence from or to the outer world. In no place are people more inclined to be sensitive over, or give importance to, trifles as here ; and important intelligence, as with the latest gossip or scandal, is ventilated at the street corners (during hours devoted elsewhere to the transaction of necessary business), rather than through the calm medium of post prandial reflection.

CHAPTER XVIII.

NATIONAL FORCES.

" Ho ! watchman, ho !
Twelve is the clock !
God keep our town
From fire and brand
And hostile hand !
Twelve is the clock ! "

IN a city consisting mainly of timber tenements, the means of preserving life and property from fire is of no ordinary consequence. Such here are entrusted to volunteer organisations, consisting of six companies, each of independent action and funds, but working harmoniously under the direction of a stipendiary fire-marshal.

The force has two steam fire-engines, two manual

ditto, a hose company, and one directing its attention to the application of hooks and ladders; and the town is apportioned to their care in five wards.

From 1846 to 1850 incendiarism was very rife; and it was not until 1850 that the city possessed a fire-engine, said to have been purchased by the Government from the wreck of the brig *Patapsco*. As in most instances, the Chinese company, with their steamer, is the best organised and most reliable, though fifth wheel in the fire brigade coach.

Other than the police there is no legalized military force whatever, the army having been abolished under the following

"*General Military Order.*

" By authority in me vested by the Constitution as Commander-in-Chief of the Military Forces of my Kingdom, I do hereby declare the organization known as the Household Troops to be, and the same hereby is, with the exception of the band, disbanded—the officers and men entitled thereto to receive an honourable discharge.

" Given under my hand and seal at Waikiki this 12th day of September, A.D. 1873.

" LUNALILO.

" By the King.

" Charles R. Bishop,

" Secretary at War."

At the commencement of the present reign (1874) the then Attorney-General, Hartwell, organised a " King's Guard," and a foreign volunteer militia, which, in its provisional organization is without proper legal sanction, and the members thereof are independent of subjection to any Articles of War.

In less flourishing times (1816) there were 400 drilled men in the fort at Honolulu, under the command of a much respected chieftain Kalaimoku ; and in 1848—when the receipts for such fiscal period are quoted at £3,132—the number of soldiers enrolled on the island of Oahu is reported as 629, irrespective of smaller forces on the other islands, the whole forming an army of about 1,000 enlisted and paid soldiery.

The present Army, or, more properly speaking, the Palace Guard, is more numerous in the commissioned ranks than that forming the file, which latter con-

sists of some fifty men, who are hired on the same
principle as other labourers, at so much a month;
and as they cannot for an instant be relied upon,
except to flaunt their braveries in support of the
enormous national emblem that is trotted out at
the opening or prorogation of Parliament, volunteer military companies have been formed to keep
them in check in case of inadvertence with their
rusty rifles. The volunteer military companies are
five in number, whose clothing evinces fertility in
imaginative tailoring. There are "The Prince's
Own"—artillery without guns! "The Leleilohoku
Guard"—cavalry without horses! two companies
of "Hawaiian Guards," and the Mamalahoas.

The commemoration of His Majesty's birthday
affords occasion for a general "turn out" of the
military and civic forces, usually taking the form of
a torchlight procession. Pursuant to resolutions
passed, and orders issued, the members of these
departments lately attended, in all their bravery of
German head-gear and Brummagem brass, at the
Fire Bell-tower, which for the nonce had been
decorated with Chinese and other lanterns.

Half-past seven P.M. being the hour appointed for
assembly, and all reported "present and correct,"

the line of march was formed, and on the occasion in witness, the torches, lanterns, and other illuminations produced a gay and picturesque parade.

The procession, headed by the Royal Hawaiian Band, and escorted by the military companies, the red and blue shirted firemen, with their engines (also illuminated), bringing up the rear, passed through the principal streets of the city, to the entrance of the Palace Yard. Arriving there, the military companies formed three sides of a hollow square, which centre was occupied by representatives of the departments interested. They, with the spectators, awaited the appearance of the King, who, in response to the wish of his assembled subjects, in due course presented himself, amid loud and prolonged cheering.

On cessation of this loud loyalty the commanders of the military and other organisations made their several addresses to the King, embodying expressions of the respect, esteem, and love "for His Majesty"; prayers for his "continued enjoyment of happiness and health," and wishing this "father of the Hawaiian race" many returns of his natal day, amid cries of "Long live our King Kalakaua!"

It was evident that His Majesty was greatly impressed by this spontaneous manifestation of good-will, and the means taken to celebrate an anniversary so interesting to him personally, and with a few well-chosen words he replied, in clear tones, and with dignified mien, to these unaffected salutations; expressing his " confidence of the love and respect of his people," and giving them his " earnest and heartfelt ' Aloha ! ' "

Renewed cheering, to the accompaniment of the " Kamehameha Hymn," before referred to, brought this part of the programme to a close. The procession then filed out of the Palace grounds, the van being led by the cavalry—in this instance mounted —followed by the " Household troops," whose domesticated aspect seems to have certainly been furthered since the days of their cannibal progenitors ; the fire brigade and gear again bringing up the rear. The military wore capes and cloaks made of yellow cloth, in imitation of those worn by Hawaiian warriors in the now ancient days of Kamehameha the Conqueror.

These uniforms, representing the costumes of the past, were fashioned for an intended exhibition of Hawaiian games and jousts during the contemplated visit of General Grant, ex-President of the United States, and were first produced on the occasion, some time ago, of a display in lance-throwing.

The procession followed a prescribed route through the principal streets of Honolulu, returning to the Bell-tower, at which point the parade was dismissed.

CHAPTER XIX.

SOURCES OF REVENUE.

" Yet wert thou as far as that vast shore, washed with the
farthest sea, I would adventure for such merchandise."

A BRIEF stay in Honolulu will more than suffice to
assure one of the hospitable intents of its residents,
and their interest in all that may, or may not,
concern a new arrival ; and when not engaged in
the self-constituted action, for the time being, in
such guardianship, the all-engrossing planting
interests are gravely discussed. Of this enterprise
all in Honolulu seem to cry " Wolf " on each and
every note of the gamut. Personal observation and
practical test of this industry gives cause for inference that the decriers generally are incompetent

to form an opinion, while the residue have an object instigating their dehortations.

In an unbiassed opinion—provided a system of irrigation be maintained—this most exuberant soil is suitable, according to elevation, to nearly every tropical or non-tropical produce ; and man has but to put forth his hand, under common-sense guidance, to be more than satisfied with the result of his investments and labour.

The wealth of this archipelago has never been developed, and is at present in embryo ; and the indolent native may be excused his ignorance and abhorrence of systematic labour in so temperate a climate and so productive a soil.

The staple exports are sugar, rice, and coffee. There is an increasing trade in bananas, fungus, tallow, hides, and wool, but there the matter ends. Sago, potatoes, cotton, hemp, the pepper-plant, and its germinated successor, the gambier, which yields terra japonica, so valuable for tanning, are yet uncultivated. Further are the gutta-percha, also the clove, unknown except through importation; and cinchona, for which, in certain districts, every-thing appears so congenial, alone suggests fortune, if not affluence, with a voracious market like San

Francisco ready to hand, and the application of moderate capital for its culture. "And why this apparent neglect?" may be questioned.

Through want of capital, energy, and system; above all, the need of labour for agricultural pursuits.

The extent of productive virgin soil on this group is great in comparison with its area of four million acres, and capable of supporting one million persons; whereas, the actual population under date does not exceed 60,000, the native contribution thereto being within 44,000, and is yearly on the decrease through immorality and inattention to the simplest matters attending hygiene.

During the early months of this year (1881) some six hundred Chinese immigrants were contracted for by private enterprise, since when, several thousands have poured in on their own account, with cases of small-pox "*en attendance.*"

Up to April some sixty fatalities from this source had been recorded; but the invasion being suppressed, it is to be hoped that the strict isolation, and quarantine regulations, somewhat tardily enforced by the authorities, may stamp out the disease, and so release the labourers waiting for hire.

The lately published policy of the Hawaiian Government is in view to recuperate the population rather than to supply commercial requirements with labour alone. This appears sound, and what has been previously advanced in these pages. But the only politic solution of the problem seems the obtination of a convention with the Government of India, on behalf of East Indian coolie immigration, including their wives, daughters, "chillumchee," and "hubble-bubble," on the lines of that done at La Hague, September 8th, 1870, between the Governments of Her Majesty Queen Victoria and His Majesty the King of the Netherlands.

There cannot be less than 12,000 Chinese on the islands at present, five-sixths of whom are, or will be eventually, employed as agricultural labourers—enough for all urgent needs. But were the British Government to allow its own subjects and British-born people to introduce and employ East Indian coolies on these islands, without the formality of a Convention, much would be gained on either hand.

CHAPTER XX.

COFFEE.

"Read o'er this; and after, this, and then to breakfast with
what appetite you have."

OF the staple exports, coffee—being a product
almost wholly in the hands of the natives—seems
to demand primary notice in that of the agricultural
industries of Hawaii-nei.

It is evidently non-indigenous to these islands,
and, seeking for the source of its introduction, we
find that Don Paulo Marin is credited with the
first effort towards its culture, A.D. 1817—from
seed probably obtained from ships touching at
Honolulu about that period. Of his successes or
reverses no record is extant, as in the case with all
early efforts of the agriculturist.

The first authentic revelation of its induction proceeds from the Manoa Valley plantation (Oahu), through plants said to have been brought from Rio Janeiro, in the *Blonde*, by Lord Byron, 1825. In August of that year a plantation was laid out on the land at Manoa, owned by General Boki, under the superintendence of Mr. Wilkinson, and to the then thorough cultivation its preservation is apparently due.

Mr. Wilkinson died in 1827—the trees grew without care or attention, and the crop was intermittently gathered. But from this one start, slips were planted in two other valleys on the island ; and about the same year, coffee plants appear to have been acquired from Manila and Batavia, that were also cultivated at Manoa.

From experienced success here, coffee was further introduced to the western side of the island of Hawaii, in the districts of Hilo and Kona (temp. 1828, 30), which situation proved still more congenial to its growth ; for the records of the Royal Hawaiian Agricultural Society state that the slips " grew luxuriantly " and " produced largely."

These successes induced others to lay out plantations at Hanalei, and Kilauea, on the island

9 *

of Kauai, A.D. 1842, the plants and seed being derived from Manoa and Kona respectively.

Another plantation was also started on Kauai, at Wailoa; but had to be abandoned—after great expenditure—the site being found unsuitable.

The first-named plantations, on Kauai, organised by the Hon. Godfrey Rhodes, seem to be the only ones upon which any system was adopted, or aim towards extension and improvement exercised. That at Hanalei afforded a model for management and an instructor in cultivation.

In almost all other districts where the attempt was made, the plants, slips, and seeds, when once committed to the soil, seem to have been discarded, to take what chance they might, until the period for gathering the berries came round—the sites usually chosen being ravines or small villages, sheltered alike from sun and wind—and where the coffee-fields are mostly found at this day.

Coffee, however, is found growing near to the sea-level; but, as in Ceylon, at an elevation of from 2,000 to 3,000 feet will be found more appropriate localities, and where cane will not so readily thrive.

As previously remarked, there are no records to

guide one as to the commercial success attending early coffee-culture ; but the most favourable districts seem to have been Hilo and Kona on Hawaii, and at Hanalei on Kauai.

Learning most from the last-quoted source, it is certain the Hanalei plantation, of about 1,000 acres, underwent a trying ordeal.

That old bug-bear, labour, was difficult to procure, and just at the cropping-season of 1847, heavy and continuous rains did great damage— causing freshets in the rivers, and forcing rocks, trees, and earth from their holdings, over the plantations.

This dearth was followed by the severe drought of 1851, seriously reducing the crops—no precautions, as now, being taken for irrigation.

Then followed a general blight throughout the islands—doubtless caused by the foregoing inundation and subsequent drought.

This blight seems to have been the smut, or species of fungus, attributed to noxious vapours from the excess of vegetation, and attacked the darker-leaved tribe of plants more virulently than others. If these be removed, those with lighter leaves seemingly recover.

It is found especially in cases of over-crowding, and prevention of the evil may be secured by clean cultivation, free circulation of air, proper drainage, and judicious pruning in season.

However, such preventions were not practised then, and are sparsely so now. All kinds of remedies receive greater favour, and I verily believe that were Mrs. Winslow's soothing syrup suggested, the planters' proclivities are sufficiently infantile to try it. In this nursery, nature seems to have been its most potential advocate : for thousands of acres are being planted at greater elevations, and promising well. Kona coffee is the choicest in the world, and is not without testimony of being superior to the far-famed "Mocha."

The district of Kau (Hawaii) also produces excellent coffee ; several tracts on Maui also give a good marketable berry. The old plantations on Kauai have been given over to the sugar enterprise. But everywhere are large tracts to select from, on excellent elevated lands.

For the last nine months of 1880, 85,333 lbs. of coffee were exported, being an increase on the corresponding period of the previous year of 31,245 lbs.

Here is a matter worthy attention, and requiring small capital.*

The foreign population are the local consumers of this beverage, and reference to the cultivation of the chief source of aboriginal sustenance must not be omitted.

Taro (*arum esculentum*) is a tuber averaging nine inches in length, and fifteen inches in circumference. Like rice, it grows under water in shallow puddled reservoirs, wherein, on isolated mounds of clay, this esculent is planted. The leaves, alone appearing above water, are broad and thick, and when boiled fairly palatable.

The root, however, is insipid to foreign tastes, something between an artichoke and a bad potatoe.

There are twenty-eight varieties; but the white is in most request by the " cognoscenti." A red kind has lately been introduced from Tahiti, and is fragrant when cooked.

Some species have a double stalk to each root. The long-leaved kinds are credited with medicinal

* Intending cultivators are recommended to peruse the Hon. G. Rhodes' *Essay on the Cultivation of Coffee;* Mr. R. Hewitt's *Coffee: its History, Cultivation, and Uses;* and *The Coffee Planter of Ceylon,* by Wm. Sabonadiere.

properties; but each and all are used in the
manufacture of " poi."

This national dish, and staple food, is prepared
by boiling the root of the taro, then mashing it up
to a pulp, and then, on a board, worked up
by hand as dough is kneaded, and called " pai
ai." On being further mixed with water or
milk, it assumes the consistency and appearance of the contents of a railway porter's paste
pot.

A poi supper in Hawaii is the synonym of 5
o'clock tea in Belgravia, and many days had not
elapsed ere we were bidden to this class of
entertainment.

Presenting ourselves, about 9 P.M., at our hostess'
domicile, we were cordially greeted by the young
ladies of the family, who at once decked our heads
and necks with sweet-scented wreaths of ginger,
stephanotis, and orange flowers.

It must be confessed the surroundings were very
agreeable—the girls being good musicians, with
well trained voices; and manners—well! just a
trifle more free than Anglican ascetics might con-
sider consistent with circumstances. But there was
an air of business about them, and a constant

endency to talk about sugar and matrimony, that
showed which way the wind was blowing.

On supper being announced we trooped into an
adjoining apartment, where a circular table groaned
under the weight of its service—sufficient to satisfy
Epicurus, and to effect disturbing influences on
digestive organs, whose experiences in varieties of
nutriment were as extensive as the countries they
had passed through.

The population of Honolulu seems no more cos-
mopolite than are its kitchens ; but on this occasion
the bill of fare consisted of salt fish, dry fish, fresh
fish, raw fish, and boiled fish ; crabs raw, crabs
cooked ; salad of vegetables, and salad of sea-weed ;
roast rat, roast dog ; taro plain, and in a pudding ;
commingling with oranges, bananas, guavas, mangoes, cocoa-nuts, and bowls of white and pink poi,
one bowl to every two guests.

Taunted with a want of appreciation of these
delicacies, I tasted them all, and can vouch to
the least nasty being the raw fish and sea-weed
salad.

Poi-eating etiquette prescribes the insertion of
two fingers into the bowl, by one person only at a
time. Its artistic conveyance to the mouth through

this means, requires considerable practice on the part of the operator, and should be commenced by motions.

At the word " one " extend the first and second fingers of the dexter hand ; thumb pressing the third and fourth fingers, which should remain closed ; head erect ; eyes and hand inclining towards the bowl.

" Two." Insert the extended fingers in the centre of the glutinous mass to a depth notexcee ding two inches, the fingers slightly curving.

" Three." Withdraw the fingers, and with a circular motion of the wrist to the left, and the elbow to the right, at the same time opening the mouth, with an under pass elevate the poi thereto, upon which close the lips without noise, eyes still inclined towards the bowl, and repeat the practice in quick time, according to etiquette.

A similar accomplishment in this series of graceful curves, may be witnessed at the Elephant House, Zoological Gardens, on the acceptance by one of its inmates of a penny bun.

CHAPTER XXI.

RICE.

"The clouds we thought would open, and show riches, ready to drop upon me."

HAWAIIAN agricultural interests, twenty-five years since, were affected (in inverse ratio) by the success of the whaling expeditions, or rather upon the number of whalers making Honolulu a port of call and recruiting district; from which source, moreover, the islanders derived their main support, and in some instances fortunes; that is to say, as the whaling business declined, so that of husbandry rose.

For several years previous to 1858 there had been a considerable decrease in the number of vessels visiting the kingdom, until trade was inflated by the advent of 536 ships during that season, and by a still larger number in the following year of 1859.

But in 1860 these visitations dropped to 325, and in 1861 to 190.

In 1862 only seventy-three vessels were noted ; and at this time, 1881, the whale-fishery in connection with the Sandwich Islands may be said to have almost altogether collapsed.

Several unsuccessful experiments in rice culture had been made by independent foreigners from time to time ; but it is to the efforts of the Royal Hawaiian Agricultural Society that the introduction of rice, as a staple article of produce, is due. During the first declination of the whaling interests, this society purchased a tract of land near the town of Honolulu, suitable for the experimental introduction of various foreign trees and plants.

A quantity of paddy having been procured from the East Indies, an old taro patch was therewith planted, and in less than four months the crop was harvested (September 14th, 1858) with a yield of three-quarters of a pound to the square yard.

This was hulled between the millstones of a flour-mill at Honolulu, but was found to be small in grain, dark in colour, and unprofitable in appearance generally.

Notwithstanding this result, and the absorbing prosperity of the whaling times of 1859, the society's manager was hopeful, and replanted, but with no better results.

Again in 1860 Mr. Holstein procured four pounds of South Carolina rice, direct from Charlestown, and, in a prepared taro patch, planted 1½ lbs. under the shade of two bread-fruit trees that still mark the spot.

The season proved inclement, and the yield therefrom of good seed rice was but 44 lbs.

With 4 lbs. of this seed the late Dr. Ford planted 1,060 square yards of a taro patch at his residence in the suburbs of Honolulu, during March 1861 ; from which was gathered no less than 1,163 lbs. of large and full-grained paddy , and Mr. Holstein's report for the same year gives the yield per acre at 1½ lbs. to the square yard, or 7,260 lbs. of paddy per acre.

This unanticipated success was electrical in its influences. The Hawaiian world "went for rice," and so contagious was this " rice on the brain " disease, that all the taro patches were transmuted

to paddy-fields, even to the dethronement of growing plants in favour of the newly-constituted idol.

Seed rice was purchased by ship-loads, and taro
patches bought or rented, and, labour hired, at
fabulous prices.

Every available spot being thus occupied a taro
famine ensued, with consequent suffering amongst
the natives, until the esculent was worth its weight
in current coin.

Spontaneous energy eventually moderated, and
while some adveturous planters incurred severe
pecuniary loss, others became dispirited.

A great drawback to successful issues super-
vened from the non-existence of rice-mills and
polishers on the islands, enforcing exportation to
San Francisco for marketable preparation. The
machines there, were moreover suffering from
repletion of consignments, which conduced to pro-
tracted storage and consequent expense and general
leakage.

Under these circumstances, a small but fairly
efficient mill was imported by Dr. Ford, leading to
the subsequent production, by the late Colonel
Prendergast, of a rice-polisher superior to that
in vogue even in California.

Owing to previous anticipations being unrealised and the losses incurred by theoretical aspirants, the enterprise languished, many rice-lands being replanted with taro. By this means that commodity was lessened in value, when a revolution in favour of rice re-occurred. Since that time (1865) the production and exportation of rice has steadily increased.

From the number of Chinese now resident, as well as the adoption of it at most meals by other foreigners and natives, the local consumption of rice is very great, about 400,000,000 lbs. per annum, and the export for the nine months of 1880 reached 3,915,640 lbs., or an increase, on the corresponding nine months of 1879, of 837,627 lbs.

This pursuit is now almost wholly in the hands of Chinese planters, who are indefatigable in their own interests and raise as many as three crops in the year.

The localities chiefly affected by them are on the islands of Oahu and Kauai, but there are hundreds of disused taro-beds of great extent available for rice culture, that could, by the application of systematic irrigation, be turned to most remunerative account. The local price is 5d. per lb., or $6 per bag of 100 lbs.

The Chinese consul, Mr. Afong, has lately set up a large and superior working rice-mill and grain-polisher at Honolulu ; and, given the water-supply, rice offers sound and fair prospects as an investment from its acknowledged reputation of being equal to that from South Carolina, its original source.

But it is conjectured this article of commerce will be expunged from any future treaties of reciprocity with the Government at Washington.

CHAPTER XXII.

CANE.

" He who would eat the sweets should taste the cane."

A VERY prominent feature of the capital is its flag-staffs, for irrespective of the crowd of consuls residing here, every other enclosure is thus armed and garnished on available occasion. One of these was, not long since, the source of considerable chagrin to a diplomatic representative on finding the emblem of his nationality alienated to a subordinate position on its own pole, in favour of that borne to the breeze by the country of a colleague.

The means of manipulation being cut off, in addition to the general amusement his discomfiture afforded, further aggravated matters.

Remedial measures lay between razing the flag-

10

staff radically, and pinning the noses of the
perpetrators to the conservative political block.

The adolescent representative in question being
more easy with the pen than handy with the axe,
said nothing, but poured forth his grievances in
floods of ink, all insufficient to allay the diplomatic
dust-storm that stifled every sentiment but merri-
ment in this mirth-loving community.

Suspicion of the offending parties fell upon the
British members of a co-operative jeunesse dorée-
hood, tenanting a retreat not inaptly styled " the
Spinster's Hope," and on this covert being drawn,
a portion of the halyard belonging to the outraged
State was found—scent good enough to justify a
"run in."

An " amende " being insisted upon, the political
malefactors were paraded *en grande tenue* by their
" chief," and marched to the scene of their late
momentary triumph. The offended dignitary received the deputation with every imaginable courtesy, and informed it that the restitution of his
flag to its proper position on the staff could alone
condone the indignity to which it had been infor-
mally subjected.

Congratulating themselves upon His Excellency's

magnanimity and the means of extrication offered
from a serious dilemma, these practical jokers
expressed their gratification to comply at once with
the conditions and, evening-toileted though they
were, proceeded to supplement such expressed
willingness with instant action.

This, however, was not so easy of accomplishment, from the fact of the pole having accumulated
certain lubricating matters towards its summit since
the previous ascent.

The absurdity of the situation, combined with
the ineffectual attempts to attain the end in view,
was ludicrous in the extreme, and convulsed the
fringe of inquisitive spectators. After a series of
slippings and slidings a composited climb was
achieved amid acclamation from the assembled
crowd, and consular honour upheld by the destruction of four hapless black suits, and score of
the odd trick in the rubber—to Dummy.

But having slipped our agricultural cable, let
us put back to pick it up again, and note what *it*
may have accumulated.

Symptoms of sugar at last!

It is asserted by the Chinese that they are the
manufacturers of this article from cane, of some

10 *

3,000 years standing, though India seems to be
the source of its previous emanation ; however,
without detraction of the *Flowery nation*, sugar-cane
is found growing now-a-days in almost every
tropical climate on the globe, and said to be indigenous to the Hawaiian islands. At all events Cook
found it here "of large size and of good quality,"
and it grew wild in almost every valley and plain ;
though no use was made of it by the natives,
except as an item of food. There seems to be a
striking similitude between the Bourbon, Tahiti,
and the so-called Native cane.

The Tahiti, or as sometimes termed here Lahaina, cane (from Maui) is of a pale-greenish hue,
deepening in the latter colour as it arrives at
maturity ; the joints are long, with the eye partly
sunken in the rind, which is somewhat soft. It
stands high, twelve to fifteen feet, and strips easily ;
arrows, or tassels, freely ; and ratoons well ; and
has a rich juice.

The varieties of cane found here are numerous,
those chiefly cultivated are herein quoted under
their native appellations, the best being the—

Manulele. Colour dark brown with large stalk,
     which sometimes is found one foot in cir-

cumference at the bottom; it is rich in juice and hardy under culture.

Ko kea. Colour yellow, very long jointed, but does not grow thickly in the stalk; rich in juice, prolific, and ratoons well.

Of the ordinary kinds are the—

Ko liea. Colour yellowish red.

Ko wala. Colour, red and yellow.

Arria. Colour, greenish red; rich, and preferred in high-land cultivation.

Pua ole. Arrowless cane; does not exhaust the soil, nor deteriorate by standing.

The richness, or density, of the juice varies throughout the islands, according to the species grown and the elevation where; but from authentic reports the average gives nine degrees by Baume's saccharometer, or 15·75 per cent. of pure sugar, about the average ascertained in Java; but far less than might be obtained under a rational system of cultivation.

To the Royal Hawaiian Agricultural Society also is this industry indebted for any statistical information as to its commencement and progress, and from such source is gathered that the earliest instance of sugar manufacture on this group was in

1802 on the part of a Chinaman, who arrived in a vessel trading for sandal-wood, accompanied by a stone mill and boilers. After grinding off a crop on the island of Lanai, he appears to have returned to China, taking his tools with him.

The authenticity of this statement is questioned, some according its primary manufacture a later period.

Among the numerously nominated claimants to the first establishment of this industry, Don Paulo Marin has recorded the fact of his having made sugar in Honolulu A.D. 1819.

Antone Catalina is credited also with being its founder, from making syrup at Waikapu (Maui); and Hungtai, a Chinaman, is said to have set up the first mill at Wailuku, on the same island.

However! Sugar was made by an Italian named Lavinia, at Honolulu, A.D. 1823, by pounding the cane on poi boards with stone beaters, and boiling the collected juice in small copper kettles; and the manufacture of sugar and molasses seems to have been pretty general about this time, chiefly in support of the then extending rum traffic.

1825 appears to be the year of inauguration in organised cane-planting; and as with coffee, an Englishman was its inductor, by name Wilkinson, who laid out 100 acres in the Manoa Valley adjacent to his coffee-fields.

He dying, as previously mentioned, in 1827, one crop of sugar only was taken off during 1828, when for want of attention the cane degenerated.

Some ten years or so elapsed, until 1835 witnessed the first regulated sugar plantation at Koloa (Kauai), where Mr. Hooper, on behalf of Messrs. Ladd & Co., with a light plough broke up land secured to them by grant from Government, for sugar and silk culture, and there established the first regular mill, of primitive structure.

The yield therefrom in 1838 is quoted at 5,039 lbs. of sugar and 400 gallons of molasses, off one acre of plant cane.

Similarly to its congenitor, coffee, the sugar enterprise seems to have had a " rough time " until after the establishment, in 1851, of the Royal Hawaiian Agricultural Society ; with marked regularity in the initiative being taken by a Celestial, and system and production being continued by an European.

The first exportation noted, appears in the year 1837, and the tabulated statement on the next page may be instructive, and of possible interest.

152   FROM SWORD TO SHARE.

YEARLY EXPORTS OF SUGAR AND MOLASSES FROM THE
HAWAIIAN ISLANDS SINCE 1837.

Year.	Sugar.	Molasses.	Year.	Sugar.	Molasses.
	lbs.	Galls.		lbs.	Galls.
1837	4,286	2,700	1859	1,826,620	87,513
1838	88,543	11,500	1860	1,444,271	108,613
1839	100,000	75,000	1861	2,562,498	128,259
1840*	360,000	31,739	1862	3,005,603	130,445
1841†	60,000	6,000	1863	5,292,121	114,413
1842‡	—	—	1864	10,414,441	340,436
1843	1,145,010	64,320	1865	15,318,097	542,819
1844	513,684	27,026	1866	17,729,161	851,795
1845	302,114	19,353	1867	17,127,187	544,994
1846	300,000	16,000	1868	18,312,926	492,839
1847	594,816	17,928	1869	18,302,110	388,311
1848	499,533	28,978	1870	18,783,639	216,662
1849	653,820	41,235	1871	21,760,773	271,291
1850	750,238	129,432	1872	16,995,402	192,105
1851	21,030	43,742	1873	23,129,101	146,459
1852	669,170	62,030	1874	24,566,611	90,060
1853	642,746	75,769	1875	25,080,182	93,722
1854	575,777	68,372	1876	26,072,429	139,073
1855	289,908	38,304	1877	25,575,965	151,462
1856	554,805	58,842	1878	38,431,458	93,136
1857	700,556	48,486	1879	49,020,972	87,475
1858	1,204,061	75,181	1880§	49,988,189	153,944

* These figures are from January to August only.

† These figures are from August 1840 to August 1841.

‡ No figures; but 1843 includes both years.

§ For first nine months only, showing increase over same period of 1879 of 10,418,636 lbs. of sugar, and 104,564 galls. of molasses. For first three months of 1881, increased export is 3,793,787 lbs. of sugar and 34,831 galls. of molasses.

Previous to 1843, the exportation of Sandwich Island sugar ·was unfavourable, from the shipment of imperfectly dried sugars ; but a noticeable improvement in cultivation, manufacture, and general consignment, was effected from the influential interest taken in its career by the Royal Hawaiian Agricultural Society.

A report made to that body by the late Mr. L. L. Torbert, in 1852, states that cane grew without culture almost everywhere on these islands, at altitudes up to 3,000 feet above sea level. At half that height it ceased to blossom, or tassel, and continued to grow on from year to year, for five or six years, without exhausting the soil, or deterioration.

In some soils, however, it appears to die out, while in others long standing seems to improve it.

Centrifugals were first used at East Maui in 1851, superseding the old perforated boxes in the process of drying.

The saving in time and labour, together with the elevation of grade in the sugar produced from this source, caused a revolution in the enterprise.

Up to 1855 the yield was small and unsteady, influenced by the drought of 1851, low prices in

California, the establishment of duties, and scarcity of labour. The importation of Chinese coolie labour in a measure gave relief; but as in 1851, so up to 1881, labour is the vexed question of these islands, and in 1857 we find the number of plantations reduced to five.

1858-59 heralded the adoption of steam as the motive power in manufacturing sugar. This progressive step was set by the Haiku plantation, on Maui, the projectors, later on (in 1876-77), of systematic irrigation by water brought in canals and through pipes from the mountains to the plantation, a distance of twenty miles.

1861 witnessed the introduction of steam strike pans and vacuum pans, as also the Sorghum pan, which acted so advantageously for the operations of small capitalists, and augmented the number of planters, bringing it up to twenty-two; nine plantations using steam, twelve water, and one animal power.

About this period a sugar refinery was started in Honolulu, but proved a signal failure, and naturally soon collapsed.

With the recent additions of good machinery and late improvements, principally introduced by

Messrs. Muirless, Tait, and Watson of Glasgow, the quality and quantity of the produce has greatly improved.

Notwithstanding the severe ordeal this industry has encountered, there is still much that is crude about the culture and manufacture. Were it not for the advantageous terms of the Treaty of Reciprocity with America, the present intermittent supply of labour, high rate of wages, and a general absence of systematic economy in working, would seriously diminish the present list of plantations engaged therein, enumerated as under.

Sugar Plantations and Mills.

Those marked * are planters only; those marked † are mills only; the remainder are plantations complete with their own mills.

Firm's Name.	District.	Island.	Agent or Broker in Honolulu.
1. Akaualiilii & Co. .	Makawao	Maui	C. Brewer & Co.
2. Beecroft Plantn. *	Kohala	Hawaii	T. H. Davies.
3. Costa „	Hilo	Hawaii	W. G. Irwin & Co.
4. East Maui „	Makawao	Maui	C. Brewer & Co.
5. Eleele „	Koloa	Kauai	F. A. Schaefer & Co.
6. Grant, Nicholson & Brigstocke	Kilauea	Kauai	E. Hoffschlaeger & Co.
7. Grove Farm Plntn.	Puna	Kauai	H. Hackfield & Co.
8. Grove Ranch „	Makawao	Maui	Ditto.
9. Haiku No. 1 „ } 10. Haiku No. 2 „ }	Haiku	Maui	Castle & Cooke.
11. Hakalau „	Hilo	Hawaii	W. G. Irwin & Co.
12. Halawa „	Kohala	Hawaii	J. T. Waterhouse.
13. Hamakua „	Hamakua	Maui	Castle & Cooke.

Firm's Name.	District.	Island.	Agent or Broker in Honolulu.
14. Hamakua Plntn* |	Hamakua	Hawaii	T. H. Davies.
15. Hamakua Mill † ∫			
16. Hana Plantation.	Haua	Maui	H. Hackfield & Co.
17. Hanamaulu ,, *	Puna	Kauai	Ditto.
18. Hawi Mill †	Kohala	Hawaii	T. H. Davies.
19. Hawaiian Agricultural Co.	Kau	Hawaii	C. Brewer & Co.
20. Hawaiian Commercial Co.	—	Maui	W. G. Irwin & Co.
21. Heeia Plantation	Kaneohe	Oahu	H. Hackfield & Co.
22. Hilea Sugar Co. .	Kau	Hawaii	W. G. Irwin & Co.
23. Hitchcock & Co. .	Hilo	Hawaii	Castle & Coode.
24. Honokaa Sugar Co.	Hamakua	Hawaii	F. A. Schaefer & Co.
25. Honomu Plantn.	Hilo	Hawaii	C. Brewer & Co.
26. Huelo ,, *	Hamakua	Maui	C. Brewer & Co.
27. Kaalaea ,,	Kaalaea	Oahu	T. H. Davies.
28. Kamaloo ,,	—	Molokai	T. McColgan.
29. Kanehoe ,,	Kaneohe	Oahu	C. Brewer & Co.
30. Kanpakuea ,,	Hilo	Hawaii	C. Afong.
31. Kealia ,,	Kealia	Kauai	W. G. Irwin & Co.
32. Kekaha ,, *	Waimea	Kauai	E. Hoffschlaeger & Co.
33. Kekaha Mill Co. .	Wainae	Kauai	H. Hackfield & Co.
34. Kilauea Sugar Co.	Kilauea	Kauai	H. Hackfield & Co.
35. Kipahulu Mill * .	Hana	Maui	T. H. Davies.
36. Kipahulu Plntn. *	Hana	Maui	H. Hackfield & Co.
37. Kohala ,,	Kohala	Hawaii	Castle & Cooke.
38. Koloa ,,	Koloa	Kauai	H. Hackfield & Co.
39. Laie ,,	Laie	Oahu	I. T. Waterhouse.
40. Lichgate & Co. Plantation. *	Laupahoehoe	Hawaii	T. H. Davies.
41. Lilikoe Plantatn.	Haiku	Maui	H. Hackfield & Co.
42. Lihue ,,	Lihue	Kauai	Ditto.
43. Makahanaloa Plantation.	Hilo	Hawaii	C. Afong.
44. Makee Plantation	Ulupalakua	Maui	W. G. Irwin & Co.
45. Makee Sugar Co.	Kealia	Kauai	Ditto.
46. Moanui Plantatn.	—	Molokai	Wong Leong & Co.
47 Montgomery & Co. Plantation	Kohala	Hawaii	T. H. Davies.
48. Naalehu Plantn. .	Kau	Hawaii	W. G. Irwin.
49. Niu ,,	Waialae	Oahu	J. C. White.
50. Niulii ,,	Kohala	Hawaii	T. H. Davies.
51. Olowalu ,,	Lahaina	Maui	H. Hackfield & Co.

Firm's Name.	District.	Island.	Agent or Broker in Honolulu.
52. Onomea Plantn. .	Hilo	Hawaii	C. Brewer & Co.
53. Ookala ,,	Hilo	Hawaii	H. Hackfield & Co.
54. Paauhu Mill † . ⎫	Hamakua	Hawaii	W. G. Irwin & Co.
55. PaauhauPlntn.* ⎭			
56. Pacific Sugar Mill †	Hamakua	Hawaii	F. A. Schaefer & Co.
57. Paukaa Plantatn.	Hilo	Hawaii	C. Brewer & Co.
58. Pioneer Mill † .	Lahaina	Maui	H. Hackfield & Co.
59. Princeville Plntn.	Hanalei	Kauai	C. Brewer & Co.
60. Spencer's ,,	Hilo	Hawaii	G. W. Macfarlane.
61. Star Mill ,,	Kohala	Hawaii	G. W. Irwin & Co.
62. Union Mill Co. Plantation.	Kohala	Hawaii	T. H. Davies.
63. WaiakeaPlantn.⎫	Hilo	Hawaii	T. H. Davies.
64. Waiakea Mill † ⎭			
65. Waialua Plantatn.	Waialua	Oahu	Castle & Cooke.
66. Waianae Sugar Co.	Waianae	Oahu	H. Hackfield & Co.
67. Waihee Sugar Co.	Waihee	Maui	W. G. Irwin & Co.
68. Waikapu Plantn.	Waikapu	Maui	G. W. Macfarlane.
69. Wailuku ,,	Wailuku	Maui	C. Brewer & Co.
70. Waimanalo Sugar Co.* · .	Waiman- alo	Oahu	H. Hackfield & Co.

In addition to these are many parties planting on shares with the mill-owners. Of the different plantations whose several extents vary from one hundred to three thousand acres under cultivation in and for cane, therefore,—

Island of Hawaii has 30 acknowledged plantations
,,   ,, Maui   ,, 18   ,,   ,,
,,   ,, Kauai ,, 12   ,,   _   ,,
,,   ,, Oahu   ,,   8   ,,   ,,
,,   ,, Molokai ,, 2   ,,   ,,
                        ——
      Total   .   .   70

The principle firms, acting as plantation agents, as also in the capacity of factors and bankers thereto, are Messrs. Hackfield and Co., Messrs. Irwin and Co., Messrs. Brewer and Co., and Mr. T. H. Davies, all of Honolulu.

Of all these planters and agents, scarcely one will co-operate with another, as in other countries, towards the acquisition of knowledge on matters relating to general welfare and advancement, or for the diffusion of such experience as they have gained.

Several attempts have been made towards the establishment of a Planters' Association, in view to acquire a cheap and permanent supply of labour, together with national and general benefit, independently of Government aid ; but contentment, derived from isolation, and the (in many cases mis-guided) propulsion of private crafts, seems incontestable up to date.

CHAPTER XXIII.

OAHU.

" We are not thieves ; but men who much do want."

CONTEMPLATION of such narrow-minded policy, through the window of wonderment, will scarcely augment one's balance at the solitary bank, especially as the sole aim and object of the commercial community here seems to be the abstraction of said balance at the least possible *quo* for a *quid*.

The actual or affected inability to afford one the slightest practical guidance is quite as astonishing as perversion of fact is lamentable, pervading so otherwise intelligent a fraternity.

The old story of " paying for peeping," we

suppose; but the practical pursuit of every man seems, Peep the most and pay the least you can. So, putting such axiom to the test, by borrowing a horse for a day or two, let us take a peep at the island, and see according to linguistic pronunciation " Who-are-who ? " (Oahu).

Ambling eastward on our Mexican saddled loan, four miles of road to Waikiki is in good order, broad, and suggestive of a capital track for a tramway, especially as the Government are finding numerous purchasers and tenants for their " Building Lots " that flank the route thereto. These are sold by auction at prices averaging £100 each, and have about 100 feet frontage, by 150 feet in depth.

Nearing the native huts, we find the paddy-fields stretching hence toward Diamond Head ; those in proximity to the tidal-way seemingly suffering from the corrupting influences of salt water. Continuous poppings of fowling-pieces, accompanied by vocal execrations from Celestial bird-scarers, give life to an otherwise somewhat dreary expanse of waving marshland, between the sea and the surrounding mountains.

Northward, is the wild and beautiful valley of

Manoa, watered by a stream much frequented by wild duck, the derivation of its name.

Within a short distance up through the spurs, shrouding this retreat, we chanced upon a pic-nic party — whose hospitality we, nothing loth, accepted; and, after a survey of the general surroundings, took the Punch-bowl Hill on our return route towards the town. On this summit, 500 feet high, is the now solitary fort of these islands, with its mediæval saluting battery of two guns. From this point the reverse view of Honolulu, to that on arrival in the harbour, is obtained; and the axis of the earth (according to residential views) observed in its entirety.

Descending, we cross a stream, and through a by-way come out upon the Nuuanu Road. Here troops of garlanded horsemen and horsewomen, attired in gayest colours, are galloping to and fro.

Saturday afternoon is usually occupied in this manner by the natives, without motive, except it be exercise, and kicking up a disagreeable dust.

Up this road, some ten furlongs from the town, is the Cemetery, with Royal Mausoleum of the Kamehamehas, containing the remains, or at least the coffins supposed to hold them, of the former

11

kings and chiefs of these islands.   Further on is
the ice and soda-water manufactory—very primitive
—and in perceptible ascent a turn of the road
brings one to Chulan and Co.'s Rice Mills.

Six miles and a half is the extent that wheels
can travel in this direction, almost reaching the top
of the volcanic precipice called the Pali.   The
present road was first opened for traffic in 1845, by
Kamehameha III., accompanied by his then First
Lord of the Treasury, John Young.   Carriages
have been known to traverse it, a considerable feat;
and in that light we should look upon it as a
pretty considerable one now.

The gorge is narrow, and the rain-clouds are
driven through with terrific force by the wind.
Railings now guard the precipice, though not put
up until the list of casualties at this point had
assumed portentous length.   Above are steep,
black, densely-wooded rocks: below, at a depth of
2,000 feet, extends, in horse-shoe form to the
sea, a picturesque verdant plain, dotted with
dwellings.

The further descent is by a very rough, sharp
turning, and somewhat dangerous pathway, and
leading one's horse becomes advisable, if not

absolutely necessary, to the fork of the Kaneohe and Waimanalo roads, a distance of half a mile.

We next came to a rice and taro patch, noted for a desperate struggle between the contending chiefs and their followers, as in later times of the murder of a Kanaka by two Chinamen. Further on is the Roman Catholic Church at Heeia.

Within another five miles we reach Kaaluea, the Hon. C. Judd's ranch, or stock farm. Making a short halt and brief inspection of the cattle stationed here affords the surmise — " Does it pay ? "

Passing two churches, we come to " Will-Ka-a-i " Mill, on the Oahu Plantation, twenty miles from Honolulu. By this peculiar nomenclature is the district known throughout the islands, as a sample of Hawaiian humour.

When digging the foundations of a mill, a one-eyed Kanaka (native), accustomed only to the use of the o-o-, twisted his neck round, while needlessly following, with his single optic, each spadeful that he threw out. Finding his neck so stiff as to be scarcely able to move it, in half-piteous accents, and with comical expression, he

11 *

exclaimed, "Will-Ka-a-i!" in translation, "This is a regular twist the neck!"

A mile further on is Kaawa, the Hon. J. Wilder's place; and arriving at the School House, some four miles on, attention is attracted towards one of the most natural curiosities extant; for standing out, in bold relief, on the top of the mountain, is the Colossal Hawaiian lion, reminding one of Landseer's *chef d'œuvres* in Trafalgar Square, and for which it might have served as a model.

The hind-legs are drawn under, fore-paws stretched out in front, and the tail curling naturally over the back.

The head is raised and turned towards Honolulu, where all his sympathies seem centred. So natural and graceful is the form and expression, that one is astonished to find he does not rise and roar.

Within a further mile we reached Punaluu Ria plantation; and as our horse showed unmistakable signs of giving in, and one's own interior economy of giving out, there seemed no help for it but to halt here for the night.

A comfortless prospect; but thanks to a courteous native, shelter against possible rainfall was secured in an antediluvian grass hut, and a cane stretcher-chair served all the purposes of the most springy mattrass. Divesting my borrowed nag of his gear, and watering him to his heart's content, further provision of sustenance was relegated to his own discrimination, a position to which he seemed quite equal; while the contents of a saddle-bag furnished an ample meal of tinned beef, with a loaf of bread, relished under the shadowy light, shed from some ignited cotton that floated by the aid of cork in a sconce of castor oil.

" Nature's sweet restorer " speedily caused oblivion of whether the tenement in dreams was the vault of heaven, or of marble halls, till aroused in harshest tones by the inevitable roosters at sunrise.

Having caught the horse, saddled up, and taken leave of our host, half-an-hour's jog in the fresh morning air brought us to Norton's, opposite Kalu-waa Falls, where a bathe was irresistible. It is in this ravine that Pagan temples were existent, and where the Hawaiian zodiacal archer held sway in feats, still the theme of many an elementary ode.

At Laie, thirty-two miles from Honolulu, we drew rein to look at the Mormon Colony, here located, and to crave a cup of coffee at the residence of

Mr. Mitchell. But resisting a hospitable request that we should stay to breakfast, our route was resumed towards the famous water-hole, into which in days gone by a woman dived and eluded the pursuit of Kamehameha's bands. Supposing her to be drowned they bathed here at their leisure, talking unguardedly of the plans of their chief. The woman was hiding the while and overheard their conversation from a cave, the entrance to which was concealed below the surface of the water. Escaping from her retreat on their departure, she traversed the mountains to the camp of her friends, to whom she revealed the intentions of their foes.

Another five miles brought us to Waianae plantation, where we arrived in time for a much needed " square meal," in the form of comfortable breakfast at Mr. Richardson's, 7.30 A.M.

This plantation may be quoted as the show one on the islands, from its readiness of access from Honolulu by road, and its equidistance from the point of departure in this circular tour.

The plantation is not so extensive, but its organisation and working is as perfect as any. Unfortunately the mill was not grinding during our visit. But the fields were clean, and the cane in the most prolific and healthy condition. The average of a subsequent crop therefrom yielded over five tons of sugar per acre, sufficient to justify the encomiums passed upon the soil of these islands, especially when under judicious culture.

A representative from the agents to this plantation was here, and having seen what was possible I took the opportunity to accompany him to Honolulu, after a noon-day dinner.

The greater portion of the distance (about forty miles) through Waimea, Ewa, and Waialua, once a populous place, comprises the alternating ascent of steep hills, and descent into valleys that are scored by ravines and watercourses; and with the exception of a few houses, one or two small rice and sugar-cane plantations, and cattle ranches *en route*, the surroundings present the aspect of a treeless waste.

Past the lunatic asylum, reformatory school, and prison, we reached the confines of Honolulu within five hours—the through circular route, without deviation, being about seventy-seven miles.

A most unwelcome scene greeted our entry of the city at the police station, for it was surrounded by a number of those unfortunate beings afflicted with leprosy, who were in attendance for registration purposes previous to the leave-taking of sorrowing relations, and departure for the leper establishment on the island of Molokai.

Such morbid exhibitions, that are of constant occurrence, cause conjecture and disgust at the supineness of the Governmental machinery (more than replete in its component parts) in not conducting such necessary regulations with greater privacy.

CHAPTER XXIV.

INTER-ISLAND TRANSIT.

" If consequence do but approve my dream,
  My boat sails freely, both with wind and stream."

AMONG my numerous commissions, before leaving England, was the presentation *in propriâ personâ* of a parcel to some people planting on the island of Kauai, within fifteen miles of the district wherein my correspondent of Chapter I. had been desirous to plant also ; but from inability to come to terms with the proprietors of the land, all negotiations had fallen through.

Ascertaining from one of the young ladies of the family, then in Honolulu, the appropriate period to present myself and parcel, it was arranged my escort would be agreeable on her return home by the

inter-island steamer sailing at 4 P.M. the following
day.

At the appointed hour I found several little
steamers, as like one crow is to another in dirty and
black appearance, puffing and whistling amidst
general admiration from a loquacious crowd; and
after strict inquiry I was directed to (if there be a
comparative degree) the dirtiest vessel, as that
bound for my destination.

Giving saddle and saddle-bags—without which no
one stirs in these parts—to the Chinese steward,
my *companion de voyage* was sought for in vain, and
anxiety anent the whereabouts of such fair charge
was exercising stirring influences, when, without
further warning, the steamer had actually started.

In considerable concern an intelligent-looking
white passenger was questioned as to our being all
right for Kauai, when to my horror, he exclaimed,
" Say, stranger, you bet we're making tracks for
Maui," just the opposite direction to that which
another similar craft was steaming.

All requests to be put on shore again were
unavailing, the commander stating the imperial
sway of time and tide made it impossible.

No way out of the dilemma presenting itself, the

best of a bad beginning was made while watching
the efforts of a row-boat, that from the wild gesti-
culations of its freight seemed desirous to attract
attention and induce the steamer to stop, though
to no purpose. This boat, I afterwards learnt,
contained my lost charge.

Someone has somewhere descanted, in more
glowing than truthful terms, upon the merits of
these steamers, together with the delights of a
passage therein—a measure, we suppose, of that
contentment previously adverted to. But for the
benefit of those preferring practicality to *persiflage*
the following is a list of the vessels registered at,
and hailing from, Hawaii ; and from which it will be
noticed the tonnage of this vessel* is figured at 190.

HAWAIIAN REGISTERED VESSELS.

MERCHANTMEN, WHALERS, AND TRADERS.

Register.	Class.	Name.	Tons.	Registered Owners.
149 new	Schooner	Giovanni Apiani	85 92.95	Jas. I. Dowsett.
150 ,,	Bark	Kale . . .	867 73.95	H. Hackfeld.
154 ,,	,,	Mattie Macleay	308 65.95	Jas. I. Dowsett.
164 ,,	Brigantine	Pomare . .	220 45.95	H.H.M. Minister of Interior.
168 ,,	Brig	Julia M. Avery	178 11.95	Chas. K. Clark.
173 ,,	,,	Eliso . .	812 77.95	Chas. K. Clark.
175 ,,	Bark	Iolani . .	924 76.95	H. Hackfeld.
192 ,,	Brigantine	Stormbird .	130 69.95	H.H.M. Minister of Interior.

Register.	Class.	Name.	Tons.	Registered Owners.
193 new	Bark .	Kalakua . .	404 89.95	P. C. Jones, jr.
202 ,,	,, .	Liliu . . .	701 71.95	Henry Cornwell.
206 ,,	,, .	Hawaii . .	417 88.95	H.H.M. Minister of Interior.
210 ,,	Schooner	Julia A. Long .	187 89.95	
211 ,,	,,	Kaluna . .	86 44.95	A. F. Cooke, W. L. Wilcox.
217 ,,	Bark .	Starlight . .	636 2.95	J. S. Walker.

COASTERS.

Register	Class	Name	Tons	Registered Owners
170 new	Schooner	Kulamanu .	96 34.95	Allen & Robinson, C. M. Cooke.
166 ,,	,,	Nettie Merrill .	158 77.95	Henry Turton.
174 ,,	,,	Catarina Apiani Long.	43 85.95	Allen & Robinson.
171 old	,,	Manuokawai .	51 45.95	Thos. R. Foster.
176 new	,,	Kekauluohi .	53 89.95	Allen & Robinson.
127 ,,	,,	Marion . .	105 49.95	Thos. R. Foster.
169 ,,	,,	Kate . . .	22 04.95	Walter Bates.
158 ,,	,,	Ka Moi . .	154 16.95	T. H. Hobron.
130 ,,	,,	Keoui Ana .	26 42.95	
131 ,,	,,	Pauahi . .	111 38.95	Allen & Robinson.
69 ,,	Sloop .	Wailelo . .	15 36.95	Ipuhao (w.).
161 ,,	Schooner	Kapiolani . .	10 78.95	H. Grube.
68 ,,	,,	Prince . .	85 41.95	Thos. R. Foster.
115 ,,	,,	Warwick . .	23 29.95	Jacob Brown.
177 ,,	Steamer	Likelike . .	596 58.95	Samuel G, Wilder.
179 ,,	Schooner	Leahi . .	103 24.95	Allen & Robinson.
180 ,,	,,	Wailele . .	75 85.95	Cooke, Alexander, Wilcox & Wilcox.
129 ,,	,,	Jenny . .	63 4.95	T. R. Foster & J. Brown, trustees.
41 ,,	,,	Rob Roy . .	25 38.95	Jas. I. Dowsett.
182 ,,	Sloop .	Kulamanu .	8 24.95	M. P. Robinson.
203 ,,	,, .	Hae Hawaii .	9 12.95	E. Kahelemake.
145 ,,	Schooner	Kauiki . .	7 64.95	Jas. I. Dowsett.
155 ,,	,,	Mile Morris .	22 32.95	Jas. I. Dowsett.
142 ,,	,,	Uilama . .	78	B. M. Allen.
117 ,,	,,	Kinau . .	41 59.95	Jas. I. Dowsett.
183 ,,	,,	Haleakala .	116 75.95	Allen & Robinson, C. Afong.

Register.	Class.	Name.	Tons.	Registered Owners.
185 new	Schooner	Mary E. Foster	116 6.95	Thos. R. Foster.
186 ,,	,,	Waioli . .	65 68.95	A. F., C. W. & C. M. Cooke, W. L. Wilcox.
187 ,,	,,	Haunani . .	130 24.95	T. R. Foster, Jacob Brown.
188 ,,	,,	Waiehu . .	60 37.95	W. L. Wilcox, W. McCandless, A. F. Cooke.
189 ,,	,,	Pato . . .	95 8.95	Reed & Sisson.
*190 ,,	Steamer	Kilauea Hou .	271 10.95	T. H. Hobron.
194 ,,	Schooner	Waimalu . .	95 97.95	A. F. Cooke, W. L. & S. W. Wilcox, S. T. Alexander.
195 ,,	Steamer	Waimanalo .	49 81.95	Waimanalo Sugar Company.
196 ,,	,,	Mokolii . .	96 78.95	S. G. Wilder.
197 ,,	Schooner	Liholiho . .	122 35.95	Thos. R. Foster.
214 ,,	,,	Liliu . .	85 69.95	C. M. & A. F. Cooke, W. L. Wilcox.
199 ,,	Steamer	Kapiolani (tug) .	24 24.95	J. S. Walker.
200 ,,	Schooner	Luka . .	122 35.95	Allen & Robinson.
204 ,,	Steamer	Lehua . .	217 91.95	S. G. Wilder.
205 ,,	Schooner	Mokuola . .	17 10.95	J. H. Black.
207 ,,	Steamer	James Makee .	244 15.95	T. R. Foster, J. Brown, Mrs. Godfrey.
208 ,,	Schooner	Malolo . .	133 65.95	Alexander, Cooke & Co.
209 ,,	,,	General Siegel .	39 12.95	A. F. Cooke, W. L. Wilcox, G. P. Castle.
215 ,,	,,	Kauikeaouli .	139 70.95	Allen & Robinson.
216 ,,	,,	Jennie Walker .	137 85.95	William Greig.
218 ,,	Steamer	C. R. Bishop .	281 36.95	T. R. Foster, G. N. Wilcox, Mrs. C. E. Godfrey, J. Brown.
219 ,,	Schooner	Mana . .	107 10.95	A. F. Cooke, W. L. Wilcox.
213 ,,	Sloop .	Sarah . .	6 21.95	W. F. Williams.

Of the steamers the *Likelike* plies between
Honolulu, Maui, and Hawaii ; the *Kilauea Hou*
between Honolulu and Maui ; the *Molokii* between
Honolulu and Molokai ; the *Lehue* between Hono-
lulu, Maui, and Lauai ; the *James Makee* between
Honolulu and north-east coast of Kauai ; the *C. R.
Bishop* between Honolulu and south and west coast
of Kauai.

They are fair sea-boats, and mostly built on the
same lines, at San Francisco ; are commanded by
whites and manned by natives ; the steward usually
being of the heathen persuasion.

The fore-deck is generally overladen with lumber,
horses, cattle, and South-Sea islanders ; the after-
deck with natives, Chinamen and sundries, huddled
in an indiscriminate mass. A small portion—over
the propeller—is awninged off for the use of *first-
class* (?) passengers ; and if the change of name
would make it sweeter, such would be more than
welcome.

The decks are filthy ; the stuffy crib called a
saloon, is of the most limited description and
flanked with six bunks on each side, that no one
desirous of health would utilise ; and the food—
well ! the least said about it the better ; and the

nearest approach to the general nausea and discomfort here found, will be met in the steerage of an Irish pig-boat.

The rate of travelling is about six knots per hour. 24s. for *first class* (?) and 8s. for deck accommodation is charged by the monopolists of these channels; while for an all-round trip, comprising Maui and Hawaii—which no one in his senses would take in these vessels for pleasure—£5 is demanded.

With the aid of a mattress and blanket on deck one essays to obtain some sleep, to which the noise and vibration of the screw, the rattling of the steering gear, to say nothing of the erratic perambulation of restless passengers, is far from conducive.

Dawn found us in the channel between Molokai and Maui, and we arrived, after a comfortless transit, at 7.30 A.M. at Kahului.

This is now the chief port of the island of Maui, and consists of an expansive coral-reefed, sandy-beached bay.

Here transhipment to a scow, or flat-bottomed oblong barge, occurs, to which passengers, freight, &c. &c., are helter-skelter consigned, and tugged ashore by one of the steamer's boats; horses and cattle having to swim in every case of transfer from ship to shore, or *vice versâ*, in these islands.

The spirit of enterprise seems more matured, by an advance of ten years at least, on Maui than elsewhere; for here is a narrow-gauged railway and the elements of a depôt for locomotion and prosperity in the planting interest, together with the establishment of telephonic communications with most districts.

The line runs to within a furlong of Wailuku (about three miles), a somewhat pretentious village having a Roman Catholic and Congregational church, and is surrounded by cane plantations with their several mills.

Having secured a room, with a bed in it, at the house of a Frenchman (M. Auguste), I was fortunate enough to find an English gentleman, lately arrived from the West Indies, occupying the adjoining apartment.

His great experience in the cultivation of the sugar-cane subsequently afforded me much aid, and from this fortuitous *rencontre* considerable practical information and advice was gained; and though he had no fault to find with the country, his opinion of the planters generally seemed to be that they knew as much about sugar-planting as a ploughman does of the sidereal system.

As previously remarked, the object of these pages being of practical rather than pictorial effect, it will suffice to observe that Maui, with its 400,000 acres, is divided into East and West Maui, of which about 300,000 acres belong to the eastern division, and on which the most wonderful, though now extinct, crater of Haleakala is situate. Its height above the sea is 10,000 feet, the bottom being 2,800 feet below that point. The greatest length of this crater from east to west is seven miles and a half, and the narrowest points are nearly three miles apart. The area is about sixteen and a half square miles, and its oval-shaped circumference is from eighteen to twenty miles.

The mountain has a circumference of ninety miles, and is divided into eight districts. That adjoining Makawao is Kula; then Hanuaulu, better known as the Ulupalakua plantation, with its soft rich soil; Kahikinui is a grazing district, and Kaupo and Kipahulu are rocky and unfit for high cultivation; Hana has good soil for sugar and tobacco, as also Koolau and Hamakua, the former

12

noted for its forests, and the latter for its well-watered plains.

The district of Makawao lies about 2,000 feet above sea-level, with a delicious climate and an extent available for agricultural purposes that cannot be far short of 100,000 acres, upon which nearly all classes of cereals and tubers could be raised under systematic irrigation.

The chief attractions of the western division centre upon Lahaina, the original source of the best species of cane grown on these islands. It was in early days the capital of Hawaii, and the harbour was much frequented by whalers. But its ancient glories have departed, and general decay seems but too all-engrossing, and even the planting interests here have a despondent air, though scholastic institutions seem to be prosperous.

The road from Lahaina to Wailuku, twenty miles, lies over a mountain track, and by a series of precipices that should never be attempted by a stranger, especially in wet weather, or unaccompanied.

It should be borne in mind that excepting the capital, hotels have no existence on these islands, and the traveller is entirely dependent for board and lodging on the first house chanced upon, whether pertaining to post-office or plantation.

It is always advisable to obtain letters of intro-duction from the agents —see list, Chapter XXII., p. 155—or someone in Honolulu before starting, when one is always welcomed ; for in most cases the traveller is considered to confer the boon on the host, especially if accompanied by a genial tempera-ment and the latest news from the outer world.

Not contemplating a visit to Maui on departure from Honolulu, I was accredited to no one ; so bethought me of the existence of one of the first and richest planters here, an ex-fellow-passenger from San Francisco.

A passable horse soon conveyed me to his residence, the most remarkable feature *en route* being the enormous growth of the cactus plants hedging the roadway, and the number of doctors pursuing their profession here, though the list of these fit for duty had been lately diminished through the incarceration of one for misdemeanour. And one may here remark that there is a fair field for duly qualified practitioners throughout the group, who would be in receipt of a subsidy from the Government and planters in, developed districts.

12 *

CHAPTER XXV.

MAUI.

" The stranger at my fireside cannot see
   The forms I see, nor hear the sounds I hear ;
   He but perceives what is, while unto me
   All that has been is visible and clear."

MINE—pre-ordained—host was from home, but
the charmingly-furnished drawing-room, in which
his wife cordially greeted me, was a model of
comfort, and European or American luxury.
" Sugar pays in these parts," was the inference
to be deduced, and the external surroundings proved
a general endorsement thereto.

At the Railway Depôt of Wailuku, early on the
following morning, another ex-fellow-passenger was
chanced upon with his family, who proffered a
pressing invitation to their plantation at Haiku,

towards which the railway had been completed some ten miles, and within seven miles of his residence.

In fulfilment of a projected inspection of the Spraekelsville plantation, the cars were quitted at that point, and nearer approach, through a continuous red-dust storm, found one amid a perfect army of white and black labourers.

Here a large 12-ton mill was in course of construction on a concrete foundation, while a not far distant site was under prospection for a similar one to be erected at an early date.

Surrounding these were fields, whose conjoint extent amounted to over 3,000 acres, with cane growing in various stages towards maturity, and a water-course thirty miles long for their constant irrigation.

Assuming the judgment of informants at the capital to be correct, and cane-cultivation to be a losing concern, what motive can induce the expenditure, in this enterprise, of so large an amount of capital as here represented ; especially when such disbursement is directed by one of the first and most shrewd merchants—a class not usually noted for its senility—in San Francisco.

Ahem! N.B. "When found, make a note of it."

Moreover, a long conversation with the resident manager elicited the opinion of his disapproval of planters on shares being admitted into the concern, as had, at the outset, in one instance occurred.

Here was food for contemplation, sufficient for most of the day, the residue being devoted to an exhaustive conference with my newly-found friend from the West Indies.

A few words with a young fellow-passenger, while using the means of locomotion adopted the previous day, proved we had met in similarity of purpose.

The train by which we travelled was made up of some dozen sideless trucks, or trawleys, on which the freight of sugar-containers, lumber, and other building material was placed. One truck only, "the Palace car," was furnished with benches and devoted to ten of the sex that, but for the sun-tint, might have been fair. The remainder of the voyagers being ensconced à *discrétion* on the trucks preceding the engine.

From various and frequent shuntings three hours were occupied in compassing the ten miles, though not without incident, from the trucks running over a Chinaman, with fatal effect.

From all accounts the average of such casualties appeared to be about two a week, and Chinamen the proverbial victims to indiscreet action.

At the extremity of the line we found horses awaiting us, and, galloping over the sandy expanse, arrived in time for dinner at an hour usually affected by " society " in European capitals for breakfast.

Fresh horses were at our disposal, on which thirty miles must at least have been covered from the various plantations and mills that were visited under the astute guidance of our host, who projected and supervised the construction of the great Haiku Ditch, previously alluded to.

In all past times the sugar industry of these islands has suffered severely from the absence of any ordinary or ingenious method of collecting, conducting, and distributing water for irrigation purposes at economical discretion.

Cane will grow prolifically and mature perfectly on these soils, provided this needful adjunct be given, and to our pioneer is due all honour for his perspicuity and persistent energy in leading the van of progress in this matter.

A grant from the Hawaiian Government to use the water streaming down the interstices of our old forest-clad friend Haleakala (House of the Sun), having been secured, the work was commenced in 1876 ; and from terrestrial difficulties surmounted, with the limited material at hand, this water-course may be classed as a stupendous and meritorious piece of engineering.

The channel, from its head to the outfalls on the plantations, is about twenty miles in length, and mostly meandering through the forests and a stratum of red clay ; but in many places tunnelling and blasting had to be resorted to.

The numerous smaller ravines and gulches are crossed by wooden flumes—longitudinal troughs— while over the larger, nine in number, the water is conveyed through 26-inch pipes.

The grade varies from twelve feet to the mile to one per thousand.

The most interesting portion is the piping that conducts the water down, across, and up the Maliko gulch—about 500 yards wide—and this inverted syphon was not constructed without considerable peril to the workmen engaged on it.

Its vertical lengths alternate between ninety feet

and 450 feet, the pipes at the bottom being thicker,
to resist the enormous pressure. The lengths are
clamped to the rocky sides of the precipices, and
a cursory glance thereat from the brink causes a
most unpleasant sensation.

The outfalls are trump-like, and fitted with
gratings and sand-boxes, the inclusive cost being
about £16,000.

This appears somewhat excessive. Other con-
duits subsequently completed cost from £150 to
£1,000 per mile, according to the physical difficulties
encountered; but the benefit derived has always
justified the outlay.

Visiting the Baldwin, Alexander, and Grove
Ranch plantations and mills, all in admirable condition, brought the sun's rays in the direction of
the dinner, or here supper, hour. Passing an
enormous dam-structured pool, in connection with
the irrigating works, we followed the example of
some native men and women in its enjoyable
depths, and witnessed several clever aquatic feats,
including leaps into the water from a height of
over eighty feet.

During the evening we were regaled with music;
the exhibition of pictures and curiosities collected

in almost every clime, and anecdotes connected with the experience of our much-travelled host, and the sugar interests generally.

Previous to turning into my most inviting bed-chamber, a meditative pipe evolved smoke-wreaths that reproduced the scenes and events lately presented to notice.

If sugar does not pay? how does this family and others, enjoy almost every luxury that had been produced?

How does it travel *en prince* almost yearly on the continents of America, Europe, and Asia? How did it construct that system of irrigation, but by sugar?

Ergo, the cultivation of sugar *must* pay, and so we'll try to make it before very long! was the result of such reflections.

The mill, close to the house, was in full operation in the morning ere I had completed a hurried toilet, and a ton of sugar was being turned out per hour from the mounds of cane-stalks floated down in a wooden flume from the upland plantations.

Breakfast and a feast of mangoes and rose-apples, off the trees in the garden, occupied the intervening period until our departure to catch the cars on their way back to Kahului, under the fullest impression that the sugar enterprise offers facilities to fortune-making, provided the elements of tact, energy, prudence, and system are at the prow, and Capital at the helm, of any-sized craft thus steered.

CHAPTER XXVI.

MOLOKAI, LANAI, KAHOOLAWE, AND HAWAII.

"Honour to those whose words or deeds
Thus help us in our daily needs,
And by their overflow
Raise us from what is low."

LEAVING all apathetic existence to the listless
aborigines, the tourist on pleasure bent and in
search of picturesque scenery, should visit the
Wailuku pass and valley; also Koolau with its
forest of ohias (native apples); and the Ulupalakua
plantation, noted for the exuberance and variety of
its vegetation, while we summarise the capabilities
of the rest of the islands in the group.

Molokai, or, as the natives style it, " the land of

precipices," has been mentioned before, as that on which the leper establishment is situated, and here, under Government restrictions, are these unfortunates settled.

Leprosy in this community differs from that of others similarly afflicted, in its constituent rather than cutaneous inoculation, the disease being more contagious than infectious, and is evidently a venene importation, intensified through indiscriminate intercourse.

Most that can be effected, in science and sympathy, is done for these poor things, who are outwardly cheerful and industrious, as their physical condition may admit.

This island is further noted for its numerous fishponds, that in former times were a source of revenue to its chiefs; and His present Majesty has an extensive cattle-ranch on the leeward side. But any adaptability of the soil for sugarcane cultivation is depreciated by the impassability of the mountains and difficulty in seaward approach.

Lanai, twenty-one miles by eight miles, has a central table-land, at an elevation of 1,500 feet, about 20,000 acres in extent, surrounded by mountains that are rich in ravines and shrubs, with a fair supply of water.   It is utilised for grazing purposes, and very sparsely cultivated.

Kahoolawe contains about 3,000 acres of table-land, leased out by the Government for the pasturing of sheep and goats. Its residents are most limited in number, and it is otherwise noted only for the peculiarity and fineness of certain brown-tinted grasses—that are plaited by the natives into hats—and the growth of the sweet potato.

The varieties of this esculent are very numerous in Hawaii nei; those indigenous to it amount to over fifty. The Waipalupalu, white and soft, seems to be a favourite amongst foreigners. The floury species are mostly of a dark colour externally, and those with an orange tint are unsavoury, if not totally unfit for human consumption.

Molokini is but a bare rock. Coastwise, as one passes through these channels, general neglect of piscation is only too conspicuous; a ready source of wealth for the indolent native to thus grasp, appears everywhere.

The passing steamer *Likelike* suggests a survey of the island of Hawaii, that, according to native notions, surpasses in extent and resources the all-accumulated British possessions ; whereas the entire acreage of the group is about equal to that of Yorkshire, Hawaii being analogous to the East and West Ridings of that county.

Hawaii apparently has a great future, especially now that the spirit of enterprise is associated with it in the construction of a railroad on the windward side. There, as elsewhere, vegetation is more abundant than to leeward, where, especially on Hawaii, it is hot, desolate, and covered with volcanic *débris*, lava being the predominant feature on this island.

The centre of attraction to most Englishmen and tourists on this part of the coast is Kaawaloa, where a plain white cone marks the spot, adjacent to that where Captain Cook fell mortally wounded. Its supporting base bears the following inscription :—

"In memory of the great circumnavigator, Captain James Cook, R.N., who discovered the Islands on the 18th of January 1778, and fell near this spot on the 14th of February 1779. This monument was erected in November, A.D. 1874, by some of his fellow-countrymen."

The cause or causes of the onslaught remain

enveloped in mystery; but, from traditional accounts, avarice and indiscipline, on either or both sides, appear to have been instrumentals.

This monument is in the Kona district, where also is Kailua, the seat of the coffee culture before alluded to, and for which it seems eminently adapted, as are thousands of unplanted acres here. Horse-hire (the only means of transport) being most expensive—16s. a day for the most sorry hack—the tourist will find it more expedient to purchase a horse or mule on landing, and part therewith on quitting the island; but better still is the plan of taking one's own horse, saddle, and bags wherever one goes, horse-freight on the steamers being £1 each journey.

Kau, to the south, is developing into a cane-growing district, of which Mr. Spencer's plantation at Naalehu is the most matured, though the eruptions of the crater of Kilauea tend to make the value and condition of property in this locality comewhat precarious.

Puna, to the south-east, is prominent in cocoa-nut groves, rough roads, and pools of tepid water, the depths of some of these being unfathomable. It has but two recognised plantations as yet, and is also in dangerous proximity to the destructive influences of Madame Pele.

Hilo, the eastern district, is the most fertile, as will be seen from the list, Chapter XXII. ; it is the most developed in cane cultivation. The Onomea plantation, and that of the Chinese Consul, Mr. Afong, at Kaupakuea, and the Kaiwiki plantation, owned by Messrs. Hitchcock & Co., three miles from Hilo, being the most considerable.

The soil appears most congenial to the cane from its general fertility and richness. It is of a dark chocolate colour, attributable to the profusion of ferns in which the district abounds.

The surrounding mountains attract a never-failing moisture, and the continuous rainfall in this part of the kingdom (averaging for twelve months ending December 1880, 155·23 inches) makes artificial irrigation quite unnecessary, and thus lessening the amount of capital required in production of cane. Yet, what is thus gained is balanced by the longer time the cane takes to mature, in most cases twenty months, as against twelve and fifteen months on the other islands, with their comparative dryness producing at least three crops to two from Hawaii.

Hilo, the capital of the island, is situated at the

18

head of Byron's Bay, and, next to Honolulu, is
the most populous town in the group, occasioned
not only by the sugar interests there involved, but
from residence of Government officials, and the
American and Roman Catholic Missions.   The
tourist will be re-paid in a visit to the novel and
attractive sight of the "Rainbow Falls," within
easy walking distance from the town; and, should the
sun be provident enough to shine, the view of a most
perfect arc in prismatic colouring will be procured.

The adjoining northward district of Hamakua
extends from the valley of Laupahoehoe to that of
Waipio, some thirty miles distant.   The latter is
one of the most fertile, rugged, and intensely
isolated spots on the globe, and contains a water-
fall, insignificant in volume, though second only
to Niagara in its depth of descent.

This tract of land has fine grazing qualities, and
is well adapted to the cultivation of cane and
coffee: but the few roads are execrable, and means
of transport laborious.   Freight and passengers are
conveyed between the cliffs and the vessels by
means of gangways, almost perpendicular in their
declination, from the heights overhanging the sea,
that vary from 200 to 2,000 feet.

Kohala is the most northern portion of Hawaii, and extends from Pololu, on the north-eastern point, to Wainanalii, adjoining Kona, with one or two indentations on its western coast, divided into North and South Kohala.   In extent it is about 300 square miles, and has signs of a large population in past times.   It is well adapted for cane, as evidenced by some eight plantations of considerable standing ; but the difficulty and expense of necessary road-making are essential drawbacks.

Fourteen miles from the port, at Kaiwaehae, is Waimea, a grazing-plain between the mountains of Kohala and Hamakua, and a district erst celebrated for its sepulchral caves, though now more favoured for its fine breed of horses.

The central portion of the island, from Waimea to Kau, is occupied by the mountains and sprays of Mauna Kea, 13,805 feet; Mauna Hualalai, 8,275 feet ; Mauna Loa, about 13,600 feet (all but as high as Mont Blanc); and the crater of Kilauea 4,500 feet.

In narrating a visit to Madame Pele during the summer of 1880, we cannot do better than quote one whose ink seems imbued with less high colouring than most enthusiasts affect in their descriptions of the indescribable.

13 *

CHAPTER XXVII.

MADAME PELE AT HOME.

" Nor could I ask a dwelling more complete,
Were I indeed the goddess that he deems me.
No mansion of Olympus, framed to be
The habitation of the Immortal Gods,
Can be more beautiful."

" It seems of little use to try to describe a trip to
the Crater of Kilauea, since words fail to express
the grandeur of the scene, or its desolate
appearance, its fires, the boiling and surging of the
molten masses, its intense heat and wonderful
powers. Like many others before us, we arrived
at Hilo with the intention of visiting the home of
the Goddess Pele, and our party of four mounted
horses, in early morning, starting off from town in

a pouring rain, for the frequency of which that part of the island is noted. After a scramble of eight or nine hours, up hill and down dale, over slippery lava-flows of known and unknown dates, through splendid tropical fern-forests, impenetrable except by trail, we reached the Volcano House at 5.30 P.M., wet through and tired, having stopped only at the half-way house for rest and refreshments. Here we found a courteous host, and a roaring fire in an old-fashioned but very smoky fireplace, around which we crowded and steamed away to our hearts' content and bodily comfort.

"Before retiring, and after our clothes had ceased to steam, we strolled out on the verandah, and before us, and nearly at our feet, obtained our first view of the volcano, a scene we never shall forget, with its fires so bright and vivid. When we first arrived, the low hanging clouds had hidden it; but now they had lifted, and the darkness of the night brought out the brilliancy in strong relief, the heavens being lighted as by some vast conflagration. Sometimes it would nearly die out, and, a moment later, flash forth in greater splendour. To the right of the main illumination were numerous smaller fires, caused by lava-flows on the more level portion of the crater, bursting forth with vivid flashes ; they would grow dimmer as it cooled off, only to break forth again in some other quarter. Sometimes the regularity of the lights made it seem as if we were looking down into some large city, with its myriads of street lamps ; then again it would change, seemingly into a train of cars, the head lights of the engine being larger and brighter than the smaller lights in the balance of the train ; we could, in fact, imagine all manner of things, as the forms and brilliancy of the fires changed position and density.

" The next day was very pleasant. We arose early, feeling much refreshed, ate a good breakfast, and with our guide and sticks set out for the crater, the brink of which was only fifty or sixty feet from the house, and which, had we known it the night before, might have made us restless ; but " where ignorance is bliss," &c.

" The first view we had of Kilauea in daylight was somewhat striking. Below us, at a depth of 600 feet, was a great black-looking field of lava, distorted into every conceivable shape, and which might be likened to an ice gorge in the northern rivers, only black in colour.

" After making the descent by a steep and zigzag path, passing the marble cross on the spot where Mr. Houlder died of heart disease in August of 1879—which, by the way, would make one of weak nerves shake somewhat as an introduction to the trip—we reached the lava, and commenced a two-mile pedestrian tour over loose slag and scoria to the new lake, which has been recently formed from a small blow-hole. Long before we reached it we could see the smoke and heat rising, and as we approached could see it also, both with feet and faces, for the heat and sulphurous flames were issuing from the many cracks in the lava, causing us to make rapid steps and occasional long jumps; but at the end, reaching the edge of the lake, its grandeur burst suddenly upon us.

" Below us some seventy or eighty feet was a lake of molten lava, boiling and bursting up to a height of thirty or forty feet, enclosed in a circular wall some 800 feet in diameter.

" In three or four places near the centre the molten mass was boiling, splashing, bursting wildly; while near the walls eruptions were taking place with great fury, the waves of lava surging from side to side, and breaking under our feet.

Now they would die down, only to be renewed again
and again, to follow in the same burning track. At
times the mass would separate in the centre,
showing a red fiery river · through the black sea of
lava, when in a great wave would rush, only to dash
up against the sides and be hurled madly back
again like the angry beating of the ocean's waves
against the cliffs.

"The wind would sometimes catch the fine lava
as it was thrown upwards into the air, and spin it
into 'Pele's hair,' so called, which resembles spun
glass, and which would be borne by the breeze
against the frowning walls, and over them on to
the surrounding lava fields.

"Here we stood for an hour on the brink of this
lake of fire, watching it in all its changeful moods.
Sometimes it would be very quiet for a spell, then
suddenly break forth again in great fury and force,
while we, chained to the spot by the magnificence
of the scene, were undergoing a process of alternate
toasting and cooling, the cool refreshing breeze on
the one hand furnishing one medium, the heat
from the burning lake on the other hand providing
the other.

"On noticing the gaping fissures near and around

us—we being between them and the lake—and re-
viewing our situation, we were somewhat forcibly
struckwith the idea that it would be well to see some
of the other wonders of the crater. Not that we
were at all fearful. Oh no! for the guide had just
comforted us with the information that since the
preceding Sunday over 100 feet of the brink had
fallen in, making the lake that much larger; and
the trembling of the place on which we stood was a
powerful argument in urging us to proceed with our
explorations.

" And we went, a sigh of relief escaping us when
we found ourselves at a safe distance. The guide
said that the new lake was the most dangerous place
in the crater, and we were glad to get away from it.

"After another pleasant (?) ramble over broken
lava, leaping from one cake to another, carefully
avoiding the holes and bubbles, we came to the old
crater of Halemaumau, and descended a nearly
perpendicular cliff of eighty feet over loose, jagged,
lava rocks, expecting every minute to get a fall, or
hit on our heads from a stone loosened by those in
the rear; but we arrived safely at the bottom with
a few contusions occasioned by the sharp stones.
Here we found " Madame Pele," very mild in

comparison with the place just left, although she was grumbling and splurging considerably.

" After gaining our breath we scrambled out again.

" From here we travelled up an easy trail along a perfect river of old lava, about twenty feet wide and half a mile long, to view the south lake ; and, as we were to the leeward of it, had the full benefit of a good dose of sulphur smoke, which came so suddenly upon us as to nearly stifle us.   We thought we had found a lucifer match factory in full blast.   We left this locality in a hurry, and it was some time before we could get a full breath again ; but we finally got out all right, inflated our lungs with purer air, and started for the north side of the crater.

For the first time, we now had a good view of our surroundings.   Here we were penned up in a crater or immense well some three by five miles in diameter, with towering perpendicular walls from 600 to 1,000 feet on all sides of us.   Under our feet was lava black and ragged, and twisted and turned in every conceivable shape.   Smoke was issuing from numerous cracks and openings, and intense heat was emitted by flowing lava which had no visible outlet.

" Our feelings may perhaps be considered to have been pleasant. They were not.

" Our guide now grew facetious, and thought to play a joke on us—a decidedly practical one too—as, without a word of warning (we trusting him implicitly because we couldn't help it), he led us over a recent flow of lava, which had partially cooled on the surface, and which was black like that around. But the red-hot kind was still flowing below, and in a very short time we perceived the point of the joke, and commenced to dance rather a lively measure, as our feet were nearly blistered by the intense heat, so we started for the cold lava without waiting for the guide to lead the way.

" The lava cools on the surface very quickly on coming in contact with the air, but inside remains in an incandescent state for some time, when the crust is strong but very hot; we did not know it then, but we do now.

" By this time we had become accustomed to our strange position and grew bolder, and approached a place where we could see the lava flowing. We found it hot enough to make its presence felt, and halted to partake of the lunch that had been

provided for us, which we did heartily, and while
eating watched the flow, ready at any moment to
travel in light order, and quickly, too, in case it
made a break towards us.   One might imagine that
it would flow rapidly, but, unless over a declivity,
it does not ; for, as before stated, it cools quickly
on the surface, while the inner and molten mass
will push through first in one direction then in
another, working its way in a winding course as
best it can.   No one can tell when or where it is
likely to break out ; consequently we watched
closely for any indications, ready at any moment to
change base.   While lunching we divided the time
in getting coin specimens, which made a pretty
memento of the visit, but found it difficult to get
one out whole, as the lava is very brittle.   We
made them by getting a lump of red-hot lava on a
stick and working coins into it, keeping them in
their places by turning up the edges of the lava
and letting them cool ; for although it looks black,
it is still very hot, and continues so for a long time.
Some, in fact, have to leave their specimens and
preserve themselves, on account of some sudden flow
taking place.

    " Having finished our lunch, and being well

toasted ourselves, we began our return journey over the desolate and black-looking mass towards the high wall and place of our descent.

"After a long, difficult, and tiresome climb, we at last reached the top and the Volcano House, very much exhausted after our jaunt of six or seven hours, covering a distance of twelve or fourteen miles, and it seemed pleasant to be in comparative safety again; we say comparative, because all around the house the steam issues in immense seams and cracks; but still the danger is not so imminent as below, where one does not know at what time an outbreak may be expected.

"During the evening we amused ourselves in looking over the registers of the house, in which nearly every visitor writes that "he arrived" at a certain hour, after a certain kind of trip, from Hilo generally; some report having had fine weather, but the majority of them bad. The specimens of wit are of all classes—good, bad, and indifferent— and the various handwritings are a study. Some of the sketches of incidents which transpired on the journey up were very amusing and well executed; and a perusal of the books well repays one for the time occupied, though some vandals have cut out leaves, either whole or in part, making it very aggravating to the reader.

" A quarter of a mile below the house is a fine sulphur bank, where one can occasionally find beautiful specimens of crystals, though the labour in getting them is great, as the steam is constantly rising, and the ground is quite hot.

" A new place for sulphur bathing has been prepared, which is said to take away the effects of lameness and fatigue. But the memory of the day's experience was so vivid we declined to try it, having had enough for one day.

" The next morning, bright and early, our breakfast was eaten with the sauce of a good appetite ; after which, our horses being saddled and brought to the door, we started on the return trip, bidding adieu to our courteous host, and arriving at Hilo at 5 P.M. tired and lame after the three days pilgrimage. We were saluted on our arrival with an earthquake, a proceeding of nature which is not frequent here, considering the great powers working within so short a distance.

" The ride from Hilo to the volcano, a distance of thirty miles over a very rough road, to one unaccustomed to the saddle will be found a trying one ;

the lava being so ragged and slippery in places, and the pathway so steep, that, unless your animal be a sure-footed one, it is a severe trial on weak nerves, and after the journey is accomplished the average traveller or tourist will be only too glad to enjoy the hospitality of the courteous host of the Volcano House. The present Volcano House,* a one-story frame building, fifty feet in length and twenty-five in width, with a spacious verandah extending along the side facing the crater, replaces the grass structure of former years, and is built a little to the south of the old site. The accommodations are good—much better than one would expect to find where everything has to be packed such a distance from the coast on the backs of horses and mules. The courtesies extended to our party, both at Hilo and the Volcano House will ever be gratefully remembered."—By " T. B. K."

* This is now gone, through Mauna Loa's lately issued writ of ejectment.

CHAPTER XXVIII.

THE GARDEN OF HAWAII.

" No greater wonders east or west can boast,
   Than yon small island on the pleasing coast,
   If e'er thy sight would blissful scenes explore,
   The current pass, and seek the further shore."

THE intelligence received from our friend Con, of
continuous inability to secure cane-land on fairly
equable terms, was far from encouraging, and
afforded anxiety anent the method of procedure,
though circumstantial evidence pointed towards
Kauai as the land of promise.

Our yet undelivered parcel forming a pretext, so
the first departing steamer—on this occasion the
right one—was boarded, for the most northern
portion of King Kalakaua's dominions.

HANALEI (DISTRICT AND PLANTATION), KAUAI, H. I.

No matter the nomenclature, or direction of the inter-island transit service, such is identical, and one descriptive passage serves for all.

We arrived by dawn at the eastern port of Nawili-wili that, surrounded by high bluffs, has all the essentials of a small but safe harbour with fair anchorage.

An element of homeliness was apparent when setting foot on shore, and a heartiness in the greetings of native and white frequenters of the diminutive log-piled jetty; and while waiting for the conclusion of the aquatic performances of the horses, some far from indifferent coffee and sardines was enjoyed at the Chinaman's store near the beach.

This island has, not inaptly, been named " The Garden of Hawaii," to which might be added "-or English Settlement," from the majority of proprietors and their white *employés* here being British born, or bearing allegiance to Her Britannic Majesty.

Owing to its situation it is less frequented by tourists than the other islands of the group; but, excepting the capital, is more civilised and compact, and claims the most agreeable climate.

Its shape is almost circular ; the western side being occupied by an impassable mountain range in abrupt elevation from the depths of the ocean, and from which the bluffs are inaccessible, except by ropes or ladders.

In proximity to the beach at Nawiliwili are extensive paddy-fields, and ascending either of the steep hills surrounding them, a ride of two miles brings one to the heart of the pioneer plantation of these islands at Lihue.

This estate is a joint-stock affair, and of about 10,000 acres in extent; is one of the most profitable extant. The soil is heavy, requiring much labour to break, and more so to make, up.

Here were observed ten yoke of oxen and four men to one plough, and still—owing to the exuberance of the soil—sugar apparently pays.

The Kekaha plantation at Waimea is the most western site of cane culture, at a point notable as that first touched by Cook in his discovery of the islands, 1778, as also of its having been a Russian settlement (temp. 1815), and locality of the final conflict between Kamehameha and Kaumuali for supremacy in 1824.

The scenery is very fine and similar to park and

pasture-land in England, between which and Lihue is the extensive enterprise of Mr. Wright at Koloa. This part is apparently too bleak for prolific produce of cane, yet the soil has encouraging composts.

From Lihue to Kapaa, fifteen miles, is an extensive tract of level grazing-land, in parts suitable for cane, backed by a range of mountains. On the inner side of this range are plateaux, also of excellent cane soil, awaiting the enterprise of man to plant and irrigate.

A second steamer calls at Kapaa once a week, to deliver freight and mails from Honolulu previous to touching at Kilauea on the way to the most northern port of Hanalei.

Kapaa is somewhat consequential from the plantations and works of the Makee Sugar Company— the Chinese hands forming quite a colony.

Four miles further brings one to the fields of the Kealia plantation, an off-shoot, on shares, of the Makee Company. From this point the road turns towards the shore, and crossing a ravine passes through the purely native cantonment of Anahola; many and thriving paddy-fields being sighted on the way. Thence two routes—one by a bridle-path

14 *

and ford, the other by a cart-track skirting the sea-shore—converge upon a level grassy expanse.

Guidance across the sands should be obtained from the inhabitants dwelling near at hand ; for the crossing is most treacherous, the quick-sand constantly shifting. The summit of the incline once gained, an extended mead greets one, most appropriate for cane (could water be provided from above or below), where an end-on four-mile gallop is too good to forego.

Crossing another gulch brings one to an exceptional country in scenery and agricultural resources as, through a park-like glade, one emerges upon the confines of the Kilauea Sugar Company's territory.

This property, some twenty miles from the shore to summit of the mountains, by five miles between the streams coursing through Panama Mor and Muahana Creek which form the boundaries, has every element to become the most advanced and remunerative in the kingdom.

Eight miles northward, through gulch and glebe, the district of Hanalei is gained. Erstwhile a coffee grove, now absorbed by the Princeville plantation, comprising 20,000 acres of fine arable soil, also a joint-stock enterprise.

Truly exquisite scenery encompasses this district, which is verdantly picturesque from innumerable streams, further advantaged by a good harbour, safe anchorage, and comparatively expansive penetrating rivers, with surrounding soil second to none for the culture of cane, coffee, indigo, and a variety of esculents, vines, and rice.

Six miles westward is the limit of achieved exploration, where stand the wonderful caves of Waiamoo and Waiakanaloa, containing subterrene and submarine chambers, whose treasures remain, as yet, uninvestigated.

Kauai possesses numerous picturesque features and waterfalls, the principal descents being those at Wailua and Hanapepe, whose volume and effect are influenced according to the rains; but this island is certainly the best watered of the group, while wheeled conveyances may be adopted from Maua point, south-west, to Hanalei, north-east, a distance along the coast of nearly seventy miles— quite out of the question elsewhere. An economical feature, moreover, is the absence of any necessity for shoeing horses or any other species of quadruped—or biped.

Niihau, fifteen miles south-west of Waimea by

sea, with its few inhabitants, requires a passing
glance from the deserving popularity of its owners
and their romantic domestic record, concerning
which they are somewhat reticent ; but it is understood that this family, of which there are three
generations enjoying providential good health, was
possessed of considerable property in New Zealand.

Being of retiring dispositions they were much
chagrined at finding a prospected railway was to
pass through their estate, though at a distance of
seven miles from their residence. This approximate invasion was deemed insupportable. The
property was sold, a vessel chartered, and to which
all their personality was transferred, and they sailed
in search of the seclusion apparently denied them
through human enterprise. Such seclusion was at
length found on the western heights of Kauai,
where they still reside, the management of a no
inconsiderable estate being personally conducted by
Madame la Grande-mère to this date ; and may
this dear old Scotch boddie continue such administration for many more years in health, happiness,
and prosperity, is the sincere wish of all who have
had the pleasure to make her acquaintance.

Niihau consists of some 70,000 acres of fine

grazing land, utilised as a sheep-walk.   It is, more-over, eminent in the production of a peculiarly-tinted and pliant grass from which the noted mats and hats are plaited, resembling those from Panama; but it is most difficult of access.

Lehua and Kaula are but sea-bird-swarmed rocks.

Thus having exhausted the islands, and delivered our parcel, let us return to Honolulu and avail ourselves of experience gained.

CHAPTER XXIX.

ALL ABOUT SUGAR.

" White-handed mistress, one sweet word with thee."
" Honey, and milk, and sugar ; there are three."

As the cultivation of taro may be safely left in
the hands of the natives ; rice and coffee of those
making such a speciality; sugar seemed to offer
itself as an enterprise with most attractions : so at
an agricultural conference it was then and there
agreed to devote our energies towards its production.

In the idea that other attention may be similarly
directed, such project will be speeded in the knowledge that every sort of sugar contains the following
properties in hydrates of carbon, viz. carbon,
hydrogen, and oxygen—the two latter in the same

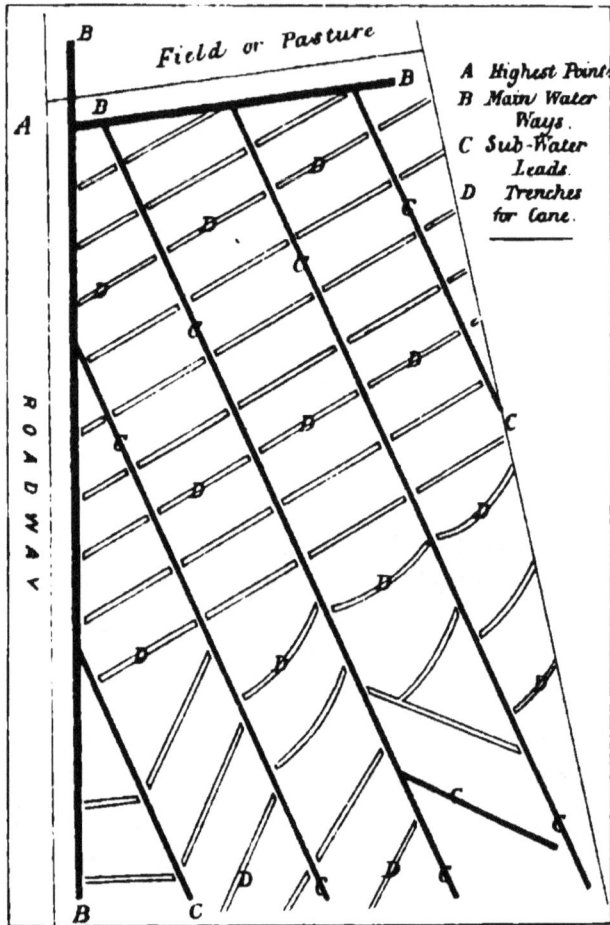

SECTION OF FIELD LAID OUT FOR CANE.

A Highest Point
B Main Water
       Ways.
C Sub-Water
       Leads.
D Trenches
   for Cane.

ratio as they form water, H_2; so that in chemical formula sugar equals C_6, H_{12}, O_6.

Almost all sugars are crystalline, and will always dissolve in warm water, but are indissoluble in alcohol; moreover all sugars are free from nitrogen.

No sugars are dissolvent in alcohol, but they are all "optical working," and the chief distinguishing feature of every sugar is its ability to undergo alcoholic fermentation.

Thus—

$$\text{Sugar.} \qquad \text{Alcohol.} \quad \text{Oxide of Carbon.}$$
$$C_6H_{12}O_6 \;=\; 2C_2H_6O \;+\; 2CO_2$$

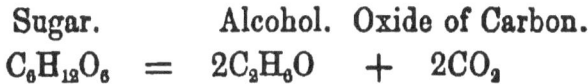

Alcohol is almost invariably produced from sugar.

Sugars may be classified according to the processes of their separate fermentation, some fermenting directly, others indirectly by changing into another class of fermentable sugar.

Those under the first group are called "glucoses," to which fruit and grape sugars belong. The second are styled "saccharoses," comprising milk sugar and cane sugar.

The purest form of cane sugar is sugar candy, in large even crystals.

It cannot withstand the working of acids or ferments—that is putrefaction, rotting, or decay—

and the sugar-cane, beet-root, maple or ahorn tree, and the areng palm—which also produces sago—are the only four plants containing sufficient " cane sugar " to extract it with advantage.

The chemical formula of " cane sugar " is $C_{12}H_{22}O_{11}$.

If cane sugar combines itself with water—sugar $C_{12}H_{22}O_{11}$ + water H_2O, it equals $2C_6H_{12}O_6$; then $2C_6H_2O_6$ is a mixture of fruit and grape sugar, viz. the two glucoses, and styled " invert sugar."

If a solution of white sugar be boiled in water, poured out into another receptacle so as to allow it to cool, an amorph (or deviation from a determinate shape or form) is obtained with transparent matter ; but if the cooling process be conducted slowly, a non-transparent matter is obtained, which process is called " sugaring."

If melted sugar be boiled for a considerable time, decomposition supervenes, molecules of water evaporate, and a substance (far richer in carbon than the original sugar) remains, called caramel, or burnt sugar, used for colouring spirits, vinegar, soap, &c. ; and the darker the sugar the richer it will be in caramel.

Caramel is very brown, and bitter to the taste, and is to be found also in the crust of bread.

All cane sugars can withstand the working of " bases " (hydroxides), or that with which acid unites to form a compound or a salt.

" Sandwich Island " sugar is extracted from the sugar-cane (*saccharinum officinarum*) which belongs to the family of grasses (*Triandria digynia*), and has a creeping root, with powerful organs of aspiration.

It is propagated by cuttings from the cane plant, the best being its upper joints or " cane tops "; but every part is good provided the joints are furnished with a perfect eye or bud, out of which the roots and shafts of cane spring, the latter attaining from eight to fifteen feet in height in from twelve to twenty months, according to the influences of soil, climate, seasons, and method of cultivation.

The best soils are those which make up into a fine friable mould, are retentive of moisture, and contain oxides of iron, alumina, and potash.

With regard to those of Hawaii, the following is an extract from a report lately issued by Professor of Agriculture E. W. Hidyard, of Berkeley, California.

" The Hawaiian soils differ widely from other known cultivated soils hitherto analysed, nearly approaching the celebrated black soils of Central Russia, the Tchernosem; but distinct in essential points. The soil is of unusual fertility and durability as regards two most important ingredients, viz. phosphates and nitrogen, which are three times in excess of ordinary soils, and it is eminently favourable for cane, where drainage is good. The requisite resuscitating fertiliser is potash, the home supply being found in the ashes of woods and weeds, and notably in the begasse."

The most congenial climate is of a warm and moist character, varied with moderate intervals of dryness, and especially when attempered by sea-borne breezes ; and cane will grow more luxuriantly on islands than elsewhere.

The seasons, as we have noticed, are all but uniform in the Hawaiian Islands; and the method of cultivation depends upon experience and common sense, guided by practical economy, tact, and temperance.

The leaves grow from each joint to from four to five feet in length, the edge cutting like a knife if improperly handled. The cane has a hardish outside bark, and a somewhat soft, white, fibrous pith, and in which pith the sugar is mostly contained.

The soil having been thoroughly ploughed, cross-ploughed, and harrowed, the fields are laid out in trenches, like asparagus-beds, from fifteen to twenty feet long, and six feet apart.

Water-ways B and C, diverging from the highest point of the field A, are then laid out with the plough, for irrigating the trenches D, as shown in the illustration given in the opposite page ; in which the portions of cane, from ten to eighteen inches in length, are placed by hand in an oblique direction to the subsoil—the eyes directed to the sides of the trench—and slightly but perfectly covered with earth.

Under proper irrigation the cane will appear above ground, like the leaves of the lily of the valley, in about three weeks from the time of planting, during which interval the fields should be securely fenced against the intrusion of cattle.

Constant weeding with hoe and cultivator is absolutely essential, together with systematic irrigation that can be pursued simultaneously. In three

months time the canes are periodically and carefully stripped of such lower leaves as have degenerated, after due performance of their functions, in
order to admit the air to permeate freely.   In
November the cane tops will throw out a feathery,
dove-coloured blossom, called tasselling, when the
limit of height is reached.

The plants are then denuded of all leaves ;
irrigation is relinquished, and the stalks cut off
close to the ground, the tops being used for replant-
ing other land.

The roots being left in the ground, speedily shoot
out again with renewed vigour, and yield an abundant harvest the following year in " Rattoon cane."

The cut cane is now conveyed to the mills and
worked as speedily as possible, for it deteriorates
if kept long.

Placed on a cane-carrier, or traversing platform,
the cane-stalks are by it conveyed to and between
three large-grooved cylinders (shown on next page),
impinging the one on the other (within the space
of one half to a quarter of an inch), which revolve
continuously and express the juice that falls through
a perforated strainer into a receptacle below.

This expressed sap is neither more nor less than

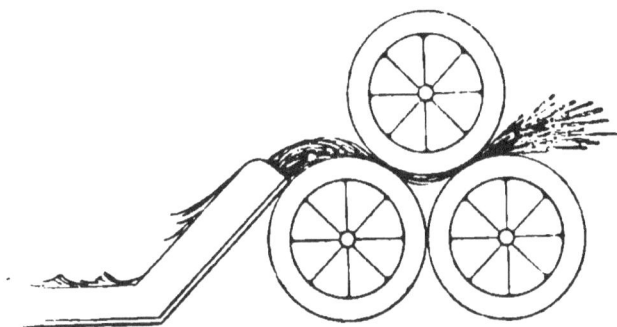

sugar-water, and in composition is, say, 72° water, 17·40° sugar, 8·40° cellulose, and 2·20° salts, albumen, &c. If 80° of sap be expressed from the cane such amount may be considered good.

This sap now passes through various stages of preparation—first into the clarifiers, where it is boiled and slaked with lime; thence it is run into the clearing pans and skimmed; and subsequently to the concentrating pans.

From these it is passed into the vacuum pans and reboiled, whence it descends to the mixing troughs.

The sugar being now, to a certain extent, crystallised, and of the consistency of thick treacle, enters the centrifugals in desired quantity.

The centrifugals are drum-shaped perforated

cylinders inserted in a stationary iron tub. The rapid and constant rotatory motion of these cylinders forces the treacle through the copper gauze, leaving the sugar in a dry crystallised condition, as found in domestic use, which is passed into the sugar-room, and there packed in bags ready for shipment.

CHAPTER XXX.

ALL ABOUT LAW.

" Is that the Law ? "
" Thyself shalt see the Act ! "

ON the decision arrived at in the opening of the
previous chapter, negotiations were at once resumed
for eligible land formerly under consideration. The
difficulties and quibblings, and little and big nasti-
nesses attendant thereon, will long be remembered ;
but, as " nothing succeeds like success," we buried
our hatchets and soon piloted ploughs in a very
favourable locality.

The policy of land-holders is to lease rather than
sell; but estates can be purchased here, as elsewhere,
on very reasonable terms, from the Government or
private freeholders. Money is monarch here ; but

15

in dealing with the question of capital, whose limit admits only of planting on shares with the proprietors of the land and mill, on terms sufficiently fair to afford encouraging prospects, the following form may serve as a guide toward an equitable covenant with reciprocal benefits.

It must be borne in mind that the miller always has the turn, and his object to grant land free is to afford supply and work for his mill for as many days in the year as possible ; and items relating to privileges of water for irrigation, seed-cane, carting, and site and extent of land for cultivation, should be distinctly embodied, as also the time for grinding the cane.

Form of Lease.

This indenture, made this
between A. of the first part, and B. and C. of the second part :

Witnesseth that, in consideration of the covenants of the said B. and C. herein-after set forth, the said A. hereby covenants to furnish to the said B. and C.   acres of cane-land on the sugar estate of the said A. on the island of   , one the Hawaiian Islands, for the term of   years

from the date hereof, with privilege of extension
for a further term of   years at the option of
the parties of the second part, under the same conditions as are herein agreed upon for the first term ;
to furnish seed-cane to the parties of the second
part for their first year's planting, and afterwards
to furnish them cane-tops for seed, at such times
as the sugar-mill of the said A. is grinding cane ; to
furnish them with water for irrigation purposes in
proportion to the area of land cultivated by them
in cane, as compared to the area of land cultivated
in cane on the rest of the said sugar estate, and
convey it to their fields ; to cart their sugar-cane
from their fields to the sugar-mill of   , and
manufacture the same in like manner as the
cane from the rest of the plantation is manufactured
into sugar during the same respective grinding
season ; and to pack and deliver at the said sugar-
mill to them, the parties of the second part, one
half of the sugar manufactured from their said
cane.   And the party of the first part further
agrees to allow the parties of the second part to
cut fuel for their own private use upon the freehold
lands of the said A. during the said term, and
also to furnish them pasturage for horses, mules,

15 *

and milch cows for their private use, and also a suitable house lot.

And the said B. and C., in consideration of the said covenants of the said A. in this agreement contained, hereby covenant to plant   acres of land with cane in the first year of the said term and not less than   acres each year after the first; to cultivate, irrigate, and strip the said crops in a thorough manner, until the same are properly matured; to conduct the water for the irrigation of the said crops from the ditches or flumes of A. at their own expense; to cut and place their cane, when mature, in a convenient manner for the carts or cars of A. at such times as the sugar-mill of   is able and ready to grind the same; to furnish containers for their own share of the sugar; to build all fencing necessary for the protection of the said crops, and the said house lot; to work their labourers the same hours as are customary on the rest of the plantation.

It is hereby mutually agreed between the parties of this Indenture—

First. That in each grinding season during the said term A. shall first grind   acres of his own plant cane, then   acres of the plant cane of the said B. and C., and so on alternately, until all the plant cane of both parties is ground and manufactured into sugar; and in the same manner shall the rattoon cane of the first and second parties be ground.

Second. That if at any time the said parties of the second part shall, in the opinion of A. or his manager for the time being, neglect the proper cultivation, irrigation, or stripping of their said cane, the party of the first part may, after four weeks' notice to the parties of the second part, specifying the neglect complained of, enter upon their cane-fields and put the same in order, at the expense of the parties of the second part, and may, upon persistence in such neglect by the parties of the second part hold possession of the said cane-fields, with option to cancel and determine this indenture.

Third. That the dwellings and fences which the parties of the second part shall build as aforesaid shall be considered as fixtures, which at the end of the said term shall be paid for by the party of the first part at a reasonable valuation, at the deter mining of this indenture.

Fourth. In case of unavoidable accident to the sugar-mill of   , whereby the same is disabled, or to the crops of the parties of the second part, whereby the same are destroyed or rendered unfit, the failure to carry out the covenants of this agreement thereby resulting, shall not be considered a non-performance of the agreement to the extent of rendering the party so suffering liable on the bond herein inserted, or to the extent of forfeiting this agreement.

Fifth. That in case of any dispute arising between the parties to this indenture, and incidental thereto, the same shall be referred to two disinterested arbitrators for settlement, one chosen by the party of the first part, and the other by the parties of the second part; the said arbitrators, if unable to agree, to choose a third arbitrator to act with them, the decision of the majority to be final.

Sixth. That the parties hereto bind themselves to each other in the penal sum of   as liquidated damages to be paid by the party failing to carry out the agreement.

Seventh, that the covenants and agreements of this indenture shall apply to and be binding upon the executors, administrators, assigns, and successors of the parties of the second part.

Witness our hands and seals the day first above written.

A.

Signed and sealed in   B.

   presence of   C.

D.

The signatories should then severally acknowledge their signatures to the document before an agent to take acknowledgments, and have the same stamped and registered at the Government buildings.

Although in the case of more than one person being a party or parties of the second part, such document would hold good as a partnership agreement, it is deemed advisable for them to subscribe to a deed of co-partnership, holding good in the Hawaiian Courts. The following, subject to necessary modifications, is that in general use and effect :—

Partnership Agreement.

Articles of agreement made and entered into this   day of   one thousand

Between A., now of   of the
first part; B., of   of the second
part; and C., of   of the
third part:

Witnesseth that the said parties hereto do hereby
mutually agree to carry on business at   in
the island of   as co-partners in
the business of planters, growers, and manufacturers
of sugar, and other products of sugar-cane, and
business connected therewith under the name, style,
or firm of

And they hereby mutually covenant, promise, and
agree with each other that they will carry on the
said business in co-partnership for the term of
          years, to be computed from the
day of   last, unless the same shall
be sooner dissolved in manner herein-after mentioned. And it is also hereby agreed that the
partnership capital or stock shall be the sum of
          to be contributed in propor-
tions   by the said partners in cash, or
by its equivalent, to the mutual satisfaction of the
said parties, and that the lease of the land known
as   held by the said
          shall be taken and held to be partnership

property, and that the said   shall
be resident managers of the said plantation, and
shall be credited with a salary at the rate of
                per annum for such term until the other
partners shall reside on, and take an active part in
the carrying on of, the said plantation.

That neither partner shall buy any goods for, or
contract with liability, on behalf of the co-partnership exceeding in amount the sum of
without the consent of the others.

That neither partner shall draw more than
                per month from the partnership
business, after said partners take an active part in
the management of the said plantation, while any
debts shall be owing by the firm.

That neither of the said partners shall draw,
endorse, or accept any bills of exchange, or promissory notes, or drafts in the name of the firm except
for partnership purposes, or become surety or bail,
or become answerable for any other person, or do
or suffer to be done any other act whereby the
partnership property or business may be prejudi-
cially affected.

Neither shall any partner absent himself from,
or cease to take an active part in, the management

of the said plantation without the consent of the others of them.

And that if any dispute or difference shall arise between the said partners, or any or either of them, touching these articles, or the said business, or the management thereof, the same shall be referred to arbitrators, one to be chosen by each, the decision of a majority of whom shall be final, such arbitrators having power to decree a winding up of the partnership in their discretion.

It is understood that this partnership cannot be dissolved unless with the mutual consent of the three partners in writing, or as herein-after provided, and that in the event of the death of either partner, his representatives shall have the right to take his share in the business and carry on the same with the survivors, according to these articles.

Proper books of account shall be kept, and shall be open to the inspection of each partner at all times and shall be balanced annually, and each party shall bear his   share of all losses incurred and shall be entitled to   share in all profits of the business.

Any partner who may give notes or other security for his share of the capital stock, and shall not meet the same when due, shall cease to be a partner; and all moneys paid in by him shall belong to the other partners, and absolutely forfeited as against the person in default.

Witness our hands and seals the date first-above written.

A.

Signed and sealed in   B.

    presence of   C.

       D.

This document should also be acknowledged and stamped, and the partnership recorded at the registrar's office.

Further, it will be necessary to appoint an agent in Honolulu to act in the capacity of commission agent, broker, banker and factor, with whom a contract also should be made, somewhat as follows :—

Agent's Contract.

This agreement, made and entered into at Honolulu, Island of Oahu, H.I., by and between A. & Co., merchants, of Honolulu aforesaid, parties of the first part, and B., C., and D., all of parties of the second part :

Witnesseth that the said parties of the first part agree to act as agents for the said parties of the second part, and are to purchase all merchandises and supplies for which the said parties of the second part are to pay them a commission of per cent., and also agree to honour all drafts drawn upon them by said parties of the second part. The parties of the first part also agree to receive and sell for account of the parties of the second part their crops of sugar, for which they are to be allowed a commission of per cent. on net sales if shipped to San Francisco, after deducting all shipping charges incurred, including a commission of per cent. of the San Francisco agents ; or if the sugars are sold in Honolulu, then the said parties of the first part are to be allowed a commission of per cent.

The said parties of the first part are to make up an account of receipts and disbursements at the end of each quarter year, and are to charge and allow interest at the rate of per cent. per annum on all accounts, both debit and credit.

The said parties of the second part agree to place their business in the hands of Messrs. A. & Co., parties of the first part; to supply them with funds

at all times, so that the said A. & Co. shall not be
called upon to make any advances; or if called
upon in accordance with mutual agreement, only
up to the sum of   , at the rate for the
period of such advance of   per cent. per
annum.

To send all orders for merchandise and supplies
to the said parties of the first part, and to pay them
a commission of   per cent. for all purchases
made by them, also to consign all sugars manufactured or produced to the said parties of the first
part, for sale, and if sold in San Francisco to allow
them a commission of   per cent. on al
net returns, allowing for all freights and shipping
charges, and a commission of   per cent. to
the San Francisco agents, or if sold in Honolulu
the parties of the first part are to be allowed a
commission of   per cent.

All orders or drafts drawn by said parties of the
second part are to be advised when drawn, and the
said parties of the first part are to be allowed
charge up to the debit of the parties of the second
part, all such drafts or orders on receipt of the
letter of advice.

It is mutually agreed by all the parties hereto,

that this agreement shall continue in force for the term of   years from the date of this contract.

Witness our hands and seals, the date first above written.

	A. & Co.
Signed and sealed in	B.
the presence of	C.
E.	D.

Part of the agents' manifold functions is to provide the plantations for whom they act with labourers. Printed forms of labour contracts, in the Hawaiian and English languages, are easily obtained at slight cost, and are signed in duplicate by employer and employed.

The usual contract is for two years' daily service of ten hours, Sundays and general holidays excepted, at wages ranging (according to supply) from ten to twenty dollars a month, and food and lodging, or say five dollars in lieu of such provisioning.

A most serious drawback in connection with the procuration of labour is the iniquitous system of advances, occasioning a deep dip into capital at the outset.

Custom makes this unavoidable, especially in the

case of outstanding emigration accounts with the shippers. These advances range from thirty to one hundred dollars per capitâ.

It is balanced, however, in course of time, provided one keeps a sharp look-out against desertion before the advance is worked off.

———————

CHAPTER XXXI.

HOW IT 'S DONE.

" So bring us to our palace, where we 'll show
What 's yet behind, that 's meet you all should know."

CONSIDERABLE anxiety, labour, and money would
be saved by the inexperienced *in embryo* planter
were he to invest his capital in an established
concern, and with someone of whose antecedents
he is aware; and although the share of incomings
would be insignificant at first, yet experience would
be gained for eventual and more profitable direction
of a similar enterprise on his own account, if so
minded, and in comparative security.

If preferring to launch at once, the allowance of
one man to every five acres under cultivation will
be found adequate; and the requisite amount of

capital should not be less than $150, *i.e.* £30, per acre.

This sum will include subsistence until the crop comes in—say fifteen months—and will be found ample for all ordinary needs.

An excellent plan, hitherto unadopted in Hawaii, is to contract with a "Boss" Chinaman for him to prepare the land, plant and cultivate the cane to maturity, and cut it, under an agreement, at so much money per ton or cwt. of sugar manufactured from the cane produced under such contract, after deducting the amounts necessarily and previously advanced to such contractor per mensem.

By such means every hand would be interested in making as much "sugar in the field" as possible. This may be open to objections, but would be a source of relief to the novice in freedom from unknown risk and numerous inevitable mistakes at starting.

As taking the bull by the horns is dear to the heart of Englishmen, whether within the confines of Madrid or the Sandwich Islands, and in the assumption that land has been secured by lease or otherwise, and labourers engaged to work it, it will be necessary to equip oneself for plantation life.

16

This, excepting draught power, may be effected in Honolulu.

Until the crop is harvested, manufactured, and sold, the outgoings for equipment and management of a plantation of 50 acres may be condensed thus:

Planting Fifty Acres—First Year.

	* $	£
Passage-money, &c. to Honolulu .	500 or	100
Wages of ten men at $20 a month for fifteen months	3,000 or	600
Maintenance of self, stock, &c., for fifteen months	750 or	150
	4,250 or	850
Capital Stock.		
1 dwelling-house . . .	1,000 or	200
1 labourers'-house . . .	125 or	25
Fencing fifty acres . . .	375 or	75
Implements, household and general necessaries	1,750 or	350
	$7,500 or	£1,500

Supposing this £1,500 to have been taken out of a 5 per cent. investment, which in fifteen months would produce £93 15s. 6d., so such sum must be made in this time not to be at a loss.

In the erection of houses, the cost of sawn

* The dollar is herein calculated at 4s. sterling.

timber and builing materials averages in Honolulu
$40 per 1,000 feet, inclusive of freight to the port
of destination, but an approximate estimate may be
arrived at from the calculation of the cubic contents
of the proposed dwellings at from 5d. to 1s. per
cubic foot, inclusive of freight, carting, and construction, according to the class of workmanship
embellishments, &c.

The necessary implements, &c. will consist of—

		$	£
1 Moline plough complete . . .			
1 light ,, ,, . . .		150 or	30
2 harrows ,, . . .			
1 cultivator ,, . . .			
Hoes, cane-knives, spades, picks, car-penters' tools, lanterns, &c. .		50 or	10
1 two-wheeled cart, with four spare wheels for hauling . . .		200 or	40
Household necessaries per capità .		50 or	10
Harness and horse-gear . . .		250 or	50
6 oxen at $150 per yoke = $450			
2 horses and 1 pony = 350			
Or ——— $800		800 or	160
8 horses at $100 = 800			
Or			
8 mules at $100 = 800			
Sundries, and depreciation . . .		250 or	50
		$1,750 or	£350

16 *

Having thus calculated in outline the cost of production by an ample margin at $150 or £30 per acre,* we will now take into consideration the return produce.

Sandwich Island sugars realise in San Francisco from £24 to £26 per ton, from which must be deducted freight, commission, brokerage, &c.

In view to make full allowance for all such contingencies, the net price obtained by the planter shall be calculated at $110, or £22 per ton.

The fertility of the soil of these islands is certainly exceptional, for it is now well established that, with irrigation and good manufacture, one acre of best cane land will produce five, six, and even so high as seven tons of good crystallized sugar.

Planters in other cane-growing countries, visiting these islands, have stated their inability to produce the crops yielded in Hawaii; but apart from such extraordinary returns, an ordinary well worked plantation will average the production of three tons of good sugar per acre without difficulty.

* Expenses in production will prove less than $100 or £20 per acre.

On the foregoing basis a further calculation may be thus made :—

FIRST SEASON.

Return Produce : Fifty acres of Plant Cane.

Grower's half-share of produce at three tons
per acre = $\frac{150}{2}$ = 75 tons—75 tons, at a
net receipt of £22 = 75 × £22 =   . £1,650

Deduct cost of production at £30 per acre
£30 × 50 acres   1,500

Or a net profit of . . £150

In addition to £150 included for maintenance during the period of realisation.

SECOND SEASON.

It is now that the planter will secure the fuller benefit of previous outlay and labour ; for, as before remarked, the canes have been cut down, and the roots are again speedily shooting forth new suckers from each hill in equal, if not greater vigour.

The absence of preparative ploughing, harrowing, trenching, and planting, together with reduced work with the hoe and cultivator, must sensibly diminish the cost of production, which will be found to average £6 per acre only, so that on harvesting the crop the following calculation is almost a foregone conclusion.

SECOND SEASON.
Fifty acres of Rattoon Cane.

Grower's half-share, as above . . .	£1,650
Deduct cost of production, £6 × 50 acres .	300
Net profit . .	£1,350

Thus the planter has lived rent and board free for two years and a half to find his banking account augmented in that period by

The first season's proceeds . . .	£150
The second season's proceeds . . .	1,350
Total . .	£1,500

or his capital fully returned to him.

But during the latter fifteen months he will have fenced, broken up, planted, and cultivated at least an additional fifty acres, that cannot well yield him a lesser profit than his first year's venture of £150; which makes his net profits amount to £1,500 + £150 = £1,650 in two years and a half; or at the rate of £44 16s. per cent. per annum.

So that sugar would seem to pay fairly well after all; but if the capital be doubled and proceeds quadrupled, a fair idea may be gathered of the *Miller's* profits.

In substantiation of such allusions, the plantation of the district adjoining that we are interested in was not long since shackled with a debt of $36,000, or £7,200. One crop not only released it of such burthen, but the proprietors found a considerable balance to the good in the hands of their agents besides.

THIRD SEASON.

The grower will now be in a position to cultivate 100 acres per annum, with a proportionate decreased expense in production estimated cost being at $100, or £20 per acre, because of having no house to build, and outset necessaries and gear to purchase; to say nothing of more economical and systematic working.

One hundred acres Plant Cane.

Grower's share on previous basis $\frac{200}{3} = 150$ tons at £22	£3,300
Deduct cost of production, £20 × 100 acres .	2,000
	£1,300
Add to which fifty acres of rattoon cane of second season's planting	1,350
Total net profit . .	£2,650

He would now be able to cultivate 200 acres a year, if so minded, but if continuing with 100 acres per annum only, the fourth season gives him—

FOURTH SEASON.

One hundred acres Plant Cane.

The same amount as the third season, viz. .   . £1,300

Add to which 100 acres of rattoon cane of
     third season's planting.   Grower's
     share $\frac{100}{2}$ = 150 tons, at £22 .   . £3,300

Deduct cost of production, £6 × 100 acres   600

                                          ——— 2,700

                          Total net profit   . £4,000

Therefore the third season's proceeds of   . £2,650
     (which he did not utilise in the cultiva-
     tion of extra land), added to that of the
     fourth season   4,000

Equal a net profit in five years of   .   . £6,650
     On a capital of £1,500.

Should he then prefer to relinquish the
     undertaking, the sale of his buildings
     and general stock-in-trade could not
     realise less than   500

So that his calibre is represented by   . £7,150

To this must not be omitted his maintenance for five years at £150 for fifteen
months = £150 × 4 seasons   .   .   £600
                                        ─────────
                                          £7,750
                                        ─────────

which gives a profit at the rate of over 93 per cent.
per annum during the five years; whereas his
£1,500, even at compound interest for the same
time, in the original investment would amount to
but £1,914 7s. 6d.   So, allowing £150 for a
luxurious passage home, where he arrives with
£7,000, and that reinvested in the Five per Cents.,
gives him £350 per annum, instead of the original
income of £75 per annum, with an enjoyable
change into the bargain—a solution consistent
with the mysterious disbursements that exercised
previous attention elsewhere.

CHAPTER XXXII.

PRACTICAL PLANTING.

"One ounce of practice is worth a ton of theory."

IT will be obvious that such issue is not attained without contention with numerous discouragements and difficulties that must be borne and surmounted on encounter, otherwise the opening would not exist.

For instance the geographical position and expensive, though enjoyable, journey, on nothing but pictorial report of the capabilities of the country, wherein (if truth abide) such is usually dove-côted with other " travellers' tales."

No! for the establishment and administration of an estate in an undeveloped country, wealth of physique, good constitution, well-balanced brains, with self-reliance, temperance, firmness mingled with courtesy and kindness; patience, untiring energy and fertility in expedients, are essential to the planter's interest; so as to enable him to cope with any circumstances under which he may find himself placed, and which may be summed up in the one word "education."

These pages have long since exceeded the limit of their first intent; yet a few additional remarks in guidance towards successful cane-culture in the Hawaiian Islands may not be *de trop*.

The *sine quâ non* is sufficient capital, according to local circumstances, at starting; herein quoted at £30 per acre.

A good description of cane, suited to the soil, should be chosen, and stimulated only with such matter as will tend to enrich the juice, the greatest fertiliser being its own leaves, and cane trash generally, which should be returned to the soil close to the roots, after the juices are expressed. This trash should on no account be needlessly burnt as fuel, coals being actually cheaper in the end.

The dwellings should be serviceable, yet plain; for

additions and embellishments can always be made.
The employés should be well housed, and treated
with considerate discipline. The fences strongly
made, five feet in height. Posts (twenty feet apart
at most) and battens are better than wire, are
more effective, tidy in appearance, and cheaper:

It will be advisable to purchase a good tent in
San Francisco, for service during the construction
of a dwelling-house ; it will always prove useful,
and can be tenanted in all weathers.

Purchases should be made to the extent only of
actual necessaries, for it is wonderful what one can
do without. " What the eye does not see the heart
does not grieve for."

Payments should be just and prompt, the
employés being paid by the month, and *advances*
only entertained for procuration of food. Systematic
book-keeping should be practised, and results
closely watched and compared.

In the schooling and general treatment of horses,
mules, and oxen the utmost patience and gentle-
ness should be exercised, addressing each by name,
and talking to them the while, in view to engross
their attention and enable them to overcome innate
nervousness. In Australia each bullock is appealed

to by words, and knows his name; and the brutality
of whipping and goading them, and twisting their
tails (as performed in India and elsewhere) should
on no account be permitted.

As an instance of what can be done, we commenced operations with ten perfectly untrained
young horses, wild as zebras, which, for the first
week, were the nuisance of our existence, as
well as our sole occupation—for the time being
—from hunting for and driving them back to
enclosed pastures, whence they had made their
escape.

These hawks of the prairie were severally
attracted to person and place, harnessed, and
performing their appointed duties within less than
twenty hours after being taken in hand. There
wasn't a whip in "the crowd," neither did we
possess a blinker.

The carts, harness, &c., should be light, yet
strong, fitted to the work required and the draught
power engaged; mule power being preferential
generally.

The hours for field labour are from 6 A.M. to
11.30 A.M., with a break for dinner, work being
resumed at 12 noon, and continued until 4.30 P.M.

But mill work should be continuous, if possible, and performed by relays.

Draught operations are best conducted between 6 A.M. and 10 A.M., with four hours interval for food and rest, and continued from 2 P.M. until 5 P.M.

When the moonlight admits, ploughing, cutting cane, and carrying, may be effected at night.

In the absence of rain, irrigation should be thoroughly conducted so as to give each acre such requisite nourishment once in eight days at least. This also can be done by the gangs at night without moonlight, as lamps, made for the purpose, are used.

One man can irrigate from one acre to ten acres in ten hours, in accordance with the flow of water at disposal, the lay of the land, and the system of irrigation adopted.

The fields cannot be kept too clean from weeds ; and terriers would be a great acquisition in antagonistic force to the rats, which infest most cane plantations.

A preparation of arsenic and flour, thinly spread upon roofing shingles which may be placed along the furrows, will do wonders towards the destruction of such vermin.

In cases where the " borer " may appear, cutting down and burning the infected stalks is the best preventative; but kerosine oil will keep off most invertebrates.

Finally, the juice should be most thoroughly expressed from the canes, and defecated and concentrated on the most approved methods.

Sugar manufacture is almost as close a trade as that pursued by the Guild of Fishmongers, and it would be judicious on the part of the intending planter to attach himself to a sugar refinery before going westward, especially as the apprenticeship would occupy but about three months, which would enable him to practice sugar-boiling as a well-remunerated profession.

CHAPTER XXXIII.

MAUNA LOA'S LATEST ISSUES.

" What should be said of him cannot be said,
    By too great splendour, is his name attended."

To touch upon the various vicissitudes of plantation
life would so trespass upon even extraordinary
interest evinced in such subjects, as to invite further fatigue from, and augment—what already is
feared to have been—importuned, attention ; but
whatever momentary concern or anxiety (insepar-
able to a planter's existence) may arise, a golden
and ludicrous infusion will be there, like the " silver
lining " accredited to the darkest cloud.

It is not long since many residents divined cause
of excitement and alarm from the sulphurous
smoke-clouds enveloping the island of Hawaii, and

even canopying the rest of the group; for, about
7 P.M. on Friday the 5th November 1880, the
" Royal Fire Mountain " of Hawaii burst forth in
majestic aspect, though comparative silence.

It is recorded of previous eruptions on Mauna
Loa that that of 1852 was magnificent and terrible;
when jets of lava and flaming matter ascended to
1,000 feet above the crater's summit, and volcanic
operations shook the island throughout.

The latest activity had many points in resem-
blance to that of 1855, which also burst out,
without previous warnings, on the side of the
mountain, and tunnelling underground as well as
flooding the surface, surrounded the adjoining
districts with masses of rock and scoriæ.

1859 witnessed a recurrence, when the molten
lava flowed in several streams full sixty miles from
the crater's topmost edge, and found its way into
the sea at Kiholo.

Twelve years then seem to have elapsed ere Pele
again sounded her detonating trump of doom, accompanied by visual manifestations in re-enkindled
embers of her wrath.

This grand eruption, reports the *P. C. Advertiser*,
commenced the latter part of March 1868 with

17

great shocks of earthquake and remarkable ebbs and floods of the sea.

" On the 2nd of April the sea rose, and swept away villages and a multitude of people. The top of the hill Ipuu, in Kau, was lifted up by a mighty steam outbreak, and whelmed almost instantly a village containing about sixty people, who lie buried as they were—eating or sleeping, with their calabashes or cooking utensils by their side—to be exhumed some day as a Hawaiian Pompeii, to satisfy future antiquarian study of this archipelago. And the mud stream of Keiwa flowed about three miles with the velocity of a fleet locomotive, as it captured and submerged fleeing animals— wild cattle and goats. At the same time great flows of lava took place in Kahuku, shocks of earthquake tossed the land to and fro, throwing down all the stone walls of Kau, and compelling Rev. J. F. Pogue to preach out on the open plain, as he had reason to fear that his church would tumble down upon the heads of himself and congregation. Then the shocks of earthquake were sensibly felt on Maui, Molokai, and Lanai. The air was also obscured with smoke, and watchers on the summits of these islands observed not only the glare of the mighty lakes and rivers of flame seventy to a hundred miles distant, but witnessed remarkable gaseous and electric phenomena, darting coruscations of light from the mighty fiery dome. And whilst the summit crater, at an elevation of 14,000 feet, and the lower flank craters were pouring forth their rivers of fiery earth, the ever-constant crater of Kilauea, at an elevation of only 4,000 feet on the flank of the same mountain, was comparatively quiet. The floor of its Halemaumau, or eternal abode of the fire goddess Pele, had sunk about 500 feet below its usual level, and was still."

And with regard to the latest volcanic phenomena the same newspaper remarks that,—

" According to all information now received, the eruption of this year breaks forth without any of the wonted terrific volcanic heraldry—yet majestically. As in 1859, the flaming reservoirs of the mountain's *enceinte* have found easy vent,—and as then, the vast volume of molten matter forming several rivers of flame are flowing in different directions, and may continue to flow for several months, as occurred during that year. The vast plain, or divide, lying between Mauna Kea and Mauna Loa, has been overflowed, overspreading

17 *

some of the land of the ranch of Mr. Gay; and
from thence rivers flow down the Waimea side and
the Kona side of the mountain. The remarkable
flow of scoriæ and rocky debris, described in the
correspondence we publish, is the effect of lava
flow in a covered or subterranean duct. You see
a mound or ridge of dark scoriæ, or debris, fifty or
a hundred feet wide, by ten to fifteen feet high,
moving along; even as someone may have observed
the effect of the underground working of a mole;
as he burrows and tunnels onwards, the observer
notes the onward movement of a miniature ridge
of earth—so the mighty volcanic mole is working a
passage through subterranean channels near the
surface; and as it marches the observer sees
the heaving movement of the surface. In places
the lava-flow is more apparent, and its white
flaming liquid is mingled with tumbling masses of
rocks and earth hurled onwards. The lava, which
sometimes is very rapid at its first issue from a
vent or crater, moving at the rate of ten or more
miles an hour, sometimes slackens its speed as it
progresses, until a sluggish course of two or three
miles a day is attained. So these rivers of molten
lava now flowing down the slopes of Mauna Loa

may continue for some time to come their flaming course, and afford an opportunity for the wonder-seekers to come from afar to witness the greatest natural wonder of the world."

Moreover, with reference to marine effects, it is from the same source quoted that,—

"Captain Kaaina of the schooner *Pauahi*, arrived yesterday morning from Hawaii, reports that on 16th instant, whilst off Honokaa, Hamakua coast, about three miles from land, the smoke was so dense that the land was entirely obscured all day, till about 4 P.M., when the smoke lifted a little, and land could be seen once in a while. The Pauahi's boat that went ashore on Monday evening, could not make its way back to the schooner on Tuesday, on account of the dense smoke and darkness.

"At 4 P.M., as the smoke had lifted, the captain and crew of the schooner saw ahead of the vessel, and not distant more than about a quarter of a mile, a submarine eruption of scoriæ and rocks, accompanied with clouds of steam. The ebullition of the sea and spout of volcanic matter lasted about three minutes. The captain in alarm ordered the man at the wheel, the vessel being then under way,

to head her off; but as she was about to wear
round, they saw astern another submarine eruption.
In this they could only perceive a great ebullition
of the ocean, and an ascending column of steam,
which continued visible till night set in. The sea
all around the vessel during this time was in a
fretful state, making a heavy chop sea, and the
schooner rolled and rocked heavily."

Having ascertained that the eruption was still
as intense as in the first stages of its flow, and
that the safest approach was from Hilo, we subsequently found a coign of vantage on the south
side of the mountains, and encamped beside some
mamani trees where, on clearance of the clouds and
fog, a panoramic exhibition beyond description
greeted us.

Here it was found that the original source was
above that of the eruption of 1855-56, and pursued
a somewhat similar course.

The whole line along the summit was environed
with torrents of fire that streamed furiously down
the slope in intense brightness, till obscured by a
huge and dense cloud and fog bank, encompassing
the low lands.

Ascending the hill towards Puna, the whole

stream lay before us, and though the moon had set, one could read with the greatest facility.

The nearest analogy to this magnificent sight may be conveyed in the microscopical medium of a British iron-foundry when, at strike time, its blast furnaces emit their liquid contents, and whose continuous course is conducted through the moulding channels.

Away in the far-above distance, towards the starlit heavens, shone the brilliant flame-head; thence streamed liquid lava, at a white heat, without a break for thirty miles.

About a mile from the point of issue a division occurred, furthering the formation of a parallelogram, and at reunition, five miles below, the stream ran down three-fourths of a mile in width, rolling along with gaseous and electric emanations flashing up, and dying down, along its whole edge.

Through the cool night air came intermittent detonations resembling explosions from the magazines of a shell-rained city; doubtless from the old lava caverns, their heated atmospheric contents bursting through lower and upper lavic crusts.

A sonorous rumbling, similar to distant heavy

artillery practice, would now and again seem to come from the mountain's deepest recesses.

Then occurred frequent cannonades as of near, then distant thunder; the fiery flood being comparable to nought but continuously fluctuating flames of frozen lightning.

Again, as rooted to the spot we watched it, another stream started from the mountain's rim, and flowed along its ridge for about two miles, in a steady rushing stream.

Mounting our horses, a toilsome progress brought us across the old flow, within twenty feet of where hell itself seemed broken forth in this ceaselessly flowing molten-massed river, that carried along its bed huge rocks and tons of petrified boulders, an they were paper boats.

Avalanche after avalanche of fire whelmed down, whose volume could not be less than from twelve feet to thirty feet deep, by one to two miles wide, of rolling, tumbling, gliding, red-hot rock, liquid lava, scoriæ, and sand, all in one continuous roar. The heat being terrific; and the surface, as it cooled, assumed a dull brick colour.

After firing sticks, &c. from the edges, this awe-inspiring scene was relinquished to its untrammelled course, and even at a distance of seventy miles was still witnessed this canopy of flaming light, that covered the mighty dome of Mauna Loa, and mountains of seething lava that poured down its flanks, whence ever and anon ascended columns of smoke and steam, until the lowering clouds obscured from our dazed sight these latest manifestoes of the King of all Volcanoes.

CHAPTER XXXIV.

A WAY-UP TIME.

" Then hurrah for the chase, the glorious chase,
    And may it for ever stand,
  As firm and strong and last full long
    In this so 'sun-kissed' land ;
  And may old England's sons have many hard runs—
    And I hope that for many a day
  Both habit and trew at the meets will accrue
    When the mule is far away."

EXCEPTING the Island of Hawaii, the Sandwich Islands may be pronounced as exempt from volcanic excesses as the European or American continents, and it would appear that such visitations are confined to districts commanded by Mauna Loa and its attendant satellite Kilauea, and even to these in less frequent recurrency; so there is no grave cause for alarm on the score of indiscriminate ebullitions, except perhaps on the part of proprietors in the immediate neighbourhood of the fire-king.

In regard to the heretofore excessive death-rate of the Hawaiian race, it is argued with much propriety that such is an incorrect view at the present time, as, notwithstanding an universally incidental epidemic, the race is not dying faster than others in reputedly healthy climates, but that it is the *low birth-rate* that is deplorable, and that too few are growing up to supply the places of those gone to the great majority. There is much in this.

The Government has had its attention drawn to the prolific tropical races of Eastern Archipelagos; and the main question appears to turn upon the probability of such continuing to labour and multiply under new circumstances and surroundings.

A source of depopulation may be extracted from an essentially native institution named " Hula Hula," erroneously termed a dance.

The pretty, yet threadbare, programme of " the quarrels of lovers being the renewal of love " is the

synopsis of this ballet, and as reflected in these
realms may—without mincing matters—be classed
amongst most disgusting of exhibitions; all in-
nocence of "poetry of motion" being supplied by
much quantity and very indifferent quality, so the
less said about it the better. All this, and more,
is anxiously occupying King Kalakaua's attention,
and on the eve of his departure* it must have been a
source of great gratification to His Majesty to
observe how his subjects rallied round him, and bid
him "Good speed." The following are the last
words on the subject, addressed to a crowded con-
course in the Stone Mission Church at Kawaihae,
after some words of warm adieux from many other
native speakers.

* " PROCLAMATION.—We, Kalakaua, by the grace of God,
of the Hawaiian Islands, King: Agreeably to Article thirty-
third of the Constitution of our Kingdom, We have this day
appointed, and do hereby proclaim and make known our
beloved subject and sister, Her Royal Highness the Princess
Liliuokalani as Regent of our Kingdom to administer our
Government in our name, during our absence from our
Kingdom. Done at Iolani Palace, in Honolulu, this 20th
day of January, in the year of our Lord, one thousand eight
hundred and eighty-one; and in the seventh year of our
reign.—KALAKAUA Rex. By the King: W. L. Green, Premier
and Minister of Foreign Affairs."

The Hon. Noble Kapena rose to reply:—

"We have heard our King tell us this evening about his intended visit abroad. He spoke to you from the same place six years ago, when he went before to visit America. It is true the King goes but for the good of his people, to make the country richer by getting more capital and people to come this way. See the result of his visit to America—before he went natives were receiving but twenty-five cents per day, now see what they get, $2·50 and $3·00 per day. This is the King's work. New houses, ships, railroads, and every new enterprise are largely due to the King's visit abroad. But all this wealth is of no use if there is to be only one *kauna* a mere handful of us left. So the King this time takes with him a commissioner to inquire into and bring other people of brown skins here to repeople these isles. The King himself would be only so in name if he had no people to rule. The King will not rest until his hope of repeopling these isles has been fulfilled. Let no one have any little feeling of jealousy about the King's going. Let no one be envious. The King goes to see how the great nations of the earth govern and rule their people, and it is well. It does not do to always

remain in the dark.   The great nations now look
with respect on this little kingdom, and will have
still more, when they see our King travelling among
them for information to benefit his people.   Let us
all pray every day for the King's health, and safe
return to his people."

Midnight serenades were also given, for the feelings of the people were not stayed from their
expression, even after churches had closed, and the
hours for slumber came ; for, all night the palace
grounds resounded with song and mele.   At midnight and afterwards a band of Hawaiian chorus
singers made the calm clear moonlight vocal with
tender and touching chant.   Some of these choruses
have a very sweet and plaintive melody ; and during
this lovely midnight hour, the soft summer air of
the walks and umbrageous foliage of Iolani Palace,
was tremulous with the tender songs of Hawaiians
bidding farewell to their King.

In the heartiest wishes for his pleasant journey
and safe return to the land of his birth and control,
let us stay over one more mail, to observe that in
the absence of any systematic survey of the surface
of his kingdom, one is not surprised at the non-
discovery of mineral deposits within its boundaries,

if existent ? And, in fact, until 1880 Artesian well-boring had never been attempted ; so far proving successful in an excellent flow of water having been obtained at and around Honolulu, from depths between 200 and 300 feet ; but demonstration of other subsidences is embedded in the womb of time.

Ferruginous superficies, however, in the form of oxide, appear to be very plentifully diffused through-out the group, and conglomerates abound rich with this material.

Stock and cattle raising is becoming a very lucrative business, and the export of wool, hides, and tallow is steadily increasing.

An inestimable boon to residents on these islands is the absence of snakes, scorpions, or other veno-mous reptile, excepting the centipede, while the hornet confines his flights within the limits of the guava bushes.

As civilisation advances, sport declines here as elsewhere ; and the Hawaiian goose—found chiefly in the neighbourhood of Mauna Loa, in Hawaii—may be said to be the only species of indigenous game.

Of imported kinds the most plentiful are the

common plover, with his "long-legged" and " lesser pied " relatives.

Ducks are fairly abundant, especially between August and April, when the "Nor-West" duck comes over in considerable flocks.

The American quail also, nearly synonymous with the British partridge, is found in proportionate quantity ; and pigeons are becoming numerous.

A few partridge and pheasant have been imported, and are said to have done well.   If extant ? they are very scarce ; but many parts of Kauai, where water is plentiful, are excellently adapted for pheasantries ; fortunately for the planters there are no hares nor rabbits.

The existence of established game laws evinces civilisation in no ordinary degree, albeit "hardly ever" enforced in their tenour of levying £1 per annum for a license to shoot game within the town of Honolulu and district, comprised under the name, style, and title of the Kona (wherever it may be), on Oahu.

No license is required to carry arms for sporting purposes ; bur during the close season the fine for killing imported insectivorous game, between the 1st of August and 1st of May, is stated to be one dollar per head.

Nevertheless the sportsman need not be anxious about what appears to be all but a *dead letter*; and if in search of keen excitement such will be found in plenty: after the wild bulls in the forests and jungle surrounding Haleakala, on Maui, and other highlands.

If anything of a horseman, which he will soon become here, he will derive intense enjoyment by joining a party of cattle-drivers in their capture, by lasso, of young stock. Such is sharp work at times; but one has yet to learn that Englishmen are much behindhand in anything that contributes to sport or profit.

If not so profitable as many enterprises in this part of the world, there is one sport affording exciting and healthful enjoyment to both sexes in " A Mule Hunt," that is generally " fixed "—don't be shocked good people !—for Sunday.

" *Qui s'excuse s'accuse* ; " but please do not for an instant imagine we planters have any intention of excusing such exercise to our " dearly beloved brethren," more favouredly circumstanced in devout occupations, and who may think proper to accuse us

18

of "the desecration," &c.; but it may be just to
observe that a planter's professional and domestic
life is peculiarly monotonous. He rises at 5 A.M.,
and after a hurried toilet catches his horse and turns
out his field, and other hands, and tells off each
gang to its several daily duties. His spirit must be
everywhere, and flesh as near ubiquity as his horse
can convey it—whether to office, fields, or mill—
from daylight till dark. If rejoicing in a resident
male partner, to work by reliefs, and share his
labours and anxieties, so much the better. And if
in a female partner, to minister to his happiness
and comfort, so much the more enjoyable for him,
and the worse for her.

The truism of "Ladies and watches not going
well together," is in a great measure applicable to
sugar plantations.

"Like likes like," 'tis said, so "Sweets go to
sweet"; but they can have too much of a good
thing; and, therefore, plantation-life is not that
adapted to a lady; and—when aware of it—nought
but innate selfishness would solicit her acceptance of
such a position.

This healthful, and in many ways enjoyable,
though rough life, is adopted only for the purpose,

we presume, of making money; and were proper domestic help obtainable, such—as a luxury—would decrease the profits.

In any case the wife—too often a delicately nurtured girl, or erst *grande dame* with growing daughters—finds herself forced to fulfil the most arduous and menial offices. Not that there is the slightest degree of derogation therein ; but though an educated man may do anything, and thrive on it, a refined woman *should* not, and it is unfair to place her in a position commanding such action.

Isolated from all congenial society, distraction is most essential; sometimes only to be obtained in a gallop with the males of the family, and their neighbourly *confrères*, as circumstances permit.

The system adopted on some plantations is, to alternately work one half of their dray and saddle stock weekly, while the passive portion is at pasture, that is collected and driven into the home paddock by Saturday night, to be there inspected and in readiness for work on Monday morning. On most of these occasions a *strayer* is reported "absent without leave," and the roll being called, he—in nine cases out of ten—proves to be next door to an ass—a source of great gratification

18 *

to the girls of the family, as favouring fun for the morrow. Such intelligence is not long finding its way to abjoining plantations, although, perhaps, twenty miles distant.

Sunday morning is devoted also to "a lay off" and late breakfast at 8 A.M. Then, perhaps, prayers are read, and these finished, a general overhauling, cleaning and oiling of saddlery comes off; and odd buttons are sewn on, with home letters to be written—the last certainly postponed in favour of a mule hunt.

It does not take long for a lady in these parts to attire herself for the chase; the difficulty is to mount each fair *equestrienne* without an argument.

"You'll ride 'Peter,' won't you, Annie?" asks Agnes.

"No! Not with his sore back!" shouts Tom from the verandah, while mending a girth.

"Let Emily ride him!—her saddle came back restuffed from Honolulu last mail-day."

"Well! I'll have 'Wall Eye!'" responds Annie; "Agnes can then ride 'Mantrap,' and——"

"What rot you girls talk," interrupts Frank, "when his girth-gall won't be healed for a fortnight."

" Well, then, I'll ride 'Naughty Boy'!" remarks
Agnes. " He'll go right straight away, if he has
his head and a breather occasionally!"

"What may I ride, Father?" asks Baby, cuddling
up to the old man; for her claims on attention,
until now, appear to have been ignored.

" Why, dear, all the cattle seem to be mono-
polised; but there's old 'Stranger,' I shan't want
him to-morrow, and it is not asking him too much
to carry your wee mitiness."

" But my saddle won't fit him, Papa!"

" Then, darling, take mine."

And matters being thus satisfactorily arranged,
the " boys" saddle-up and fasten the nags to the
hitching post to be ready for action.

" We won't start till eleven!" appoints Ernest
who, having given the horses some corn to play
with, follows his brothers into the house, intent
upon " bossing the crowd" to-day at all events.

" I wonder if 'the boys' from Ratapa will come
over, and how many shall we muster?" soliloquises
Tom.

" Here they come! Here they come!" shouted
" Baby," running up the steps.

Out comes " Mama," followed by Annie and

Agnes *en déshabille* of riding bodices and every-day continuations.

" Yes ! there 's Maurice and Mr. Manners on the top of the hill, and there comes Mrs. Manners with Jack, and Kitty Couran with Dick Dooner ! " she exclaims; while they all wave hands and handkerchiefs, and Tom goes just frantic over his not-too-gifted girth.

The guests are dismounted, warm welcomed and " liquored-up,"—the ladies being refectioned somewhere in the back slums—when Ernest insists that it is full time to be off.

The ladies appear, using their pocket-handkerchiefs unmercifully—goodness knows why? for none wear moustaches, even if they had them—and there is a strong perfume of lemon pervading the atmosphere; however, they are all soon settled on their apportioned steeds ; and " Baby " is to be observed bestriding old " Stranger," toes in stirrup-leathers, as if, like Topsy, " guessed she was raised there " —perhaps she was ! for although still bearing her *soubriquet*, she must be, like " Stranger," rising nine at least.

" Here we are, a baker's good dozen," remarks Tom. " This is *way up*, and no mistake ; friend

Jacko will have a regular rattling and a rough time, I guess; you bet!"

It should be understood by the uninitiated that the mule inherits from the paternal side the greater portion of intelligence directing him to the shady and succulent cane-fields, and no matter how carefully fenced such may be, a mule will get through wire or make a gap if in any way possible.

The hunt, therefore, makes for such coverts intent upon a draw. Many miles are sometimes traversed and many blanks drawn before the quarry is viewed; when maternal instincts incite him— when thence driven—to go at a good round canter o'er hill and dale, for miles and miles, without a check.

A crack of the whip, like a pistol-shot, is heard from the extreme right of the line of mounted skirmishers—a shrill whistle followed by the shout of " Gone away! "—and then the fun commences in earnest.

By the time all are clear of the cane-fields, " Jacko " has put a considerable distance between himself and pursuers, and unhampered with freight and full of cane-tops and his week's recuperated energies, he goes express, and gives sport such as the " Master of the buckhounds " cannot afford.

On symptoms of *quantum suf.* from the hunt, and " Jacko's " flight still pointing from home, the best mounted are directed to make a *détour* as opportunity offers, so as to eventually head him ; when, by the rest of the party, Jacko is driven home, after having been the occasion to cure much dyspepsia, to unearth wells of sympathy, and to awaken sentiments of regard, only to be obliterated when we forget that,—

" That's why we often joined the mule hunt on a Sunday,
　To keep us right, and make us bright, for the canework on
　　the Monday.
　As on we flew, a jovial crew, may its members ne'er be
　　fewer,
　Yoiks ! ' Hoopilikia ua (h)oki ano, Likapu Mamua ! ' "

APPENDIX.

Holidays observed at the Hawaiian Islands.

*New Year	Jan. 1	American Anniversary	July 4
Chinese New Year	Jan. 29	*His Majesty's Birthday	Nov. 16
*Good Friday		*Recognition of Hawaiian	
Birth of Queen Victoria	May 24	Independence	Nov. 28
*Kamehameha Day	June 11	*Christmas	Dec. 25

Those prefixed by a * are recognized by the Government.

Members of the Royal Order of Kamehameha I., instituted by Kamehameha V., 1865.

Knights Grand Cross.

His Majesty the King.
Charles R. Bishop, Chancellor of the Order.
E. H. Allen.
H.R.H. Prince Alfred, Duke of Edinburgh.
H.R.H. Frederick, Grand Duke of Baden.
H.I. and R.A.M. Francis Joseph, Emperor of Austria and King of Hungary.
H.M. Louis II., King of Bavaria.
H.M. Charles I., King of Wurtemburg.
H.R.H. Louis III., Grand Duke of Hesse.
Don Manuel Rances Villanueva, of Spain.
Don Juan Tomas Comyn, of Spain.
Don Bonifacio de Blas, of Spain.
Marquie D'Azeglis.
A. S. Cleghorn.
John O. Dominis, Secretary and Treasurer of the Order.
H.R.H. Thomas, Duke of Genoa.
C. C. Harris.
H.M. Wilhelm I., Emperor of Germany.
H.I.H. Frederick Wilhelm, Crown Prince of Germany.
H.M. Humberto I., King of Italy.

Knights Commander.

Charles G. Hopkins.
C. de Varigny.
William Martin, H.M. Charge

d'Affaires and Consul-General at Paris.

Manley Hopkins, H.M. Charge d'Affaires and Consul-General at London.

Alfred Blanche de Billing, of France.

Ferd. W. Hutchison.

Baron von Petz, Admiral Austrian Navy.

Von Wiplinger, Captain Austrian Navy.

Stephen Spencer.

Dr. Edward Hoffmann, Consul for Austria and Hungary.

Don Enrique Martos.

E. von Hasslocher.

M. de Moltke, of Denmark.

M. de Stackleburg, of Denmark.

C. E. De Long, late U. S. Minister Plenipotentiary in Japan, and Minister Plenipotentiary for His Hawaiian Majesty in Japan.

H. A. Widemann.

J. Mott Smith.

Paul Kanoa.

Count Cam. Candiani d'Olivola, of Italy.

M. le Chevalier Raffaele Volpe, of Italy.

John H. Gossler, H.H.M. Charge d'Affaires, Germany.

Baron Leop. Frederick Hoffmann, of Austria.

Joseph Chevalier de Schwegel, of Austria.

Rear-Admiral John J. Almy.

Captain Wm. E. Hopkins.

Captain G. E. Temple.

H. A. P. Carter.

W. F. Allen.

General Edward M. McCook.

Baron de la Roncere le Noury, Vice-Admiral, France.

Mons. Charles Maunoir.

F. A. Schaefer.

Captain Graf von Monts.

Captain Fricherr von Reibnitz.

Hermann Schulze.

J. C. Glade.

Charles H. Judd.

George Paul Andreas Humbert, Actual Chancellor Legation, &c., Berlin.

Sir Thomas G. F. Hesketh, Bart.

Knights Companion.

J. C. Pfluger, Vice-Consul for Russia.

Stephen H. Phillips.

Rt. Rev. T. N. Staley.

W. W. F. Synge, late H.B.M. Commissioner and Consul-General.

Thomas Spencer.

William C. Parke.

William Hillebrand.

Robert Stirling.

V. Schonberger, H.B.M. Consul at Vienna.

Joseph Hugo Schonberger, of Austria.

John Kleissl, of Austria.

Adolph Plason, of Austria.

Lieut. Com. William Henry Whiting.

Colonel William N. Wherry.

J. M. Kapena.

Mons. le Baron Rene Reille.

R. A. Lyman.

Franz Edouard Gottlieb Loss, Aulic, Chancellor, &c., Berlin.

F. W. Neff, Aulic. Chancellor, &c., Berlin.

Members of the Royal Order of Kalakaua, instituted 1876.

Knights Grand Cross.

His Majesty the King.
His Excellency J. O. Dominis, Chancellor.
His Excellency E. H. Allen.
Honourable C. C. Harris.
Honourable C. R. Bishop.
Honourable A. S. Cleghorn.
H.M. Francis Joseph of Austria.
H.R.H. Prince Henry of Prussia.

Grand Officers.

His Excellency W. L. Green.
His Excellency H. A. P. Carter.
Prince R. Giedroye, Chamberlain to H.I.M. the Emperor of Russia.
Honourable A. F. Judd.
Honourable J. Mott Smith.
Honourable J. M. Kapena.
Archibald MacLean, Captain in the German Navy.
William C. Martin, Hawaiian Charge d'Affaires, Paris.
Dr. Johannes Rosing, Sup. Privy Councillor, Germany.
Herr Heinrich von Kusserow, Privy Councillor of Legation, Germany.

Knights Commander.

Honourable S. N. Castle.
Honourable A. S. Hartwell.
Honourable E. O. Hall.
Honourable S. G. Wilder.
H. W. Severance, Hawaiian Consul, San Francisco.
Edward Reeve, Hawaiian Consul-General, Sydney.

Honourable W. F. Allen, Secretary and Treasurer.
Honourable H. A. Widemann.
Claus Spreckels.
Baron Albert von Seckendorff, of Prussia.
Hans Kaester, Captain German Navy.
Charles de Livron, Captain Russian Navy.
H. A. Berger, Hawaiian Consul-General for Sweden and Norway.

Knights Companion.

Honourable John P. Parker.
Honourable Charles H. Judd.
Pitkin C. Wright.
C. Van Dyke Hubbard, of California.
Major C. T. Gulick.
Honourable H. Kuihelani.
Honourable A. Fornander.
Guido von Usedorn, Lieutenant German Navy.
August von Heerigen, Unter-Lieutenant German Navy.
Nichalaus Reitzenstein, Lieutenant Russian Navy.
George W. Macfarlane.
William D. Alexander.
Honourable Walter M. Gibson.
William H. Dimond.
John D. Spreckels.
Henry Reimenschneider.
Da Fonsaca Wollheim, Lieutenant Russian Navy.
Albrecht Heinrich Paul Landt, Privy Registrar Foreign Office, Berlin.

The Court.

His Majesty, Kalakaua, b. November 16, 1836 ; elected February 12, 1874, and inaugurated February 13, 1874. Son of Kapaakea and Keohokalole.

Her Majesty the Queen, b. December 31, 1835.

Her Royal Highness the Princess Liliuokalani, Heir Apparent, b. September 2, 1838 : m. September 16, 1862, to His Excellency John Owen Dominis, Governor of Oahu, K.G.C. of the Royal Orders of Kamehameha and Kalakaua ; Kt. Com. of the Orders of Francis Joseph and Isabella Catolica ; Member of the House of Nobles and of the Privy Council of State, &c. Proclaimed Heir Apparent to the Throne, April 11, 1877.

Her Royal Highness the Princess Likelike, b. January 13, 1851 ; m. September 22, 1870, to the Honourable Archibald Scott Cleghorn, K.G.C. of the Royal Orders of Kamehameha and Kalakaua ; Member of House of Nobles and of the Privy Council of State ; has issue Her Royal Highness the Princess Victoria - Kawekiu - Kaiulani - Lunalilo-Kalaninuiahilapalapa b. October 16, 1875.

Her Majesty the Dowager Queen Emma, b. January 2, 1836 ; m. to Kamehameha IV. June 19, 1856.

Her Royal Highness Ruth Keelikolani, sister to Their late Majesties Kamehameha IV. and V. ; b. February 9, 1818.

His Majesty's Chamberlain, Hon. C. H. Judd.

His Majesty's Staff.

Colonels W. F. Allen, Ed. Hoffmann, C. H. Judd, C. P. Iaukea, and J. H. Boyd.

Staff of the Governor of Oahu.

Majors Geo. W. Macfarlane, Chas. T. Gulick, and Capt. Antone Rosa.

House of Nobles.

His Ex. J. O. Dominis ; Hons. S. K. Kaai, J. M. Kapena, S. G. Wilder, P. Kanoa, C. R. Bishop, H. A. Kahanu, W. T. Martin, J. P. Parker, H. Kuihelani, J. Moanauli, J. I. Dowsett, A. S. Cleghorn, P. Isenburg, S. N. Castle, G. Rhodes, J. M. Smith, C. H. Judd, J. E. Bush.

The Cabinet Ministers hold seats in the House of Nobles *ex officio*.

The King's Cabinet.

His Majesty, the King.

Minister of Interior, His Ex. H. A. P. Carter.

Minister of Finance, His Ex. J. S. Walker.

Minister of Foreign Affairs, His Ex. W. L. Green.

Attorney-General, His Ex. W. N. Armstrong.

Privy Council of State.

His Majesty, the King.

Their Exs. W. L. Green, H. A. P. Carter, J. S. Walker, W. N. Armstrong, J. O. Dominis ; Hons. S. G. Wilder, J. M. Kapena, S. K. Kaai, P. Kanoa, E. H. Allen, E. O. Hall, J. M. Smith, W. J. Smith, C. C. Harris, A. F. Judd, C. R.

Bishop, A. S. Cleghorn, S. N. Castle, W. C. Parke, C. H. Judd, W. P. Wood, G. Rhodes, H. A. Widemann, H. M. Whitney, H. A. Kahanu, J. U. Kawainui, J. Moanauli, L. McCully, R. Stirling, W. F. Allen, D. Kahanu, M. Kuaea, D. Leleo Kinimaka, M. Mahuka, William Buckle, J. E. Bush, W. M. Gibson, C. H. Judd, Secretary.

Department of Judiciary.

Chief Justice, Hon. C. C. Harris.
First Associate Justice, Hon. A. F. Judd.
Second Associate Justice, Hon. L. McCully.
Clerk, J. E. Barnard.
Deputy Clerk, A. Rosa.
Terms of Supreme Court.—Sitting at Honolulu, First Monday in January, April, July, and October.

Circuit Judges.

1st Circuit, Oahu: One of the Judges of the Supreme Court.
2nd Circuit, Maui: Hon. A. Fornander.
3rd Circuit, Hawaii: Hons. F. S. Lyman, C. F. Hart.
4th Circuit, Kauai: Hon. J. Hardy.

Terms of Circuit Court.—2nd Circuit (Maui), 1st Tuesday of June and 1st Tuesday of December; 3rd Circuit (Hawaii) at Waimea, 1st Tuesday of November; at Hilo, 1st Tuesday of May; 4th Circuit (Kauai) 1st Tuesday of February and August.

Clerks of Circuit Court.—W. O. Atwater, 2nd Circuit; D. H. Hitchcock, 1st Clerk 3rd Circuit, F. Spencer, 2nd Clerk; F. Bindt, 4th Circuit.

District Justices.

OAHU.

R. F. Bickerton, P.J.; W. L. Wilcox, Deputy, Honolulu.
W. G. Needham, Ewa.
S. W. Kaaiholei, Waianae.
J. Kaluhi, Waialua and Koolauloa.
J. L. Kaulukou, Koolaupoko.

MAUI.

H. Kuihelani, P. J.,* Wailuku.
W. F. Mossman, Makawao.
S. W. Kaai, Hana and Kaupo.
D. Kamaiopili, P.J., Lahaina.
M. Kealoha, Honuaula.
S. K. Kupihea, Molokai.
S. Kahoohalahala, Lanai.
* E. H. Rogers, acting.

KAUAI.

R. S. Hapuku, Lihue.
A. W. Maioho, Koloa.
J. Kakani, Hanalei and Anahola.
F. Sinclair,* Niihau.
J. Kauai, P.J., Waimea.
Jas. K. Kaiwi, Kawaihau.
* G. Gay, acting.

HAWAII.

P. Haupu, North Hilo.
G. W. A. Hapai, P.J., Hilo.
J. P. Miau, Hamakua.
J. Makaimoku Naeole, Puna.
J. H. S. Martin, Kau.
J. G. Hoapili, North and South Kona.
P. Kamakaala,* North Kohala.
S. H. Mahuka, South Kohala.
* D. S. Kahookanu, acting.

Governors.

Governor of Oahu, His Ex. J. O. Dominis. Residence, Washington Place, Honolulu.
Governor of Maui, His Ex. J. O. Dominis.
Governess of Hawaii, H. H. Kekaulike. Residence, Hilo.
Clerk, F. S. Lyman.

Governor of Kauai, His Ex. F. W. Beckley.   Residence, Koloa, Kauai.

Interior Department.

Minister of Interior, His Ex. H. A. P. Carter.

Chief Clerk of Department, J. A. Hassinger.

Clerks: J. S. Smithies, J. H. Boyd, S. Weynton.

Registrar of Conveyances, T. Brown.

Assistant Registrar, G. Brown.

Surveyor-General, W. D. Alexander.

Assistant Surveyor, C. J. Lyons.

Postmaster-General, A. P. Brickwood.

First Clerk, P. O., L. P. Du Bois.

Supt. Public Works, R. Stirling.

Supt. Waterworks, G. D. Freeth.

Clerk of Waterworks, W. Auld.

Board of Health.

His Ex. H. A. P. Carter, President.

Members: His Ex. J. S. Walker, Hon. C. H. Judd, Hon. J. Moanauli, Hon. S. G. Wilder.

J. A. Hassinger, Secretary.

Port Physician, F. B. Hutchinson, M.D.

Travelling Physicians: Kohala, Hawaii, L. S. Thompson; Physician to the Leper Settlement, Molokai, Dr. Chas. Neilson; Kau, H. N. Vineberg; Hamakua, G. B. Greenfield; Wailuku, F. H. Enders; Lahaina, ——; Makawao, A. C. Standart; Kauai, J. K. Smith; Honolulu, N. B. Emerson.

Agents: T. W. Everett, Maui. L. Severance, Hawaii. S. W. Wilcox, Kauai. D. Dayton, Oahu. J. H. Brown for Honolulu. R. W. Meyer, Molokai.

Hawaiian Board of Health.

Colonel C. H. Judd, President.

Members: E. P. Edwards, J. Moanauli.

Commissioners of Crown Lands.

H. A. P. Carter, J. S. Walker. C. H. Judd, Agent.

Appraisers of Lands subject to Government Commutation.

Hawaii: R. A. Lyman, J. H. Nawahi.

Maui: Molokai, and Lanai: T. W. Everett, L. Aholo, D. Kahaulelio.

Oahu: J. S. Smithies, C. Brown, R. F. Bickerton.

Kauai: J. Hardy, P. Kanoa, J. H. Wana.

Commissioners of Boundaries.

Hawaii, R. A. Lyman.

Maui, Molokai, and Lanai, L. Aholo.

Oahu, R. F. Bickerton.

Kauai, J. Hardy.

Road Supervisors.

Hawaii: Hilo, J. F. Jordan. North Kohala, J. Smith. South Kohala, S. P. Wahinenui. North Kona, J. W. Smith. South Kona, H. Cooper. Kau, W. T. Martin. Hamakua, Charles Williams. Puna, J. F. Jordan.

Maui: Lahaina, D. Taylor. Wailuku, H. A. Luscomb. Hana, Makawao, J Keohokaua.

Molokai, J. Lima.

Lanai, Henry Gibson.

Oahu, Kona, C. W. Hart.

Kauai: Waimea and Niihau, V. Knudsen. Koloa, J. Hardy.

Lihue and Kawaihau, S. W.
Wilcox.
Hanalei, C. Bertleman.

Commissioners of Fences.

HAWAII.

Hilo: C. E. Richardson, J. Keahi,
S. L. Austin, R. A. Lyman, K.
Paulo.
Hamakua: J. R. Mills, J. K.
Kaunamano.
North and South Kona: M. Bar-
rett, H. Cooper, Kapae, J. W.
Smith.
North Kohala: Kamahu, J.
Wood.
South Kohala: J. Parker, S. H.
Mahuka.
Kau: W. T. Martin, C. N. Spencer,
S. Kawaa, D. W. Kaaemoku.

MAUI.

Makawao: C. H. Dickey, D.
Crowningburg, P. Nui.
Hana: C. K. Kakani, M. Pupuhi,
D. Puhi.
Molokai: R. W. Meyer, S. Paulo,
R. Newton.

OAHU.

Kona: C. J. Lyons, J. Moanauli,
D. Kahanu, J. S. Smithies.
Ewa and Waianae: Kaikanahaole,
S. Previere, S. Gandall.
Waialua: H. Warden, J. Amara,
J. F. Anderson.
Koolauloa: Kaluhi, Naili, W. C.
Lane.
Koolaupoko: W. E. Pii, G. Ba-
renaba, C. H. Judd.

KAUAI.

Moloa and Lihue: W. H. Rice, S.
Kaieo, Pahuwai.

*Agents to Acknowledge Contracts for
Labour.*

Oahu, Honolulu: C. T. Gulick, J.
U. Kawainui, J. A. Hassinger,
W. Auld, S. M. Carter.
Waialua: C. H. Kalama, S. N.
Emerson, H. N. Kahulu.

Koolauloa: W. C. Lane
Koolaupoko: G Barenaba, E.
P. Edwards.
Ewa and Waianae: S. Kaanaana,
J. D. Holt.
Hawaii, Hilo: L. Severance, J. H.
Pahio, S. K. Mahoe, D. K.
Pa.
Kona: K. Kamauoha, J. W.
Smith.
Hamakua: J. K. Kaunamano,
R. P. Kuikahi, G. W. Wilfong,
S. F. Chillingworth.
North Kohala: Chas. L. Hop-
kins, John Maguire.
South Kohala: G. Bell, J.
Jones.
Kau: J. Kauhane, J. N. Ka-
pahu, W. W. Goodale.
Puna: J. N. Kamoku.
Maui, Lahaina: K. Nahaolelua,
L. Aholo.
Wailuku: J. W. Kalua, G. E.
Boardman.
Makawao: G. Glendon, Jas.
Smyth.
Hana: Kahele opio, J. K.
Hanuna.
Molokai and Lanai: J. W. M.
Poohea, G. Kekipi.
Kauai, Koloa: J. D. Neal, W. H.
Deverill, Ku.
Lihue: J. B. Hanaike.
Hanalei: J. Kaae, J. W. Loka.
Waimea: M. Kamalenai, J.
Neddles.
Kawaihau: T. Kalaeone, J. M.
Kealoha, J. Mahoe.
Niihau: Kaomea.

Board of Education.

President, Hon. C. R. Bishop.
Members: J. M. Smith, Hons. G.
Rhodes, E. O. Hall, J. U.
Kawainui.
Inspector-General of Schools, D.
D. Baldwin.
Secretary, W. J. Smith.

Agents to take Acknowledgments to Instruments.

Hawaii—W. C. Borden, Hilo district; J. W. Smith, C. N. Spencer, J. Kauhane, F. Spencer, L. E. Swain, Ili, Kahookano, J. R. Mills, G. Bell, C. Meinecke, Kapahu.

Maui — H. Dickenson, T. W. Everett, C. K. Kakani, P. N. Makee, J. D. Havekost, T. N. Birch, R. Newton, Kalua.

Molokai—R. W. Meyer, S. K. Kupihea, J. W. Nakuina.

Oahu—W. C. Lane, S. N. Emerson, G. Barenaba, C. Brown, J. S. Kaamaana, Kaliko.

Kauai—F. Bindt, S. W. Wilcox, G. N. Wilcox, C. Bertlemen, W. H. Deverill.

Niihau—C. Kahele.

Commissioners of Private Ways and Water Rights.

HAWAII.

Hilo : D. Keawehano, Kamai.

Hamakua : T. F. Mullis, J. K. Kaunamano, J. R. Mills.

North and South Kohala : J. Smith, S. C. Luhiau, Z. Kalai.

Kau : C. N. Spencer, J. Kauhane, J. H. S. Martin.

MAUI.

Lahaina : Makalua, L. Aholo, D. Taylor.

Wailuku : H. W. Daniels, N. Kapoikai, H. Kuihelani.

Makawao : J. Keohokaua, Kekaha, J. M. Alexander.

Hana : O. Unna, C. K. Kakani, S. W. Kaai.

Kaanapali : J. A. Kaukau, J. F. Kaulia, D. H. Kaialiilii.

MOLOKAI : F. W. Beckley, L. Leparte, D. Kailua.

OAHU.

Kona : D. Kahanu, J. Moanauli, D. K. Fyfe.

Koolaupoko : C. H. Judd, Kane, G. Barenaba.

Koolauloa : W. C. Lane, Naili, J. Kaluhi.

Waialua : J. F. Anderson, S. M. Emerson, J. Kaiaikawaha.

Ewa and Waianae : S. Kaanaana, A. Kaoliko, H. U. Maki.

KAUAI.

Puna : S. W. Wilcox, D. Kealahula, A. W. Maioho.

Waimea : G. B. Rowell, V. Knudsen, Kahaoa.

Hanalei : C. Titcomb, A. S. Wilcox, Z. Seka.

Board of Immigration.

His Excellency H. A. P. Carter, President.

Members—Their Excellencies J. S. Walker, W. L. Green, Hon. A. F. Judd, J. M. Kapena, W. J. Smith.

J. S. Smithies, Secretary.

Notaries Public.

Hawaii – Hilo : D. H. Hitchcock.

Maui—Haiku : C. H. Dickey.
        Makawao : W. H. Halstead.

Oahu—Honolulu : J. H. Paty, T. Brown, C. T. Gulick, C. Brown, W. R. Castle.

Kauai—Waimea : V. Knudsen.

Chamber of Commerce.

President, S. N. Castle.

Vice-President, C. R. Bishop.

Secretary and Treasurer, A. J. Cartwright.

Department of Foreign Affairs.

Minister of Foreign Affairs, His Excellency W. L. Green.

Secretary of Department, Curtis P. Iaukes.

HAWAIIAN DIPLOMATIC AND CON-
SULAR AGENTS.

Minister Resident.

Washington, D. C., His Excellency E. H. Allen.

*Charges d'Affaires and Consuls-
General.*

New York—E. H. Allen, jun.
London, England—M. Hopkins.
Paris, France—W. W. Martin.
Germany—J. C. Pfluger.
Lima, Peru—R. H. Beddy.
Valparaiso, Chili—D. Thomas.

Consuls-General.

Hong Kong and Macao, China—
W. Keswick.
Sydney, N.S.W.—A. S. Webster.
Yokohama, Japan—H. P. Lilli-
bridge.
Sweden and Norway — H. A.
Bürger.
Brussels, Belgium—Ferdinand de
Cannart d'Hamale.
Copenhagen, Denmark — Julius
Holmblad.

Consuls, &c.

San Francisco, California—H. W.
Severance.
Portland, Oregon—J. McCraken.
Boston, Massachusetts—E. M.
Brewer.
Liverpool, England—R.C. Janion.
Falmouth, England—W.S.Broad.
Ramsgate, England—A.S. Hodges,
Auckland, N. Z.—D. B. Cruick-
shank.
Melbourne, Victoria—G. N. Oak-
ley.
Newcastle, N.S.W.—E. A. White.
Otago, N.Z.—H. Driver.
Panama—H. E. Cooke.
Victoria, British Columbia—R. P.
Rithet.
Vienna, Austria—V. Schonberger.
Glasgow, Scotland—J. Dunn.

Cork, Ireland—W. D. Seymour.
Marseilles, France—A. Couve.
Havre, France—L. de Mandrot.
Bordeaux, France—E. D. Bois-
sac.
Genoa, Italy—R. de Luchi.
Callao, Peru—S. Crosby.
Yokohama, Japan—Vice-Consul
R. W. Irwin.
Hiogo, Japan—Vice-Consul B. R.
Lewis.
Nagasaki, Japan—C. L. Fisher.
Kobe and Osaka, Japan—Vice-
Consul S. Endicott.
Edinburgh and Leith, Scotland—
E. G. Buchanan.
Grand Duchy of Baden Baden—
H. Müller.
Queensland, Australia — H. A.
Thompson.
Hamburg, Germany — F. W.
Weber.
Antwerp, Belgium—V. Forge, jr.
Rouen, France—C. Schœssler.
Bremen—J. F. Müller.
Singapore—M. Suhl.
Madeira—J. Hutchison.
Fayal, Azores—T. F. Serpa.
Tasmania—A. Coote.
Hull, England—W. Moran.
Cardiff and Swansea—H. Gold-
berg.
Lysckil, Sweden — Vice-Consul,
H. Bergstrom.
Jaluit—Commercial Agent, J. H.
Hernshein.
Ghent—Ernest C. Delebecque.

*Foreign Representatives—Diplo-
matic.*

United States, Minister Resi-
dent, His Excellency Jas. M.
Comly. Residence, corner of
Judd and Liliha Streets.
England, Commissioner and Con-
sul General, James Hay Wode-
house. Residence, Emma
Street.

19

290

FROM SWORD TO SHARE.

France, Acting Consul and Commissioner, J. L. Ratard. Residence, School Street.
E. Purvis, Acting Chancellor
French Legation.

Foreign Consuls, &c.

United States (Acting)—F. P.
Hastings.
United States Vice-Consul—F. P.
Hastings.
British Vice-Consul — T. H.
Davies.
Austro-Hungarian—E.Hoffmann,
M.D.
Netherlands } J. H. Paty.
Belgium (acting) }
Italy—F. A. Schaefer.
Peru—A. J. Cartwright.
Chili—C. S. Bartow.
German Empire—J. C. Glade.
Sweden and Noway—J. C. Glade.
Russia, Vice-Consul—J. W. Pflu-
ger.
Portugal—J. Perry.
Japan Commercial Agent—J. O.
Carter.
Denmark (Hana, Maui)—A.Unna.
Denmark (Acting)—H. R. Mac-
farlane.
United States Consular Agent
(Hilo)—T. Spencer.
Spain—R. W. Laine.
Chinese Commercial Agent—
Chung Fong.
United States Consular Agent
(Kahului)—A. F. Hopke.

Department of Finance.

Minister of Finance—His Excel-
lency J. S. Walker.
Registrar of Public Accounts—
G. Brown.
Collector-General of Customs—
W. F. Allen.
Deputy Collector—E. R. Hendry.
Harbour Master of Honolulu—
Capt. A. Fuller.

Pilots in Honolulu—Capts. A.
McIntyre, W. Babcock, and P.
P. Shepherd.
Port Surveyor—W. A. Markham.

Honolulu Fire Department.

Organized 1851. Annual Elec-
tion of Engineers First Monday
in June. Officers for 1880–81.
Chief Engineer, G. Lucas.
First Assistant Engineer, J. Nott.
Second Assistant Engineer, Jas.
Dodd.
Secretary and Treasurer, C. T.
Gulick.
Fire Marshal, J. W. McGuire.
Annual Parade Day of Depart-
ment, February 3rd.
Honolulu Engine Company No. 1
(steam), formed 1850, organised
July 18, 1855. Annual election
of officers, first Wednesday in
July.
Mechanic Engine Company No. 2,
organised December 1850, ad-
mitted February 3, 1850. An-
nual election of officers, first
Wednesday in February.
Hawaii Engine Company No. 4,
organised February 1861.
Annual election of officers, first
Tuesday in February.
China Engine Company No. 5
(steam), organised February
1879.
Pacific Hose Company No. 1,
organised January 1861, as
Engine Company No. 3,
changed to a Hose Company
December 14, 1863. Annual
election of officers, second
Monday in January.
Protection Hook and Ladder
Company No. 1, re-organised
September 1857. Annual elec-
tion of officers, first Monday in
September.

FIRE WARDS OF HONOLULU.

Ward No. 1—Comprises all that portion north of Fort Street, and *makai* of Hotel Street.

Ward No. 2—Comprises all that portion south of Fort Street, and *makai* of Hotel Street.

Ward No. 3—Comprises all that portion north of Fort Street, and *mauka* of Hotel Street.

Ward No. 4—Comprises all that portion south of Fort Street, and *mauka* of Hotel Street.

Ward No. 5—Vessels in Harbour of Honolulu.

Department of Attorney-General.

Attorney-General, His Excellency W. N. Armstrong.

Clerk to Attorney-General.

Marshal of the Hawaiian Islands, W. C. Parke.

Deputy Marshal, David Dayton.

Sheriff of Hawaii, L. Severance.

Sheriff of Maui, T. W. Everett.

Sheriff of Kauai, S. W. Wilcox.

Jailor of Oahu Prison, D. K. Fyfe.

School Agents in Commission.

HAWAII.

Hilo, L. Severance.

Puna, W. H. Shipman.

Kau, G. W. C. Jones.

South and North Kona, H. N. Greenwell.

South Kohala, Rev. L. Lyons.

North Kohala, E. N. Dyer.

Hamakua, Rev. J. Bicknell.

MAUI.

Lahaina and Lanai, R: Newton.

Wailuku, H. A. Kinney.

Hana, S. W. Kaai.

Makawao, H. P. Baldwin.

Molokai, R. W. Meyer.

OAHU.

Honolulu, Ewa, and Waianae, W. J. Smith.

Waialua, J. F. Anderson.

Koolauloa, W. C. Lane.

Koolaupoko, Rev. J. Manuel.

KAUAI.

Waimea and Niihau, V. Knudsen.

Koloa, Rev. J. W. Smith.

Koloa, Koolua, and Hanalei, S. W. Wilcox.

Life, Fire, and Marine Insurance Agencies.

Firemen's Fund, Bishop and Co.

Liverpool and London and Globe, Bishop and Co.

Equitable Life, A. J. Cartwright.

Imperial Fire, A. J. Cartwright.

New England Mutual Life, Castle and Cooke.

Union, San Francisco, Castle and Cooke.

British and Foreign Marine, T. H. Davies.

Northern Fire and Life, T. H. Davies.

Rheinish Wesphalian Lloyd, J. C. Glade.

Aachen and Leipsic, J. C. Glade.

California Marine, H. Hackfeld & Co.

North German Fire, H. Hackfeld & Co.

Trans-Atlantic Fire, H. Hackfeld & Co.

Swiss Lloyd Fire, H. Hackfeld & Co.

New York Life, H. Hackfeld & Co.

North British and Mercantile Fire and Life, Hoffschlaeger & Co.

North-Western Mutual Life, J. S. Walker.

Swiss Lloyd Marine, J. S. Walker.

Union Fire of New Zealand, J. S. Walker.

19 *

Hamburg-Magdeburg Fire, A. Jaeger.

Magdeburg General Marine, A. Jaeger.

Manhattan Life, J. H. Paty.

Hamburg-Bremen Fire, F. A. Schaefer & Co.

German Lloyd Marine, F. A. Schaefer & Co.

Fortuna Marine, F. A. Schaefer & Co.

Mutual Life of New York, Wilder & Co.

On Tai Marine, Chulan & Co.

Sailors' Home Society.

Organised 1853. Meets annually in December.

President, S. N. Castle.

Secretary, F. A. Schaefer.

Treasurer, C. R. Bishop.

Executive Committee, E. O. Hall, P. C. Jones, S. C. Damon.

Volunteer Military Companies.

Prince's Own, Artillery — His Majesty, Major ; C. P. Iaukea, Adjutant ; H. Kaaha, Captain.

Leleiohoku Guard, Cavalry — Makanui, Captain.

Hawaiian Guards, Co. A—C. T. Gulick, Captain.

Hawaiian Guards, Co. B—C. B. Wilson, Captain.

Mamalahoa—W. P. Wood.

Queen's Hospital.

Erected in 1860.

President, His Majesty the King.

Vice-President, C. C. Harris.

Secretary, F. A. Schaefer.

Treasurer, J. H. Paty.

Auditor, E. P. Adams.

Physicians—R. McKibbin, F. B. Hutchinson.

Executive Committee — C. R. Bishop, J. H. Paty, F. A. Schaefer, A. J. Cartwright, A. S. Cleghorn.

Lodges.

Le Progres de l'Oceanie, No. 124, A. F. & A. M.? meets on King St., on the last Monday in each month.

Hawaiian, No. 21, F. & A. M.; meets in its Hall, corner Queen and Fort Streets, on the first Monday in each month.

Royal Arch Chapter ; meets in the Hall of Le Progres de l'Oceanie, every third Thursday of each month.

Commandery No. 1 Knights Templar ; meets at the Lodge Room of Le Progres de l'Oceanie, second Thursday of each month.

Kamehameha Lodge of Perfection, No. 1, A. & A. S. R.; meets in the Hall of Le Progres de l'Oceanie, every fourth Thursday of each month.

Nuuanu Chapter of Rose Croix, No. 1, A. & A. S. R., meets at the Hall of Le Progres de l'Oceanie, first Thursday in the month.

Alexander Liholiho Council of Kadosh ; meets on the third Monday of alternate months from February.

Excelsior No. 1, I. O. of O. F.; meets at the Hall in Odd Fellows' Building, on Fort St., every Tuesday evening.

Harmony Lodge, No. 3, I. O. of O. F.; meets each Thursday, in the Hall of Excelsior Lodge.

Polynesian Encampment No. 1, I. O. of O. F.; meets at Odd Fellows' Hall, first and third Fridays of each month.

Oahu Lodge No. 1, K. of P.; meets every Wednesday at Hall on Hotel St.

Hawaiian Tribe, No. 1, Imp. O.

APPENDIX.

293

R. M; meets at the Hall of
Oahu Lodge, K. of P., every
Friday evening.
Court Lunalilo, No. 6600, A. O.
of Foresters; meets at Hall
of Oahu Lodge, K. of P., on
second and fourth Tuesdays of
each month.

Strangers' Friend Society.

Organised 1852. Annual Meeting
in June.
President, Mrs. S. C. Damon.
Vice - Presidents, Mrs. C. R.
Bishop and Mrs. T. H. Hobron.
Secretary, Mrs. L. Smith.
Treasurer, Mrs. S. E. Bishop.
Directress, Mrs. A. Mackintosh.

British Benevolent Society.

Organised 1860. Meets annually
May 24.
President, J. H. Wodehouse.
Vice-President, Rev. A. Mackintosh.
Secretary, J. S. Smithies.
Treasurer, A. S. Cleghorn.
Executive Committee: G. Rhodes,
G. Lucas, A. Young.

British Club.

Organised 1852. Premises on
Union St., two doors below
Beretania.
President, A. S. Cleghorn.
Secretary, G. Brown.
Treasurer, H. May.
Managers—A. S. Cleghorn, Godfrey Brown, H. Macfarlane.

American Relief Fund.

Organised 1864. Meets annually
February 22.
President, A. J. Cartwright.
Vice-President, Rev. S. C. Damon.
Secretary and Treasurer, C. R.
Bishop.

Mechanics' Benefit Union.

Organised 1856.
President, R. Grey.
Vice-President, J. W. McGuire.
Secretary, Wm. Auld.
Treasurer, J. S. Lemon.

German Benevolent Society.

Organised August 22, 1859.
President, H. W. Schmidt.
Secretary, Max Eckart.
Treasurer, J. F. Hackfeld.

Library and Reading Room Association.

Organised March 1, Incorporated
June 24, 1879.
President, A. S. Hartwell.
Vice-President, Dr. C. M. Hyde.
Secretary, H. A. Parmelee.
Treasurer, A. L. Smith.
Directors—A. J. Cartwright, T.
G. Thrum, Dr. C. T. Rodgers,
H. R. Hollister, W. Hill, R. F.
Bickerton, S. B. Dole, J. Ashworth, W. Johnson.

St. Antonio Benevolent Society.

Organised December 1876.
President, J. Perry.
Vice-President, M. B. Silvara.
Secretary, Joe Enos.
Treasurer, J. Robello.

German Benefit Union.

Organised February 1880.
President, M. Eckart.
Secretary, H. J. Nolte.
Treasurer, C. Bolte.

Deutscher Verein.

Organised 1879.
President, J. C. Glade.
Vice-President, H. W. Schmidt.
Sec. and Treasurer, P. Opfergelt.

Hooulu Lahui Benevolent Society.
Organised 1878.
President, H.M. the Queen.
Treasurer, Mrs. J. G. Dickson.

Amateur Musical Society.
Organised 1851. Reorganised 1878.
President, Dr. J. M. Smith.
Vice-President, J. C. Glade.
Musical Director, A. T. Atkinson.
Leader, H. Berger.
Treasurer, C. M. Cooke.
Secretary, W. W. Hall.

Oahu College.
Located at Punahou, two miles east of Honolulu.
President, Rev. W. L. Jones, A.M.
Instructor in Languages, F. E. Adams.
First Assistant, Miss Winter.
Second Assistant, Miss Royce.
Teacher of Music, Mrs. J. E. Hanford.
Teacher of Drawing, Miss E. C. Jones.
Matron, Mrs. W. L. Jones.

Board of Hawaiian Evangelical Association.
Originally organised 1823.
Constitution revised 1863.
Annual Meeting in June.
President, Rev. T. Coan.
Vice-President, Rev. W. Frear.
Corresponding Secretary, Rev. A. O. Forbes.
Recording Secretary, Rev. C. M. Hyde, D.D.
Treasurer, E. O. Hall.
Auditor, P. C. Jones.

Ladies' Benevolent Society of Fort Street Church.
Organised 1853. Meets annually in April.
President, Mrs. W. F. Allen.
Vice-President, Mrs. W. W. Hall.

Secretary, Miss H. S. Judd.
Treasurer, Mrs. P. C. Jones.
Directress, Mrs. E. O. Hall.

Young Men's Christian Association.
Organised 1869. Annual Meeting in April.
President, Dr. J. M. Whitney.
Vice-President, E. C. Damon.
Secretary, W. Kinney.
Treasurer, Charles Peterson.

Mission Children's Society.
Organised 1851. Annual Meeting in June.
President, Prof. W. D. Alexander.
Vice-President, Hon. A. F. Judd.
Recording Secretary, F.J. Lowrey.
Corresponding Secretary, Miss M. A. Chamberlain.
Home Corresponding Secretary, Mrs. M. Benfield.
Elective Members—Mrs. S. E. Bishop, P. C. Jones.
Treasurer, W. W. Hall.

Boards of Underwriters—Agencies.
Boston, C. Brewer & Co.
Philadelphia, C. Brewer & Co.
New York, A. J. Cartwright.
Liverpool, T. H. Davies.
Lloyds—London, T. H. Davies.
San Francisco, H. Hackfeld & Co.
Bremen, Dresden, Vienna, F. A. Schaefer.

Anniversaries.
New Years, January 1.
Birth of the Queen of Great Britain, May 24.
In Memory of Kamehameha I., June 11.
American Independence, July 4.
Birth of His Majesty the King, November 16.
Recognition Hawaiian Independence, November 28.
Christmas, December 25.

Packet Agencies.

Boston Packets, C. Brewer & Co.
Planters' Line (S. F.), C. Brewer & Co.
Spreckels Line, W. G. Irwin & Co.
Merchants' Line (S. F.), Castle & Cooke.
New York Line, Castle & Cooke.
Liverpool and Glasgow, G. W. Macfarlane & Co.
Pacific Mail S.S. Co., H. Hackfeld & Co.
Bremen Packets, H. Hackfeld & Co.
Hawaiian Packet Line, H. Hackfeld & Co.

Maile Social Club.

Organised January 10, 1878.
President, E. R. Hendry.
Vice-President, E. Holdsworth.
Secretary, W. M. Giffard.
Treasurer, J. I. Dowsett, Jun.

Places of Worship.

Bethel Church (Congregational), corner of King and Bethel Streets, Rev. S. C. Damon, D.D., Pastor. Services every Sunday at 11 A.M. Sunday-school meets at 9.45 A.M. Prayer Meeting, Wednesday evenings at 7.30.
Fort Street Church (Congregational), corner of Fort and Beretania Streets, Rev. W. Frear, Pastor. Services every Sunday at 11 A.M. and 7.30 P.M. Sunday-school meets one hour before morning service. Prayer meeting Wednesday evenings at 7.30, and Sunday evenings at 6.45.
Roman Catholic Church, Fort Street, near Beretania; Right Rev. L. Maigret, Lord Bishop of Arathea; Rev. Abbe Modeste and Rev. Father Hermann

assisting. Services every Sunday at 5 and 10 A.M., and at 4.30 P.M. Low Mass every day at 6 and 7 A.M. High Mass Sundays and Saints' days at 10 A.M.
Christian Chinese Church, Fort Street, Sit Moon, Acting Pastor. Services every Sunday at 10.30 A.M. and 7.30 P.M. Prayer Meeting Wednesdays at 7.30 P.M.
Episcopal Church, Emma Square; Right Rev. Bishop of Honolulu officiating, assisted by Rev. A. Macintosh and Rev. T. Blackburn. Services in English every Sunday at 6.30 and 11 A.M., and 7.30 A.M. Services in Hawaiian every Sunday at 9 A.M. and 3.30 P.M. Sunday-school meets one hour before English morning service.

Native Churches.

Kawaiahao Church (Congregational), corner of King and Punchbowl Streets, Rev. H. H. Parker, Pastor. Services in Hawaiian every Sunday at 11 A.M., and at 7.30 on Sunday evenings, alternating with Kaumakapili. Sunday-school at 10 A.M. Prayer Meeting every Wednesday at 7.30 P.M.
Kaumakapili Church (Congregational), Beretania Street, near Maunakea. Rev. M. Kuaea, Pastor. Services in Hawaiian every Sunday at 10.30 A.M., and at 7.30 P.M. on Sunday evenings alternating with Kawaiahao. Sunday-school at 9.30 A.M. Prayer Meeting every Wednesday at 7.30 P.M.

Publications.

The *Gazette*, issued every Wednesday morning. R. Grieve, Publisher and Proprietor.

The *Saturday Press*, issued every Saturday morning. Thomas G. Thrum, Business Manager. The *Friend*, issued on the first of each month. Rev. S. C. Damon, Seamen's Chaplain, Editor and Publisher. The *Hawaii Pue Aina* (native), issued every Saturday morn-ing. J. U. Kawainui, Publisher and Editor. The *Advertiser*, issued every Saturday morning. W. M. Gibson, Editor and Publisher. The *Kuokoa* (native), issued every Saturday morning. Rev. H. H. Parker, Publisher and Editor.

Mission Directory, Hawaiian Islands.

The different denominations are indicated in the following manner : Congregational in Roman ; EPISCOPAL IN SMALL CAPS ; *Roman Catholics in italics ;* * indicates temporary supply, and † licensed preachers. All others are ordained pastors.

HAWAII.

Hilo, T. Coan, A. O. Forbes, *P. Charles.*

Onomea, J. H. Pahio.

Hakalau, Kukahekahe. *

Laupahoehoe,

Kapaliiuka, J. Kauhane.

Puna District, *P. Clement.*

Puula,   †

Kalapana and Opihikao, Kamelamela.

Hamakua, J. Bicknell, S. Kaaua.

Kohala, E. Bond, S. Aiwohi, C. S. Luhiau ; *P. Fabien.*

Waimea, L. Lyons.

Kona—Kekaha, G. P. Kaonohimaka.

Kailua and Helani, J. Waiamau.

Central Kona, Makaike. †

Kealakekua, S. Papaula ; *P. Stanislas, P. Regis.*

Onouli, S. H. DAVIS.

Kau—Waiohinu, J. Kahuila ; *P. Nicaise.*

Kapalilua, Waiau. †

Pukaana (Congregational Church without pastor).

MAUI,

Lahaina, A. Pali ; *P. Aubert, P. Gregoire.*

Lahainaluna, S. E. Bishop.

Wailuku, W. P. Alexander, W. P. Kahale ; J. BRIDGER ; *P. Leonor.*

Waikapu, J. M. Kealoha.

Waihee, O. Nawahine.

Makawao, J. S. Green.

Oloalu, Keaupuni. †

Hana, E. Helekunihi ; *P. Boniface.*

Kaupo and Kipahulu, D. Puhi ; *P. Isidore.*

Huelo, Kaanapali, Honokohau and Lanai (Congregational churches without pastors).

MOLOKAI.

Halawa, Paulo.

Kaluaaha, E. Kekoa.

Pelekunu and Wailau, N. Pali.

Siloama, Holokahiki * ; *P. Damien.*

OAHU.

Honolulu : Seamen's Bethel, S. C. Damon, D.D. ; Fort Street Church, W. Frear ; Kawaia-

hao, H. H. Parker; Kaumaka-
pili, M. Kauea; St. Andrew's
Cathedral, Rt. Rev. Alfred
Willis, D.D., Bishop, Robert
Dunn, A. Mackintosh; *Roman
Catholic, Rt. Rev. L. Maigret,
Bishop, P. Modeste, P. Hermann.*
Kalihi and Moanalua, S. Paaluhi.
Ewa, *P. Raymond.*
Waianae, P. W. Kaawa. *
Waialua, J. N. Paikuli; *P. Des-
vault.*
Kahuku, J. Kekahuna.

OAHU.
Kakana and Hauula, D. Kekio-
kalani.

Kaneohe, J. Manuela.
Waimanalo, S. Waiwaiole.
Koolau District, *P. Martial, P.
Mathias, P. Lievin.*
Ewa and Wailupe (Congregational
churches without pastors).

KAUAI.
Anahola, G. M. Keone. †
Koolau, *P. Denis.*
Lihue, G. Puuloa.
Kona, *P. Eustache.*
Koloa, J. H. Mahoe.
Waimea (without pastor).
Waioli, Puiki. *
Moloaa, *P. Hubert.*

Marquesas and Micronesian Islands.

MARQUESAS.
Hivaoa, J. Kekela and wife, Z.
Hapuku and wife.
Uapou, S. Kauwealoha and wife.

GILBERT ISLANDS.
Tapiteuea, B. W. Kapu and wife,
H. B. Nalimu and wife.
Nonouti,
Maiana, W. N. Lono and wife.
Apaiang, H. J. Taylor, G. Leleo
and wife.
Tarawa, W. Haina and wife.
Marakei, D. Kauoho and wife,
Kabure.
Butaritari, J. Kanoa and wife, R.
Maka and wife.
Apemama, Moses Kanoaro.

MARSHALL ISLANDS.
Ebon, B. G. Snow and wife, J. F.
Whitney and wife.
Namarik, Marshall Islander.

Jaluit, D. Kapali and wife.
Mejuro, S. W. Kekuewa and
wife.
Arno, D. P. Kaaia and wife.
Mille, S. Kahelemauna and wife.

CAROLINE ISLANDS.
Kusaie—Strong's Island, Libilao
Sa.
Mokil—Wellington's Island, Po-
nape Teacher.
Pinlap, Ponape Teacher.
Ponape—Kiti, A. A. Sturges and
wife.
Ponape—Oua, F. E. Rand and
wife.
Ponape—Kenan U, and Auak, R.
W. Logan and wife.

MORTLOCK ISLANDS.
Satoan, Obedia and wife, Barne-
bas and wife.
Lukunor, Tepit and wife.

Algæ of the Hawaiian Islands.

BY J. E. CHAMBERLAIN.

Seaweed, or as the Hawaiians call it, *Limu*, abounds here. It is mostly of medium size. No varieties are gigantic. Some are woody, A great number need to be pressed immediately to preserve them. while many so prepared cannot be identified, as they must be examined with a microscope while freshly gathered.

Waialua, Kailua, Waikiki, on Oahu; Kalaupapa, Kaluaaha, on Molokai; Kahului on Maui; Kahalepalaoa on Lanai; Hilo and Kawaihae on Hawaii; Hanalei and Waimea on Kauai, and the Island of Niihau, have beaches favourable for stranded limu. Yet stranded sea-weed varies with every tide, and satisfactory work can only be done by watching for smooth low water, to go out on the reefs and wade on the rocks.

From Andrew's Hawaiian Dictionary, and other sources, the following native names of Algæ are gathered, forming a part of the whole. The names vary on different Islands. The kinds of Algæ are not equally or similarly distributed. Very few of the young natives are acquainted with more than a small stretch of sea coast. Indeed, only the older women have any comprehensive knowledge of limu. The men regard its collection and preparation for food as rather beneath their dignity.

Limu alaalaula,	Limu kahakala,	Limu lipuupuu,
aupupu,	kala,	limuloloa,
akiaki,	kalalauliilii,	lupe,
akiula,	kalalaunuinui,	mauauwea,
alani,	kumulimukala,	makaloa,
ehau,	kele,	maneoneo,
ekahakaha,	kiki,	nanoo,
iliohaa,	koeleele,	nanue,
oohiea,	koiale,	paakaiea,
ohiohio,	koko,	paakai, [hale,
okupe,	koloa,	pahapaha o poli
opai,	lipahapala,	pahapaha,
oaoaka,	lipakai,	pakeleawaa,
uaualoli,	lipalao,	palahalaha,
ulaula,	lipalawai,	palawai,
hinaula,	lipehu,	pepeiao,
holomoku,	lipoa,	pepeulu,
huahuakai,	kumulipoa,	pehu,
huluilio,	lipupu,	pupukaneilio,
huna,	lipewale,	pipilani,
hune,	lipuula,	wawahiwaa.
hunehune,		

The collection of Hawaiian Algæ was undertaken at the desire (as reported) of Dr. Asa Gray, the distinguished American botanist, because the field was said to be new and then unexplored. The collector had no knowledge of the science, and is under obligations to Prof. W. G. Farlow, of Harvard University, and Prof. Daniel C. Eaton, of Yale College, for the identification of the following catalogue.

Many specimens are not yet identified, and the list of Hawaiian Algæ may reach two hundred or more varieties when accurately and absolutely complete. We only report progress and leave to some successor to report again and in full.

Actinotrichia rigida,
Ahufeltia polyides (*Areschong*),
      concivina,
Amansia glomerata,
Ascothamnion intricatum,
Asparagopsis Sanfordiana,
Asperococcus sinuosus,
      ramorissimus (*Ag.*),
Bryopsis plumosa,
Caulerpa clavifera,
Caulerpo taxifolia,
      aspleniades,
      chemnitzii,
Ceramium (many var. undetermined),
Centrocerus clavulatum,
Chœtomorpha elevata,
Chondria Baileyana (*Haw.*),
      tenuissima,
Chryrimenia uvaria,
Chuoosphora fastigata (*Ag.*),
Chondrus affinis (*Haw.*),
Cladhymenia,
Cladophora fusca (*Martens*),
      composita (*H.*),
Chylocladia rigens,
Champia parvula,
Codium tomentosum,
Dasya mollis (*Harvey*),
      Pacifica (*Harv.*),
      villosa,
Delessira quercifolia,
Derberia marina,
Desmia ambigua,
Dictyosphœria favulosa (*Decaione*),
Dictyota Bartaryesiana,

Dictyota denticulata,
      cronulata,
      Sandvicensis,
      dichotoma,
      obtusangula (*Harv.*),
Ectocarpus siliculosus,
Entromorpha compressa,
Galaxaura marginata (*Lam.*),
Gelidium intricatum,
      cartilaginum,
      corneum,
      sesquipedale,
      amaresii,
      rigidum,
      felicinum (*Bory.*),
      radicans,
Gigartina flabellata (*Ag.*),
Griffithoia,
Gracilaria confervoides (*Ag.*),
      coronopifolia (*Ag.*),
      enchenmoides (*Harv.*),
Grateloupia filicina,
      dichotoma,
Hypuea nidifica (*Ag.*),
      pannosa (*Ag.*),
      divaricata (*Ag.*),
      corinta,
Hydroclathrus cancellatus (*Bory.*)
Hallymenia formosa (*Harv.*),
Hallyseris plagiogramma (*Mont.*),
      Australis,
Halimeda tuna,
Jania cuvieri,
Kallymenia,
Laurentia paniculata,
      perforata,
      obtusa,

Laurentia virgata,
    nidifica,
Liagora Cheyneana (*Harv.*),
    leprosa (*Ag.*),
    fragilis (*Zanadini*)
Lyngbya semiplena,
Martensia denticulata,
    flabelliformis (*Harv.*),
Neomeris dumetosa,
Nitophylum,
Notheia anomala,
Nostoc commune,
Polyriphonia (*Ag.*),
    mollis (*H. and H.*),
Phyllitis Fascia,
Polyzonia jungermannioides,
Plocamium Chamberlainii,
    abnornæ,
Potamogeton
Padina pavonia,

Rhodymenia,
Sargassum polyphyllum,
    echinocarpum,
    cymosum,
Scinaia moniliformis (*Farlow*),
Suhria pristeides,
Spiridia spinella,
    filamentosa.
Scytosephon conentarius,
Taonia solierii,
Toemoma perpusillum,
Ulva latissima,
Valonia ægagrophila,
    confervoides (*Harv.*),
    macrophysa (*Kiitznig*),
    Forbesii (*Harv.*),
Vanvoorstia coccinea (*Harv.*),
Vidalia obturiloba,
Wrangelia pencillata (*Ag.*),
Zonoria.

List of Hawaiian Ferns, compiled by Charles Derby, Esq.

Gleichenia—*glauca*, Hook. ; *glabra*, Brack.; *Owhyhensis*, Hook.; *dichotoma*, do. ; *emarginata*, do.

Cibotium—*glaucum*, Hook. ; *Chamissoi*, Kaulf.; *Menziesii*, Hook.

Deparia—*prolifera*, Hook. and Arn.

Odontoloma—*repens*, Hook. ; *Macræana*, var. Brack.

Microlepia—*tenuifolia*, Metten ; *hirta*, Presl. ; *polypodioides*, do.; *Mannii*, Eaton.

Davallia—(Stenoloma) *Alexandri*, sp. nov. Hillebrand.

Cystcpteris—*Douglassii*, Hook.

Adiantum—*capillus veneris*, Linn.

Pellæa—*ternifolia*, Fee.

Pteris—*cretica*, Linn. ; *irregularis*, Kaulf.; *excelsa*, Gaud. ; *aquilina*, Linn.; (Litobrochia) *decipiens*, Hook. ; (Litobrochia) *decora*, do.

Sadleria—*pallida*, Hook. and Arn.; *squarrosa*, Gaud. ; *cyatheoides*, Kaulf.

Doodia—*Kunthiana*, Gaud.

Lindsæa—(Diellia) *erecta*, Brack. ; (Diellia) *falcata*, do.; (Diellia) *pumila*, do.

Asplenium—(Thamnopleris) *nidus*, Linn. ; (Neottopteris) *nidus*, Brack. ; *obtusatum*, Forst.; *lucidum*, do. ; *gemmiferum*, Schrad. ; *enatum*, Brack. ; *Kaulfussii*, H. Mann; *erectum*, Bory ; *resectum*, Smith *trichomanes*, Linn.; *monanthemum*, do.; *fragile*, Presl.; *caudatum*, Forst.; *horridum*, Kaulf.; *contiguum*, do.; *falcatum*, Lam.; *furcatum*, Thunb.; *nitidum*, Hook.; *spathulinum*, do.; *acuminatum*, do.; *adiantum nigrum*, Linn.; *dissectum*, Brack.; *Macræi*, Hook. and Grev.; *strictum*, Brack.; *deparioides*, do.; *Poiretianum*, Gaud.; *multisectum*, Brack.; *Sandwichianum*, Metten; *polypodioides*, do.; *arborescens*, do.

Aspidium—aculeatum S.W., Hook.; *Haleakalense*, Brack.; (Cyrto-mium) *carytoideum*, Wall.; (Sagenia) *cicutarium*, Hook.; (Nephrodium) *Hudsonianum*, Brack.; (Nephrodium) *cyatheoides*, Kaulf.; *unitum*, Metten; *B. hirsutum*, do.

Nephrodium—patens, Hook.; (Lastrea) *globuliferum*, do.; (Lastrea) *Filix mas*, do.; (Lastrea) *latifrons*, do.; (Lastrea) *rubiginosum*, do.; (Lastrea) *squamigerum*, do.; (Lastrea) *glabrum*, do.

Nephrolepis—exaltata, Schott.

Phegopteris—Honolulensis, Mann, enum; *crinalis*, do. do.; *unidentata*, do. do.; *Sandwicensis*, do. do.; *Keraudreniana*, do. do.; *procera*, do. do.; *microdendron*, Eaton.

Polypodium—pseudo-grammitis, Gaud.; *Hookeri*, Brack.; *serrulatum*, Metten; *subpinnatifidum*, Blume, enum; *adenophorus*, Hook. and Arn.; *sarmentosum*, Brack.; *pellucidum*, Kaulf.; *Hillebrandii*, Hook. sp. nov.; (Adenophorus) *hymenophylloides*, Kaulf.; (Adenophorus) *tamariscinum*, do.; (Adenophorus) var. Hillebrandii, Hook.; (Adenophorus) *tripin-natifidum*, Presl.; (Adenophorus) *abietinum*, Eaton; *atropunctatum*, Gaud.; *spectrum*, Kaulf.

Gymnogramme—Javanica, Hook.

Vittaria—rigida, Kaulf.

Acrostichum—squamosum, Hook.; *micradenium*, do.; *conforme*, do.; (Olfersia) *gorgoneum*, Kaulf.; (Chrysodium) *reticulatum*, do.

Hymenophyllum—recurvum, Gaud.; *obtusum*, Hook.; *lanceolatum*, do.

Trichomanes—meifolium, Bory; *Draytonianum*, Brack.; *radicans*, Hook.; *parvulum*, Poir.

Ophioglossum—ellipticum, Hook. and Grev.; *concinnum*, Brack.; *pendulum*, Linn.

Botrychium—daucifolium, Hook.; var. *subbifoliatum*, do.

Marattia—alata, Hook. and Arn.; *Stibasia Douglassii*, Presl.

Schizæa—australis, Gaud.

Lycopodiaceæ Mann, Muen.

Psilotum—triquetrum, complanatum.

Lycopodium—polytrichoides, varium, pachystachyon, nutans, phleg-maria, fastigiatum, venustulum, cernuum, Haleakalæ, erubescens, volubile.

Selaginella—arbuscula, Springii, Menziesii, deflexa.

List of Hawaiian Mosses and Hepaticae.

PREPARED BY D. D. BALDWIN, ESQ.

The Hawaiian group possesses as great and fine a variety of mosses and hepaticae as any part of the world, its high altitudes and deep shaded ravines furnishing retreats well suited to the secluded habits of this order of nature. But until recently our mosses have been but little investigated, only about 55 species of mosses and 45 of hepaticae being described as coming from these islands. Of these we find in the *Bulletin of the Torrey Botanical Club*, of April 1874, published in New York city, a list of 34 species of hepaticae collected by Dr. Hillebrand, among them four new species. Also in the same periodical is a list of 61 mosses and hepaticae collected by Mann and Brigham, among them 13 new species. Since then others have entered the field of discovery, and the number now reaches over 300 distinct varieties, many of them new species. Further research will doubtless swell the number to 450 or 500 species.

The following list comprises all those which have been so far determined :

Hawaiian Mosses.*

Gymnostomum—Haleakalae (n. sp. C. Muller).
Octoblepharum—albiduen (an interesting moss—rare).
Racomitrium—lanuginosum; fasciculare.
Orthodon—serratus.
Fessidens—bryoides (Mungo Park's moss in the old story); Mauiensis (n. sp. C. Muller).
Rhizogonium—spiniforme; pungens; pumilum (n. sp. C. Muller), Baldwini (n. sp. C. Muller).
Rhacopilum—tomentosum ; cuspidigerum.
Dicranum—praemorsum ; Sandwicensis; robustum; breviflagellare (n. sp. C. Muller).
Dicranella—exilis.
Leucobryum—gracile; falcatum ; candidum ; Martianum; Baldwini (n. sp. C. Muller); serundifolium (n. sp. C. Muller).
Ceratodon—purpureus.
Trematodon—longicollis.
Campylopus—flexuosus ; exasperatus ; lamallatus ; Baldwini (n. sp. C. Muller).
Tricostomum—subglaurescens (n. sp. C. Muller).
Barbula—Mauiensis (n. sp. C. Muller).
Polytrichum—Junghuhnianum.
Macrometrium—piliferum ; Reinwardtii.

* I am indebted to Prof. D. C. Eaton, of Yale College, for the identification of a large portion of the mosses and hepaticae in this list ; also to Dr. Carl Muller, of Halle, Germany, and to Mr. C. F. Austin, of America, for the determination of the new species.

Pilotrichella—trichophora.
Encalypta—ciliata.
Orthotrichum—leiocarpum.
Bartramia—rigida; patens; Marchica; Baldwini (n. sp. C. Muller);
Sullivanti (n. sp. C. Muller); ressicantis (n. sp. C. Muller).
Mnium—giganteum; rhynchophorum (a delicate vine-like moss).
Bryum—argenteum; coespiticium; giganteum (a curious moss);
plumaefolium (n. sp. C. Muller).
Funaria—hygrometrica.
Neckera—dendroides; Lepineana (a beautiful moss); aquatilis (n. sp. C. Muller).
Meteorium—trichophorum; illicebrum; Mauiense.
Hypnum—cymbifolium (a splendid moss); delicatulum; muricatulum; tricostatum; Dratoni; Wilkesianum; opoeodon: plumosum;
gracilisetum; pungens; Bonplandii; paucipilum; Pickeringii; mollioulum; apertum; flammeum (n. sp. C. Muller); selaginellifolium (n. sp. C. Muller); recurvirameum (n. sp. C. Muller); limbatulum (n. sp. C. Muller); Baldwini (n. sp. C. Muller); condensatulum (n. sp. C. Muller).
Cladomnium—Sandwicense (n. sp. C. Muller).
Entodon—reflexisetus (n. sp. C. Muller).
Hookeria—acutifolia; ligularea (n. sp. C. Muller).
Mniadelphus—Freycinetii; paradoxus; cuspidatus; Kalakauae (n. sp. C. Muller); Baldwini (n. sp. C. Muller); Riemenschneideri (n. sp. C. Muller).
Hypopterygium—Brasiliense (a beautiful, delicate moss).

HAWAIIAN SCALE-MOSSES OR HEPATICAE.

Anthoceros—Vincentinus; vesciculosus; Baldwini (n. sp. Austin).
Dendroceros—Clintoni.
Dumortiera—hirsuta; trichocephala; denudata.
Marchantia—disjuncta; innovans; polymorpha; crenata.
Metzgeria—furcata.
Aneura—pectinata; pinguis; pinnatifida; palmata; multifidus.
Steetzia—cylindrica.
Symphogyna—Semi-involucrata.
Plagiochasma—cordatum.
Frullania—Hutchinsiae; ptychantha; apiculata; squarrosa; Kunzei; arietina.
Cephalozia—connivens.
Lejeunia—subsquarrosa; elongata; Mannii; cucullata; longifolia.
Omphalanthus—Baldwinii (n. sp. Austin).
Radula—reflexa; Mannii; pallens.
Sendtnera—juniperina; gracilis; tristicha.
Trichocolea—tomentosa.
Physiotium—conchaefolium; sphagnoides.
Mastigobryum—falcatum; patens; cordistipulum; minutum; parvistipulum; Brighami.

Lepidozia—Sandvicensis.
Calypogeia—bidentula; bifurca.
Lophocolea—connata; Orbigniana; Gaudichandii.
Jungermannia—coriacea; minuta; rigida; piligera; robusta! cal-
lithrix; nana; Bolanderi.
Scapania—planifolia; Oakesii.
. Plagiochila—frondescens; adiantoides; patens (n. sp. Austin);
oppositifolia; variegata; flexuosa; Baldwinii (n. sp. Austin); Eatoni
(n. sp. Austin); flava (n. sp. Austin); complanata (n. sp. Austin).

List of Birds of the Hawaiian Islands.

BY SANFORD B. DOLE,

*Member of the Hawaiian Natural History Society; Corresponding Member
of the Boston Society of Natural History.*

In compiling the following list, all authorities on this subject have
been consulted, and it is believed that it includes all species that have
been described, and all that have been noticed by naturalists as
belonging to the Hawaiian Islands. As by far the greater number of
birds are found in the mountain regions of the interior, and thus have
escaped the naturalists of various exploring expeditions, whose limited
time has been spent near the shores, or on the lowland, the list shows
a large preponderance of shore and water birds, and probably comprises but little more than half the avi-fauna of the group. And yet
our Museums, and those of Europe as well, have so few specimens,
even of the species here enumerated as peculiar to the islands, that it
seems well to print the brief characteristics given in the original descriptions, which it is hoped that a further study may supplement or
correct. Of the endemic species little is known in regard to their
habits or times of incubation, and few eggs are ever found, as their
nests are mostly in the jungle, or on the mountain plateaux where no
person resides, and where few go. In former times, when feathers
were demanded as a tax by the king and chiefs, many natives made a
practice of snaring birds, generally with bird-lime made from the
juice of lobeliaceous or other plants; and so common was this occupation that peculiar trees were transplanted to new places in the
forests, and well armed with the bird-lime, that the curiosity of the
birds might cause the loss of their much prized feathers. Now few
know the haunts of the birds, and the art has almost fallen into dis-
use. Messrs. Brigham and Mann, during their recent visit to the
islands, found great difficulty in obtaining specimens of the mountain
birds, of which they saw great numbers, and only procured some four

or five species. The former found a bird on Molokai, which the natives said was a " malihini," or stranger, and portions were placed in the collection of the Society, but have not yet been identified.

The compiler has made a few additions to the birds already noticed. He would here acknowledge the material assistance in this work, rendered him by Wm. T. Brigham, Esq., of Boston, whose notes were placed at his disposal.

Since the first edition, I have had increased opportunities of exam ining and comparing specimens, and have thereby been able to correct some of the mistakes of the first list, and to increase the number of described birds from 48 to 53. One of the birds on the old list, *Charadrius Hiaticula*, is dropped out of the numbered birds. Of the six additions, two, numbered 33 and 49, are birds well known to naturalists; while four, numbered 5, 9, 28 and 40, are new to the books.

FALCONIDÆ.

1. PANDION SOLITARIUS. Cassin, U. S. Expl. Exped., Mam. and Ornith. p. 97. Atlas, pl. IV. Adult. (Polioaëtus)—*Buteo solitarius* Peale, Zoölogy, U. S. Expl. Exped., Birds, p. 62 (Edit. 1848). Osprey, or Fish Hawk.

Bill rather long, compressed, conspicuously lobed and attenuated at the end; wing long with the third, fourth and fifth quills longest and nearly equal; tail rather short, containing 12 feathers; tarsi robust, covered in front and behind with broad transverse scales; toes strong, long, their under surfaces strongly corrugated; claws very large, long and curved.

Length about seventeen inches.

Head and under parts and upper tail coverts yellowish white. Occiput and neck behind with longitudinal spots of umber brown, which is the colour also of all the upper surface of the body, wings and tail. Bill and claws dark.

Habitat Hawaii, Molokai and Niihau. (Cassin.)

It is probable that this bird inhabits all of the Hawaiian Islands, but as it frequents the most inaccessible coasts it is rarely noticed. The only one I have ever seen was while I was passing the southern shore of the Island of Niihau in a sail-boat some years ago; and I will quote from my published account of that experience: " In wide, graceful circles the Fish Hawk swept into view from the upper air, and hovering for a moment over the shore, settled himself upon the crest of the rocks nearly opposite to us in the boat, and first glancing around with out-stretched head and half-lifted wings,—his shaggy legs apart—the picture of watchfulness, he finally, as if satisfied with his position, shook down his ruffled feathers, and folded his wings; and as we passed, calmly turned upon us the gaze of his piercing yellow eyes.

" Though the smallest of his genus, he is a powerful and splendid

20

306 FROM SWORD TO SHARE.

bird, a perfect eagle in appearance. His body is supported in the air by a spread of wings of three feet or over, giving him great power of flight. His movements are bold and graceful, and like others of the rapacious birds he has the power of resting motionless in the air for a considerable time."

2. ACCIPITER HAWAII. *Io.* 14 in. long. Dark brown above; throat dull white; breast mottled brown and white; dull white feathers on legs and abdomen. Legs feathered below tarsi. Strong back claw. Legs and feet light and scaly. Never before described. Confounded with Strix delicatula of Samoa and Fiji Islands in previous lists. Sparrow-hawk. Similar to young Accipiter rufitorques of Fiji Islands. Habitat, Hawaii, rare on the rest of the group.

Preys on small birds, chickens and mice, and probably larger animals, as the following incident would suggest. Mr. G. H. Dole, while riding one day in Koloa, Island of Kauai, accompanied by a Scotch terrier, noticed one of these birds, and was led by his peculiar movements to watch him carefully. The bird appeared much disturbed by the presence of the dog, and after circling about him a few times flew to a pile of stones, and took one in his claws and flew back with it to his old position over the dog, and balanced himself in the air as if intending to drop it on to the dog's back, but after some apparent hesitation he gave up whatever he was intending to accomplish with the stone, and carrying it back, he placed it on the pile whence he had taken it. This manœuvre would seem to show that the bird was accustomed to use stones in this way for killing or disabling its prey, and possibly its enemies, and especially for beginning the attack on animals too large for him otherwise to cope with. I suggest the above name for this bird. Mounted specimen in Mills' collection, Hilo, Hawaii.

STRIGIDÆ.

3. BRACHYOTUS GALLAPAGOENSIS. *Pueo.* Gould, Proc. Zoöl. Soc. London, 1837, p. 10. Cassin, U. S. Expl. Exped., Mam. and Ornith., p. 107. *Strix sandwicensis* Bloxham, Voyage of the Blonde, p. 250 (1826?), Gould, Voyage of the Beagle, III., p. 82 (1841). Owl.

Fascia circa oculos fuliginosa; striga superciliari plumis nares tangentibus et circa angulum oris, gula et disci fasciatis margine albis; vertice corporeque supra intense stramineo fuscoque variegatis; primariis intense fuscis ad apicem, stramineo fasciatis ad basin; corpore subtus stramineo notis irregularibus fasciisque fuscis ornato; femoribus tarsisque plumosis rufescenti-stramineis; rostro et unguibus nigris. Longus totus 13·5 in.; rostri 1 in., alæ 11 in., caudæ 6 in., tarsi 2 in. (Gould.)

Identical with the bird from the Gallapagos Islands, also with an Owl in western South America. (Cassin.) Food: Rats, mice, chickens and lizards. Frequents open country. Flies about in the daytime, but seeks its prey mostly in the late afternoon and at night.

Utters a harsh scream when excited. Makes its nest on the ground. Very common.

Habitat, all the Hawaiian Islands.

PROMEROPIDÆ.

4. DREPANIS COCCINEA. *Iwipolena.* Cassin, U. S. Expl. Exped. Man. and Ornith., p. 177. COCCINEA Merrem. *Mellisuga coccinea* Merrem, Beyt. Bes. Gesch. Vögel, p. 17, pl. IV. *Certhia coccinea* Gmelin, Syst. Nat., I., p. 470 (1788). *C. vestiaria* Latham,' Ind. Ornith., I., p. 282 (1790). Shaw, Nat. Misc., III. pl. LXXV; Vieillot, Ois. dor., pl. LII., LIII. 6 in. long. Wings and tail, black; all the rest bright scarlet; feathers on edge of shoulder white; last of the secondaries white. Bill 1 in. curved, deep rose. Toes, 3 forward, 1 back. Feathers formerly used for borders and trimming of feather cloaks. Food: Honey; especially fond of that from Lobelia flowers. Habitat, whole group. Specimen in Mills' collection.

5. DREPANIS ROSEA. *Iwipopolo.* Not previously described. Similar to the latter in appearance, habits and food. 6 in. long. Wings and tail, dark brown. Last secondaries white; upper and lower tail coverts, greenish yellow; general plumage bright scarlet, interspersed with masses of greenish yellow feathers mottled with black. Bill 1 in. curved, white. Habitat, whole group. Specimen in Mills' coll.

6. DREPANIS SANGUINEA. *Apapane.* Gmelin, Syst. Nat. I., p. 479. 5 in. long. Bill ¾ in., curved, sharp; bill and legs brown; wings and tail, black; under tail coverts, white; abdomen, brown; all the rest rich crimson. It seems probable that this bird may be Myzomela Nigriventis Cassin U. S. Expl. Exped., Mam. and Ornith., p. 175. Atlas, pl. XII., fig. 1, instead of D. Sanguinea. Habitat, whole group. (*Certhia* Sanguinea.) Specimen in Mills' coll.

Gmelin gives *D. virens* as possibly the female of this species; the edges of the secondaries are yellow, and the "pedes obscuri."

7. DREPANIS FLAVA. *Amakihi.* Bloxham. Voyage of the Blonde, p. 249. 5 in. long. Bill dark brown, curved sharp, ½ in. Upper mandible longer than the lower; tongue tubular, divided at extremity into minute filaments; neck, breast and belly, greenish yellow, upper parts yellowish olive green; male of a deeper colour than female; legs brown; toes 3 forward, 1 back; middle one connected with outer one as far as first joint. Classed by Gray as female of D. Sanguinea. Habitat, whole group. Specimen in Mills' coll.

8. DREPANIS PACIFICA. Gmelin, Syst. Nat., I., p. 479 (*Certhia pacifica*).

D. nigra, subtus obscura, humeris, dorso inferiore, uropygio crissoque flavis, tectricibus alarum inferioribus niveis, caudæ superioribus et nonnullis alarum interioribus flavis; rostro valde curvato fusco, basi pallidis; pedibus ex atro fuscis. Long 8 pollices. Hab. Hawaii and Kauai.

9. DREPANIS AUREA. *Akakane.* Genus probably Drepanis. Not

described in previous lists. 3½ in. long. Bill sharp, slightly curved. Plumage, except wings and tail, orange; wings and tail dusky brown. Bill and legs brown. Toes 3 front, 1 back. M. Ballieu has observed a brown variety, which may be the female. Habitat, Hawaii. Specimen in Mills' coll.

10. HEMIGNATHUS OBSCURUS. *Akialoa. (Iwi.)* Cassin, U. S. Expl. Exped., Mam. and Ornith., p. 178. *Certhia obscura* Gmelin, Syst. Nat., I., p. 470. Aud. et Vieill., Oiseaux dor., II., pl. LIII., Latham, Gen. Syn., I., pl. XXIII., fig. 1. *Drepanis Ellisiana* Gray, Cat. Birds of Trop. Islands of the Pacific, 1857, p. 9.   6½ in. long. Wings rather long, third quill slightly longest. Tail short, even. Legs rather long. Toes, 3 front, 1 back. Primaries and tail, brown. Upper parts olive green, tinged with yellow; under parts, greenish yellow; lighter on throat and under tail coverts; line over eye pale greenish yellow; spot in front of eye dark. Bill and legs brown. Bill 1¾ in., curved, sharp. Supposed by Gray to be the female of D. Coccinea. Food, honey. Habitat, whole group. Specimen in Mills' coll.

11. HEMIGNATHUS LUCIDUS. Cassin, U. S. Expl. Exped., Mam. and Ornith., p. 180. *Nectarina lucida* Lichtenstein, Mém. Acad. Berlin, 1839, p. 451, pl. V., figs. 2, 3. Voyage Vénus, Oiseaux, pl. I. *Vestiaria heterorhynchus* Lesson, Rev. Zool., 1842, p. 209. *Drepanis lucida* G. R. Gray, Gen. of Birds, I., p. 96. Habitat, Oahu.

12. HEMIGNATHUS OLIVACEUS. Cassin, U. S. Expl. Exped., Mam. and Ornith., p. 179. *Heterorhynchus olivaceus* Lafresnaye, Mag. de Zool., 1839, p. 17, pl. X. *Certhia Olivacea* Gmelin, Syst. Nat., I., p. 473.

H. olivaceus, subtus fuscus, orbitis albicantibus; rostro nigro; rectricibus extimis apice albis, ceteris cum remigibus fuscis, tinctu olivaceo; pedibus pallide fuscis. (Gmelin.)

13. MYZOMELA NIGRIVENTRIS. Peale, Zool. U. S. Expl. Exped., Birds, p. 150. Cassin, U. S. Expl. Exped., Mam. and Ornith., p. 175. Atlas, pl. XII., fig. 1.   Adult. Hartl., Weigm. Arch. f. Naturgeschichte, 1852, p. 109. *M. melanogastra* Bonaparte, Comptes Rendus, 1854, p. 263. Finsch und Hartlaub, Ornith. Central Polynesiens, p. 56, pl. VII., fig. 3, adult; fig. 4, young,

Wings and tail rather long, the latter rounded. Head, neck, breast, middle of the back, and rump, fine, bright scarlet; spot immediately in front of the eye, black; all other parts, above and below, rich, brownish black; bill and feet, black; the latter yellow underneath; iris brown. Length, 4½ in. Wing, 2¾ in. Tail, 1¾ in. Sexes alike in plumage. Habitat, dense forests in Hawaiian and Samoan Islands. Specimen in Smithsonian Inst. (Cassin.)

MELIPHAGIDÆ.

14. MOHO NOBILIS.   *O-o.* Cassin, U. S. Expl. Exped., Mam. and Ornith., p. 170. Moho niger Gmelin, Syst. Nat., I., p. 465. *Mohoa Nobilis* Merrem, Beyt. zur Besond. Gesch. Vögel, p. 8, pl. II. Cassin. 14 in. long. Plumage, bill and legs, deep, glossy black. Tuft of long,

golden yellow feathers under each shoulder; tail long; middle
feathers of tail twisted; under tail coverts golden yellow. Food:
fruit, honey, and flies. The yellow feathers under the shoulder are
used in making the royal feather cloaks. Habitat, Hawaii. Specimen
in Mills' coll.

15. Moho Apicalis. *O-o.* Gould, Proc. Zool. Soc. London, 1860,
p. 381. Dixon's Voyage round the World, plate opposite p. 357.
12 in. long. Wing, 4¾ in.; tail, 6¾ in.; tarsi, 1½ in. Head, neck,
breast, and forward part of back jet black; wings and tail brown;
flanks, upper and under, tail coverts golden yellow; shoulders tipped
with white and yellow; outside marginal wing coverts white; bill
and legs black. Bill 1¾ in. long, much curved. Habits and food same
as last. Habitat, Hawaii. Specimen in Mills' coll.

16. Moho Braccata. *O-o.* Cassin, Proc. Phil. Acad. Nat. Sci.,
Vol. VII., p. 440.
Smaller than Moho Nobilis, bill less curved, tail moderate, central
feathers longest. Tibiæ yellow. Head above black; throat and
breast with every feather having a terminal spot of ashy white;
back, rump, and under parts dark chocolate brown, with a few
longitudinal lines of white on the back. Wings and tail brownish
black, the former edged with white at the shoulder. Bill and feet
dark. Total length, 8·5 in.; wing, 3·67 in.; tail, 3·5 in. (Specimen in
Mus. Acad. Philad. male.) A good singer.

17. Moho Angustipluma. *Kiowea. Entomiza.* Cassin, U. S. Expl.
Expd., Mam. and Ornith., p. 168. Atlas pl. xi., fig. 1. Entomiza.
Angustipluma, Peale, Zool. U. S. Expl. Expd. Birds, p. 147 (1848).
12 in. long; slender. Bill 1¾ in. long, curved. Wings rather long.
fourth and fifth primaries longest. Tail 6½ in. long, wedge-shaped,
Feathers of head, neck and breast, with webs of few filaments;
feathers of throat terminating in bristles; filaments of tail feathers
next the body stand apart. Head and neck above dark brown, each
feather having central stripe of dull white tinged with green. Other
upper parts, including wings and tail, brown; wing and tail feathers
edged with green; feathers on the back with central longitudinal
stripes of white; wide black stripe from base of bill under the eye,
ending in large black spot on the cheek; throat, dull white tinged
with yellow; breast and abdomen, dull white feathers margined with
brown. Habitat, Hawaii and Molokai. Specimens in Smithsonian
Inst. and Mills' coll.

TURIDÆ.

18. Tartare Otaitiensis. Lesson, Traité d'Ornithologie, I., p. 317
(1831). Cassin, U. S. Expl. Expd., Mam. and Ornith., p. 159. *Sitta,
otatare* Lesson, Voyage Coquille, Zoologie, I., p. 666, plate xxiii., fig. 2.
Tatare fuscus A. Lesson, Rev. Zool., 1842, p. 210. Lafresnaye, ibid.
1845, p. 449. *Turdus longirostris?* Gmelin, Syst. Nat., I., p. 823,
Tatare longirostris Pelzeln, Novara Expd., Vögel (1865), p. 60. Finsch

und Hartlaub, Ornith. Central Polynesiens, p. 66. Thrush. The most usual colour is pale buff beneath, brown wings and tail, the feathers of the latter tipped with buff, and the back and head mottled with brown and buff. We have not seen any two specimens exactly alike; they vary from a chocolate brown to white; in fact they vary in markings, colour, and size almost as much as domestic poultry, but their sprightly, wren-like actions and sweet song are the same in all. They visit close bushy patches of vegetation, and sometimes reedy marshes. (Peale.) Length, 8 inches. Habitat, Hawaiian, Poumotu and Samoan Islands, and at Tahiti, Tongatabu, and other places in the Pacific. Specimens in the Smithsonian Inst. and Phil. Mus. Acad.

19. TURDUS SANDVICENSIS. *Amaui.* Gmelin, Syst. Nat., I., p. 813. Latham. Syn., II., I., p. 39. *Colluricincla? sandvicensis.* Gray, Cat. Birds of Trop. Islands of Pacific, p. 24.

T. supra et abdomine fuscescens; subtus et fronte ex cinereo albus; rostro pedibusque atris; cauda æquale. Longus 5.5 pollices. (Gmelin.)

MUSCICAPIDÆ.

20. TAENIOPTERA OBSCURA. Cassin, U. S. Expl. Exped., Mam. and Ornith., p. 155. Atlas, plate IX., fig. 3. Male. *Dusky fly-catcher. Muscicapa obscura.* Gmelin, Syst. Nat., I., p. 945 (1788). *Phæornis obscura,* Sclater, Ibis, 1859, p. 327. *Chasiempsis obscura,* Finsch und Hartlaub. *Eopsaltria obscura,* Gray, Cat. Birds of Trop. Islands of Pacific, p. 22. 7 in. long; wing, 5 in.; tail, 3 in.; tarsus, 1¼ in. Upper plumage slate; under parts light ashy. Bill dark, short, strong, ¾ in. long. Legs brown, tarsi lighter. Female, bright fulvous band across folded wing; under parts nearly white. Specimens in Mills' coll.

21. MUSCICAPA MACULATA. Gmelin, Syst. Nat., I., p. 945.

M. ferruginea, subtus dilute spadicea, remigibus atris, tectricibus alarum macula prope apicem ex ferruginea alba, rectricibus fuscis, extimis intus apice albis; rostro nigro. This is perhaps an uncertain species.

AMPELIDÆ.

22. EOPSALTRIA SANDVICENSIS. *Elepaio.* Bloxam, Voyage of the Blonde, p. 250. 5¼ in. long. Gmelin, Syst. Nat., I., 945 (*Muscicapa sandvicensis*). Latham, Gen. Syn., II., p. 344. Cabanis. Ornith. Notiz., I., p. 208. *Chasiempsis sandvicensis.* Finsch und Hartlaub. Bill ¼ in. long, straight, black. Plumage light brown; throat and wing coverts mottled with white; tail coverts white. Tibia feathered. Habitat, whole group. Specimen in Mills' coll.

CORVIDÆ.

23. CORVUS HAWAIIENSIS. *Alala.* Peale, Zool. U. S. Expl. Exped., Birds, p. 106 (1st Ed., 1848). Cassin, U. S. Expl. Exped., Mam. and

Ornith., p. 119, Atlas, pl. vi. *C. tropicus* Gmelin, Syst. Nat., I., , 572. Crow. Length of male, 18¾ in.; wing, 12 in.; tail, 8 in.; bill, 2¼ in.; tarsus, 2¼ in. Female, length, 17½ in. Plumage, fuliginous brown with a slight tinge of cinereous. Quills, light reddish brown, with their shafts white on their under surfaces; all the plumage dark cinereous at the bases of the feathers. Bill and legs black, the former lighter at the tip. (Cassin.) Several of these birds were seen by Messrs. Brigham and Mann in the forests of Kona, at an elevation of six thousand feet. All specimens have hitherto come from Kealakeakua in this district of Hawaii. The caw is not unlike that of the American species. Probably no other Corvus exists on the Hawaiian group, and this species is by no means abundant.

FRINGILLIDÆ.

24. Hypoloxias coccinea. *Akepa.* Gmelin, Syst. Nat., I., p. 921 (*Fringilla coccinea*). *Scarlet Finch* Latham, Syn. II., i., p. 270. *Loxops coccinea* Gray, Cat. of Birds of Trop. Ids. of Pacific, p. 28. Cabanis Ornith. Notiz., p. 330.

H. ex coccineo aurantia, alis caudaque æquali atris, remigum margine exteriore aurantio primorumque apice nigro; rostro fuscescente; pedibus nigris. Longa 4.5 in.

25. Psittirostra Psittacea. *Ou.* Latham, Syn., II., i., p. 108. *Loxia psittacea* Gmelin, Syst. Nat., I., p. 844. *P. icterocephala* Gray, Cat. of Birds of Trop. Ids. of Pacific, 1859, p. 28. 7 in. long. Bill thick, light coloured, lower mandible shorter than the upper. General plumage olive green; wing and tail feathers brown, edged with green; head yellow, tail short, even. Toes 3 front, 1 back. Female head dull green. Food, fruit. Musical. Habitat, Hawaii. Specimen in Mills' coll.

26. Emberiza sandvicensis. Gmelin, Syst. Nat., I., p. 875. Latham, Syn., II., p. 363.

E. fusca, subtus exalbida fusco maculata, superciliis flavis temporibus atris; rostro pedibusque atris; linea subocularis obscura; abdominis medio exal bido non maculato. (Gmelin.)

27. Emberiza atricapilla. Gmelin, Syst. Nat., I., p. 875. Latham, Syn., II., p. 202.

E. spadicea, pennarum singularum stria media fusca, subtus cinerea, vertice flavo, fronte et fascia oculari nigra, mento exalbido, occipite cinereo; rostro atro; uropygio pallide olivaceo, tectricibus alarum remigibusque margine pallidis; abdominis pennis medio pallidissime flavicantibus; cauda æquale, pedibus fuscis, unguibus atris. (Gmelin.)

28. Fringilla Anna. *Ulaaihawane.* Not previously described. 5¼ in. long. Bill short, straight. Toes 3 front, 1 back. Wing coverts and breast red; throat, primaries and tail, black; secondaries white; head grey, merging into white on the upper part of the neck, and

312 FROM SWORD TO SHARE.

grey again on the back. Habitat, Hawaii. Probably belongs to the genus Fringilla.

This is a bird of remarkable beauty, its peculiar combination of colours producing a most harmonious and elegant effect.

PSITTACIDÆ.

Psittacus pyrrhopterus Vigors, Zool. Journ., II., p. 400, pl. iv., Suppl. *Conurus pyrrhopterus* G. R. Grey, List of Psitt. Brit. Museum, p. 46. Is mentioned by various authors as belonging to this group, but, so far as I know, does not occur.—It is a native of Guayaquil.

Ceriphilus Kuhlii Wagl., Monogr. Psitt., p. 566.   Gray, Cat. of Birds of Trop. Ids. of Pacific, 1859, p. 32.   *Psittacula Kuhlii* Vigors. Zool. Journ., I., p. 412, pl. xvi.; Lears, Parr., pl. xxxviii.

Ceriphilus fringillaceus Bonaparte, Rev. et Mag. de Zool., 1854, p. 157.   Gray, Cat. of Birds of Trop. Ids. of Pacific, 1859, p. 33. *Psittacus australis* Gmelin, Syst. Nat., I., p. 329.

C. viridis, vertice cæruleo pennis elongatis cristato, gula et abdomine medio rubris, femoribus purpureis, fronte pallide viridi; rectricibus duobus intermediis viridibus, apice flavis, reliqiis flavicantibus, margine et apice viridibus, pedibus obscuris, unguibus nigris. (Gmelin.)

It is very doubtful whether any of the Psittacidæ occur. M. Prigham saw none in a very extensive journey over the Group.

CHARADRIADÆ.

29. CHARADRIUS FULVUS. *Kolea*. Gmelin, Syst. Nat., I., p. 687. Latham, Ind. Ornith., II., p. 747.   C. *xanthocheilus* Wagler, Syst. Avium, 1827. Cassin, U. S. Expl. Exped., Mam. and Ornith. p. 325. C. *Pluvialis* Pelzeln, Novara Exped., Vögel, p. 115. Gould, Birds of Australia, V., pl. xviii. Golden Plover.

Ad. supra nigro, albido et flavescente maculatim varius, fronte et superciliis latis utrinque per colli latera juxta nigredinem colli antici decurrentibus pure albis; genis, regione parotica, colli lateribus jugulo, pectore abdomineque mediis nigerrimis; hypochondriis albo, nigroque fasciatis; subcaudalibus mediis nigris; rostro nigro; pedibus fuscis; iride fusca; ƒ supra distinctius flavido nigroque maculata; jugulo pectoreque flavido-griscescentibus, obscurius nubilatis; abdomine medio et subcaudalibus albis. Long, 8.5 in. Hab., whole group.

This bird migrates from the Islands about the first of May, and returns about the end of August. It probably goes to the north-west coast of America for breeding purposes. They always assemble at the eastern or north-eastern shore of the Islands, preparatory to starting, and are frequently seen from vessels in mid-ocean. Before leaving the Islands they are very fat, and have glossy black feathers underneath.

30. STREPSILAS INTERPRES. *Akekeke.* Cassin, U. S. Expl. Exped., Mam. and Ornith., p. 322. Finsch und Hartlaub, Ornith., Central-Polynesiens, p. 197. Baird, Birds of North America, p. 701. *Tringa oahuensis* Bloxham, Voyage Blonde, p. 251. Gould, Birds of Australia, VI., pl. XL. *Cinclus interpres* Gray, Cat. of Birds of Trop. Ids. of Pacific, p. 48. Turnstone.

Length 8½ in.; spread of wings 17½ in.; bill, straight, 1 in.; 3 toes front, 1 behind. First primary longest. Central tail feathers longest; tail rounded. Body, above and below, and back of wings, white; upper wing coverts mottled, with white tips; lower wing coverts white; head, neck, and breast mottled; throat white; upper and lower tail coverts white; tail feathers dark, tipped with white; legs orange. The bird from which this description was taken was shot at Kapaa, on the Island of Kauai. They frequent the shores, but are often found on grass lands.

Charadrius hiaticula. Latham, Syn., III., I., p. 202. Gmelin, Syst. Nat., I., p. 683.

. C. pectore nigro, fronte nigricante fasciola alba; vertice fusco, pedibus luteis; rostro fulvo, versus apicem nigro; iride avellanea, mento, gula, pectore et abdomine albis. (Gmelin.)

I have never noticed this bird, and doubt if it is to be found in the Group.

SCOLOPACIDÆ.

31. NUMENIUS AUSTRALIS. Gould, Proc. Zool. Soc. London, 1837, part v., p. 155. *N. tahitiensis* Gray, Cat. of Birds of Trop. Ids. of Pacific, p. 49. *Scolopax tahitiensis* Gmelin, Syst. Nat., I., p. 656.

Summo capite nuchaque nigro-fuscis, singulis plumis cervino marginatis; dorso nigrescenti-fusco, singulis plumis rubescenti-cervino ad marginem irregulariter maculatis; tectricibus alæ nigro-fuscis, cinereo marginatis; tertiariis brunneis, marginibus pallidioribus irregulariter maculatis; uropygio tectricibusque superioribus caudæ nigro-fuscis, singulis plumis cinerescenti-cervino ad marginem fasciatis; tectricibus majoribus alarum, nigro-fuscis, ad apicem albis; 1, 2, 3, 4 et 5, primariis brunneis, stemmatibus albis, reliquis cum secondariis irregulariter albo fasciatis; lateribus faciei, gutture, corporeque, infra pallide seminis, singulis plumis, linea centrali nigrescenti-fusca; rostro ad basin flavescenti-brunneo, ad apicem nigrescenti-brunneo; pedibus olivaceis. Long. tot. unc. 20; rostri 5.7; alæ 11; caudæ 4·5; tarsi ·4.

Curlew. Not very common.

32. ACTITIS INCANUS. *Ulili.* Finsch und Hartlaub, Ornith., Central-Polynesiens, p. 182. *Scolopax incanus* Gmelin, Syst. Nat., I., p. 658. *Totanus brevipes* Cassin, Proc. Acad. Nat. Sci. Phil., VIII., p. 40 (1856); ibid, 1862, p. 321. *Totanus oceanicus* et *brevipes* Cassin U. S. Expl. Exped., Mam. and Ornith., pp. 318, 319. *T. Polynesiæ* Peale,

Zool. U. S. Expl. Exped., Birds, p. 237, pl. LXV.   *T. brevipes* Pelzeln, Novara Exped., Vögel, p. 129.   Ash-coloured snipe.

Colli laterali et antico, capitis lateribus, pectore, epigastrio, subcaudalibus et hypochondriis in fundo albo irregulariter obscuro cinereofasciatis ; abdomine medio pure albo.   (Summer.)   Long. 12 in.

Frequent the shores singly or in pairs.   Are called *Ulili* by the natives, from their note, which is a clear utterance of that word.

33. HIMANTOPUS CANDIDUS.   *Kukulu aeo.*   Stilt Plover.   Length 13 in.   Back and wings deep black with a gloss of green, the rest of the plumage white.   Bill black ; legs very long, and bright pink in colour. Common in ponds and swamps all over the group.   Generally wades, but is able to swim.   Is not very shy, and often troubles sportsmen by keeping just out of gunshot, and warning other birds away by its peculiar cry of defiance.   It carries its legs straight out behind when it flies.   Not noticed in the old lists.

ARDEIDÆ.

34. ARDEA SACRA.   *Auku.*   Gmelin, Syst. Nat., I., p. 640.   Finsch und Hartlaub, Ornith.   Central Polynesiens, p. 201.   *A. vulgaris* Forster, Desc. An., p. 172 (1844).   Cassin, U. S. Expl. Exped., Mam. and Ornith., p. 296.

A. saturate cinereo-cærulescens, abdomine subfuscente, linea a mento per mediam gulam decurvente lata nivea ; cristæ, tergi et pectoris plumis elongatis, apice ligulatis ; rostro supra fusco, infra et apice flaviscente ; pedibus flavidis ; iride flava.   Long. 24 pollices. (Finsch und Hartlaub.)

The young birds are wholly white, and the female whiter than the male.   Iris yellow.   Common all over the group.

I regret the loss of measurements and description of a fine specimen of these handsome birds, which was shot near Honolulu. When in full plumage the long feathers on the crest and back are bluish purple, and from the back of the head three long narrow feathers, of the purest white, hang half hidden among the thick dark feathers of the head and neck.   When excited, these white feathers are raised, and stand out by themselves.   They lay two eggs, which are mottled, and about the size of hens' eggs ; addicted to standing on one leg ; nocturnal in their habits.   Night Heron.

35. ARDEA EXILIS.   *Auku.*   Gmelin, Syst. Nat., I., p. 645.   Latham, Syn., III., I., p. 66.   Gray, Cat. of Birds of Trop. Ids. of Pacific, p. 49.

A. capite lævi et corpore supra ex rufo-badio, subtus albo, colli lateribus rufis, remigibus caudaque nigris : rostro virescente, iridibus stramineis ; colli pennis lateralibus et inferioribus prælongis et laxis ; pectore ex fuscescente nigro ; tectricibus alarum mediis ferrugineis ; remigibus nonnullis apice badiis ; pedibus viridis. (Gmelin.)

Habitat, all the group.   Heron.   Smaller than the last, and less showy in appearance. Plumage mottled brown. Both varieties prey on water insects, shrimps, small fish, and lizards.

RALLIDÆ.

36. ORTYGOMETRA SANDVICENCIS. Gmelin? *Rallus quadristrigatus* Horsfield, Trans. Linn. Soc., XIV., 1620, p. 96. *R. sandvicensis*, var. *b.*, Gmelin, Syst. Nat., p. 717. *O. quadristrigata* Finsch und Hartlaub Ornith. Central-Polynesiens, p. 164. *Porzana sandvicensis* Hartlaub, Weigm. Arch. für Naturg., 1852, p. 137.

Adul. Supra griseus; fronte cinereo-fuscescente; tergo et uropygio griseo-fuscis; linea a basi rostri ad supercilia ducta alba; gastræo cinereo-albicante; crisso pallide ochroleuco; alis fuscis, pellis pallide marginatis; pedibus viridi-olivaceis; rostro fusco-luteo; iride sanguinea. Long. 6·5 in., alar. 3·5 in.

37. ORTYGOMETRA OBSCURA. Gmelin, Syst. Nat., II., p. 718 (*Rallus obscurus*). Latham, Syn., III., i., p. 237, n. 16. *Prcana obscura* Hartlaub. Weigm. Archiv für Naturg., 1852, p. 137.

Fuscus nigro-striatus, subtus ex ferrugineo fuscus, rostro nigro; pedibus spadiceis; mandibularum acies flavicans. Longus 6 pollices. (Gmelin.)

38. GALLINULA CHLOROPUS L. *Alae. Rallus aquaticus* Gmelin, Syst. Nat., I., p. 712. *S. chloropus* Pelzeln, Novara Exped., Vögel, p. 135. Iris cherry red; cere and bill scarlet; bill lemon yellow at the tip; feet and legs greenish yellow; claws light brown; general plumage nearly black; breast and neck irridescent. Tail short, sharp, upturned. Toes with narrow swimming flanges. Habitat, whole group. Specimen in Mills' Coll. Frequents swamps, ponds, streams and kalo patches. By tradition of the natives, the discoverer of fire, by which its forehead was burnt red; hence its name—*a lae*—burnt forehead. Mud-hen.

39. FULICA ALAE. *Alae keokeo.* Peale, Zool. U. S. Expl. Exped., Birds, p. 224. Cassin, U. S. Expl. Exped., Mam. and Ornith., p. 306. Atlas, pl. xxxvi. Adult.

F. americana minor, rostro gracilliore. Tota profunde cinerea, capite et collo propo nigris. Long. tot. 13 pollices. (Cassin.) Specimen in Mus. Bost. Nat. Hist. Soc.

Larger than the last; similar in its habits. The frontal knob ivory white, instead of pale blue as Peale gives it. Coot.

40. PENNULA MILLEI. *Moho.* Not previously described. 6½ in. long. Bill ⅜ in. long, black, straight, sides compressed, curved at tip. Tail not visible. Wings rudimentary, hidden in the long, loose, hairy feathers. Plumage dark, dull brown, ashy under the throat; feathers loose, hairy, long. Lower part of tibia naked. Legs long, set far back. Toes, 3 front, 1 back, Habitat, uplands of Hawaii. Nearly extinct. Specimen in Mills' Coll.

I feel confident that this remarkable bird belongs to the Rallidæ, but am unable to fix its place more definitely. It is the only bird which the natives call *Moho*, which word is nearly synonymous with the New Zealand word *Moa*, which is their name for the gigantic wingless bird of that country. Regarding it as a new genus, I have taken the liberty of naming as above, gladly thereby recognizing Mr. Mills' valuable services in preserving specimens of this bird, and giving others opportunities of studying it.

ANATIDÆ.

41. BERNICLA SANDVICENSIS. *Nene*. Vigors, Proc. Zool. Soc. London, 1834, p. 43. Cassin, U. S. Expl. Exped., Mam. and Ornith., p 338. *Anser hawaiiensis* Eydoux et Souleyet, Voy. Bonite, Oiseaux, p. 104. Atlas, pl. x. Peale, Zool. U. S. Expl. Exped., Birds, p. 249.

Hab. Highlands of Hawaii ; rare in the rest of the group. Common in flocks of 3 to 7.

This bird is seldom seen near water, living almost constantly on the high lava fields, at an elevation of five to seven thousand feet, where it finds abundant food in the ohelo (*Vaccinium penduliflora*), and a species of Sonchus (*S. asper*). It builds its nest in the grass, and lays two or three eggs, white, and about the size of those of the common goose. Plumage similar to that of the Chinese goose. Smaller than a common goose. Easily domesticated. Hawaiian goose.

42. ANAS SUPERCILIOSA. *Koloa*. Gmelin, Syst. Nat. I., p. 537. Latham, Ind. Orn., p. 852. Var. *sandvicensis* Bonaparte, Compt. Rend., 1856, p. 649. Var. *A. superciliosa* G. R. Gray, Cat. Birds Trop. Ids., 1859, p. 54. Finsch und Hartlaub, Central-Polynesiens, p. 213. Duck.

Ad. Fusca, notaei et grastaei plumis pallidius marginatis ; pileo fusco-nigricante ; collo-pallidiore, ochroleuco, fusco striolato, postice longitudinaliter obscuro ; superciliis, fascia lata infraoculari gutture colloque antico unicoloribus, ochroleucis ; fascia lata utrinque per oculum ducta alteroque stricta ad rostri basin orta fuscis ; speculo alari pulchro viridi, late nigro-marginato ; rostro nigro ; pedibus brunneis ; iride areo-flava. Long. 23 in.

Plumage mottled brown, light below, darker above ; blue speculum on wing coverts. Bill flat, dark brown, laminated at the sides. Feet webbed, dull orange. Habitat, whole group. Frequents fresh water only.

43. ANAS CLYPEATA. *Moha*. Gmelin, Syst. Nat. I., p. 518. Audubon, Birds of America, VI., p. 293 ; *Spatula clypeata ?* Gray, Cat. of Birds of Trop. Islands of Pacific, 1859, p. 55. Shoveller Duck.

Larger than the last; the males brilliantly marked with bright irridescent green, white, and chocolate brown. Bill spoon-shaped. They spend the winter months at the Islands, and migrate in the spring to the North-west coast of America, returning late in the fall. Frequent fresh water.

PROCELLARIDÆ.

44. THALASSIDROMA ——. An unnamed species from the Hawaiian Islands is in the Smithsonian collection. Petrel.

45. PROCELLARIA ALBA. *Uau.* Gmelin, Syst. Nat., I., p. 565; *Æstrelata leucocephala ?* Bonaparte, Consp. Avium, II., p. 189. Petrel.

P. ex. fusco nigra, gulæ area, pectore, abdomine et crisso albis; tectricibus caudœ inferioribus ex cinereo et albo mistis; rostro nigro; cauda rotundata, 16 pollices longa. (Gmelin.)

LARIDÆ.

46. STERNA BERGII. Lichtenstein, Verz. Doubl. Berlin Mus. (1823), p. 80. Finsch und Hartlaub, Ornith. Central-Polynesiens. p. 216. *S. rectirostris* Peale, Zool. U. S. Expl. Exped., Birds, p. 281, pl. LXXV., fig. 2. *S. poliocerca* Cassin, U. S. Expl. Exped., Mam and Ornith., p. 384. *Thalasseus Bergii* Blas. Cal. y. f. Ornith (1866), p. 81. *S. (Sylochelidon) poliocerca* Gray, Cat. Birds Trop. Ids. Pacific (1859), p. 58. Tern, or Sea Swallow.

Ad Dorso, alis et cauda dilute cærulescente-canis; fronte, capitis lateribus, collo toto corporeque subtus pure albis; vertice et nucha subcristata nitide et circumscripte nigris; remigibus majoribus pogonio externo toto obscure cinereis, interno pro majore parte scapisque albis; sub alaribus albis; rostro flavissimo; pedibus nigris; iride nigra.

Jun. Supra sordide cinerea plus minus infuscata; pileo cinereo et nigricante vario; crista fusco-nigricante; colli lateribus in fundo albo cinereo-maculatis. Long. 23 in. (Finsch und Hartlaub.)

47. STERNA PANAYA. *Kala.* Finsch und Hartlaub, Ornith., Central Polynesiens, p. 228, pl. IV., figs. 1, 2, 4. Eggs. *S. panayensis* Gmelin, Syst. Nat., I., p. 607. Latham, Ind. Ornith., II., p. 808. *S. oahuensis* Bloxam, Voyage Blonde, p. 251. *Haliplana panayensis* Bonaparte, Compt. Rend., 1856, p. 772. *H. panaya* Coues, Isis, 1864, p. 391. *S. serrata* Gray, Cat. Birds Trop. Ids. Pacific 1859, p. 59. Forster. Descript. &c., p. 276. Tern.

Ad. Supra fuliginosa; pileo nuchaque fusco-nigris; fronte, superciliis brevibus, margine alari et gastraeo toto pure albus; fascia per oculum ducta late nigro-fusca; remigibus majoribus nigris versus marginem interuum albicantibus; cauda fuliginosa; rostro et pedibus nigris; iride fusca.

Jun. Notæi plumis margine pallide rufescentibus; pileo albo et nigricante longitudinaliter vario; gastraei albidine minus pura. Long. 13 pollices; caud. 5 pollices. (Finsch und Hartlaub.)

48. GYGIS ALBA. Cassin, U. S. Expl. Exped., Mam. and Ornith., p. 389. Fig., Egg. Finsch und Hartlaub, Ornith., Central-Polynesiens, p. 232. *Sterna alba* Sparrman, Mus. Carls. No. XI. (1786). *S. candida* Gmelin, Syst. Nat., I., p. 607 (descr. fals.). Latham, Ind. Ornith., p. 807. Gould, Birds of Austr., VII., pl. XXX. White Tern.

Ad Tota sericeo-alba, unicolor; rostro nigro, basi pulchre violascente cæruleo; pedibus pallide cæruleis, membranis interdigitalibus flavis; iride fusco-nigra. Long. 10·5 pollices; caud. 3·5 pollices. (Finsch und Hartlaub.)

A single egg is laid on the bare branch of a tree, a knot or slight cavity being its only protection. It is 1·5 in. long and 1·2 in. in diameter, the ends nearly alike in form ; colour brownish white, sprinkled with thread-like spots and patches of burnt umber. (Peale.)

Doubtful whether it frequents the Hawaiian Islands.

49. DIOMEDEA BRACHYURA. Cassin, U. S. Expl. Exped., Mam. and Ornith., p. 398. Birds of Cal. and Texas, pl. 35. Gould, Birds of Aust., VII., pl. 9. Temm. Pl. Col. 5, pl. 554 (liv. 75). Temm. and Scleg. Faun, Japon, pl. 87. Short-tailed Albatross. Brown changing almost to white in old age. Spread of wings 7 ft. 3 in. Lays one egg, which is white, and 4$\frac{2}{10}$ in. long. Habitat, nearly all the Pacific Ocean. Common about the Hawaiian Islands, where it is seen following vessels. Distinct from the wandering Albatross, *Diomedea Exulans*.

50. ANOUS STOLIDUS. *Oio.* Cassin, U. S. Expl. Exped., Mam. and Ornith., p. 391. Finsch und Hartlaub, Ornith., Central-Polynesiens, p. 234. Wood's Nat. Hist. Birds, p. 755. *A stolidus* et *frater* Coues, Proc. Acad. Nat. Sci. Philad., 1862, p. 558. Baird, Birds of North America, p. 865. Gould, Birds of Austr., pl. xxxiv. *A. pileatus* et *stolidus*, Pelzeln, Novara Exped., Vögel, p. 155. *A. niger* Stephens, Gen. Zool., XIII., p. 140 (1825). Sperm-whale bird. Noddy.

Ad. Pulchre fuliginosus ; remigibus majoribus et cauda fere nigris ; pileo albicante-cano ; loris nigricantibus ; rostro et pedibus nigris ; iride fusca. Long. 20 pollices. (Finsch und Hartlaub.)

The differences between the American and Pacific forms of this bird are thus tabulated by Dr. Coues, *loc. cit.*

American.	*Pacific.*
Length of wing, 10 to 10·5 in.	Length of wing, 11 to 11·25 in.
Length of tail, about 6 in.	Length of tail, about 7 in.
Height of bill at base, ·38 in.	Height of bill at base, ·43 in.
Length of tarsus, 1 in.	Length of tarsus, 1 in. (same).
Length of middle toe and claw, 1·45 in.	Length of middle toe and claw, 1·60 in.
Middle toe and claw, 1·45 length of tarsus.	Middle toe and claw, 1·60 length of tarsus.
Central tail feathers but slightly shorter than the next.	Central tail feathers half an inch shorter than the next.
Occiput bluish plumbeous, becoming pure white on the front. Sides of head and neck all round with a decided wash of bluish plumbeous. Feet nearly black in dried specimen.	Occiput brownish ash, becoming ashy white (not pure) on the front. Sides of head and neck not notably different from general fuliginous. Feet reddish brown in dried skin.

The dimensions of a specimen I obtained in lat. 20° 30′ N., long. 154° W., were as follows : Total length 13 in., spread of wings 22·77 in., length of bill 2 in. Flight rapid and unsteady. Breeds on the sea cliffs on the Hawaiian Islands.

Eggs three in number, of a dark orange colour, splashed and spotted with red and purple. They are very good eating. (Wood's Nat. Hist.)

PELICANIDÆ.

51. PHAËTON RUBRICAUDA. *Kaula.* Boddaert, Tabl. Pl., Enl., p. 57. Finsch und Hartlaub, Ornith. Central-Polynesiens, p. 248. Cassin, U. S. Expl. Exped., Mam. and Ornith., p. 395. *P. phœnicurus* Gmelin, Syst. Nat., I., p. 583. Wood's Nat. Hist. Birds, p. 756. Gould, Birds of Austr., VII., pl. LXIII. Roseate Tropic Bird.

Ad. Totus sericeo-albus, rosaceo, tinctus; remigibus concoloribus; rectricibus duabus intermediis longissimis, intense rubris, scapis nigris; rostro rubro; pedibus flavis, membranis nigris. Long. cor. 3 pollices.

Quite common throughout the group, especially on Niihau and Kauai. The natives climb the almost inaccessible cliffs to get the rose-coloured tail-feathers, which they pull from the birds on their nests.

52. PHAËTON ÆTHEREUS. Linnæus, Syst. Nat., p. 219 (1766). Cassin, U. S. Expl. Exped., Mam. and Ornith., p. 394. Finsch und Hartlaub, Ornith. Central-Polynesiens, p. 250. Tropic Bird, Boat-swain Bird.

P. albus dorso, nigro-fasciolate et undulate; rostro læte rubrio; iride flava. (Finsch und Hartlaub.)

Length 2½ feet, tail 15 inches. It has great power of flight; has been seen a thousand miles from land; lives on fish.

53. TACHYPETES PALMERSTONI. Cassin, U. S. Expl. Exped., Mam. and Ornith., p. 359. Proc. Acad. Nat. Sci. Philad., 1856. *Pelecanus Palmerstoni.* Gmelin, Syst. Nat., I., p. 573 (1788). *Atagen Aquilus.* Gray, Cat. Birds Trop. Ids., 1859, p. 61. Frigate Pelican, Man-of-War Bird. Confounded in the first edition, and by Finsch and Hartlaub and others, with the *Tachypetes aquila*, a similar but much larger bird of the Atlantic Ocean. Male—plumage black, with green, blue, and purple metallic lustre on the upper parts; under parts paler and without lustre; large gular pouch on the throat at certain seasons, of a blood-red colour. Female—breast white, without the gular pouch, larger than the male; lays one egg of a bluish white colour 2$\frac{7}{10}$ inches long; bill long and hooked. Mr. G. N. Wilcox shot two of these birds on the island of Kauai, which measured 6 ft. 10 and 11 in. spread of wings. Lives on fish captured from other birds. Habitat, tropical belt of the Pacific and Indian Oceans.

Hawaiian Tariff and Digest of the Laws and Regulations of the Customs, Pilot and Harbour Regulations, &c.

ORIGINALLY PREPARED BY JOHN A. HASSINGER, AND COMPARED WITH RECENT LAWS.

Free Imports.

Animals, Birds, Bees, intended for improving the breeds.

Bags and Containers (old) returned, when accompanied by certificate of Hawaiian Consul.

Books printed in Hawaiian.

Catechu. (*See* Tanning.)

Coals.

Copper Sheathing, and all descriptions of Sheathing Metal.

Diplomatic Representatives. All goods imported for their private use and consumption.

Foreign Navies. All supplies when imported and used as such.

Foreign Whalers. Merchandise imported by them in accordance with the provisions of Sec. 569 to 573 of the Civil Code.

Gold and Silver Coins.

His Majesty. All goods or other articles imported for his use.

Hawaiian Government. All goods or other articles imported for the use of the several departments of the Government.

Hawaiian Whalers. Oil, bone, fish, or other products of the sea, being the catch of duly registered Hawaiian vessels.

Household Effects, old and in use, of persons arriving from abroad. Also the effects, not merchandise, of Hawaiian subjects dying abroad.

Iron. All Pig Iron and Plate Iron of ⅛ of an inch in thickness and upwards.

Models of Inventions, if not fitted for use.

Oak Bark. (*See* Tanning.)

Oil, Bone, &c. (*See* Hawaiian Whalers.)

Plants and Seeds, when not intended for sale.

Philosophical, Chemical, and other Apparatus for the Schools and Colleges.

Returned Cargo, being Merchandise exported to a foreign country and brought back in the same condition as when exported, accompanied by certificate of Hawaiian Consul.

Specie. (*See* Gold and Silver Coins.)

Specimens of Botany, Mineralogy, Geology, and other Natural Sciences imported for the use of Schools and Colleges.

Tanning. Certain material used in. Oak Bark, Catechu, and other substances containing "tannin."

Tools of Trade, Professional Books and Implements in actual use of persons from abroad.

Yellow Metal. (*See* Copper.)

Free Imports from the United States by Treaty.

Agricultural Implements, Animals.

Bacon, Beef, Books, Boots and Shoes, Bullion, Bran, Bricks, Bread and Breadstuffs of all kinds, Butter.

Cement, Cheese, Coal, Cordage, Copper and Composition Sheathing, Nails and Bolts; Cotton and Manufactures of Cotton, bleached and unbleached, and whether or not coloured, stained, painted or printed.

Doors, Sashes, and Blinds.

Eggs; Engines and parts thereof.

Fish and Oysters, and all other creatures living in the water, and the products thereof; Fruits, Nuts, and Vegetables, green, dried or undried, preserved or unpreserved; Flour, Furs.

Grain.

Ham, Hardware, Harness, Hay; Hides, dressed or undressed; Hoop Iron.

Ice; Iron and Steel, and manufactures thereof; Nails, Spikes and Bolts, Rivets, Brads or Sprigs, Tacks.

Lard; Leather, and Manufactures thereof: Lumber and Timber of all kinds, round, hewed, sawed, and manufactured in whole or in part; Lime.

Machinery of all kinds; Meal and Bran; Meats, fresh, smoked or preserved.

Nails; Naval Stores, including Tar, Pitch, Resin, Turpentine, raw and rectified.

Oats.

Paper, and all manufactures of Paper or of Paper and Wood; Petroleum, and all Oils for lubricating or illuminating purposes; Plants, Shrubs, Trees and Seeds; Pork.

Rice.

Salt; Shooks; Skins and Pelts, dressed and undressed; Staves and Headings, Starch, Stationery, Soap; Sugar, refined or unrefined.

Tallow; Textile Manufactures made of a combination of wool, cotton, silk or linen, or of any two or more of them, other than when ready-made clothing; Tobacco, whether in leaf or manufactured.

Waggons and Carts for the purposes of agriculture or of drayage, Wood and manufactures of Wood, or Wood and Metal, except Furniture, either upholstered or carved, and Carriages; Wool and manufactures of Wool, other than ready-made clothing.

Dutiable Imports.

Alcoholic, and other Spirits of the strength of Alcohol, per gall. . . . . $ c. 10 0

Alcohol. Provided that security be given that the same is intended for Medicinal, Mechanical, or Scientific purposes, upon application in due form, per cent. ad val. . . . 50

21

Ale, Porter, Beer, Cider, and other fermented beverages
below eighteen per cent. of alcoholic strength, per dozen $ c.
quarts   40
    Per dozen pints   20
    Per gallon in bulk   15
Ammunition, per cent. ad valorem 0 10
Bitters. (See Brandy and Wine.)
Brandied Fruits. (See Brandy.)
Brandy, Gin, Rum, Whiskey, Liqueurs, Cordials, Bitters,
Brandied Fruits, Perfumery, and other articles of mer-
chandise, sweetened or mixed, containing alcohol or spirits,
of the strength of thirty per cent. or upwards, and not ex-
ceeding fifty-five per cent. of alcohol, per gallon . . .   3 00
Britannia Ware and Fancy Metal Ware, per cent. ad val. .   10
Candles, per cent. ad val.   10
Carriages of all descriptions, per cent. ad val.. . . .   10
Clothing, ready-made, and Wearing Apparel of every descrip-
tion, made up in whole or in part, per cent. ad val . .   10
Crockery and Glassware of all descriptions, per cent. ad val.   10
Cigars and Cheroots, per M. 10 00
Coffee. The product of any country with which this Govern-
ment has no existing treaty, per lb.   03
    All other, per cent. ad val.   10
Cordials. (See Brandy and Wine.)
Drugs and Medicines, patent and other, per cent. ad val .   10
Firearms, per cent. ad val.   10
Furniture of all kinds, if upholstered or carved, manufac-
tured in whole or in part, per cent. ad val.   10
Gimps for Clothing, per cent. ad val   10
Gloves and Mitts not otherwise provided for, per cent. ad val.   10
Gin. (See Brandy.) Liqueurs. (See Brandy.)
Hats and Caps of all kinds, per cent. ad val. . . .   10
Hooks and Eyes, per cent. ad val.   10
Hoop Skirts, per cent. ad val.   10
Insertions, Laces and Lace Goods of all descriptions, per cent.
ad val.   10
Jewellery, and all descriptions of Metal, Glass or Stone Beads,
per cent. ad val.   10
Linens, and all Manufactures of which Flax, Grass Cloth or
a similar material shall form the principal part, per cent.
ad val.   10
Matches of all kinds, per cent. ad val.   10
Millinery Goods, Beads, Braids, Bonnets, Buttons, Corsets,
Collars, Sleeves and Cuffs, Edgings, Flowers (artificial),
Feathers (fancy), Fringes for clothing and upholstery, per
cent. ad val.   10

Molasses and Syrups of Sugar, the product of any country with which this Government has no existing treaty, per gall. . . . . $ o. 10
  All other, per cent. ad val. 10

Paintings, Pictures, Engravings, Statuary, Bronzes, Ornamental Work of Metal, Stone, Marble, Plaster of Paris or Alabaster, and all imitations thereof, per cent. ad val. . 10
Perfumery (other than that which pays a spirit duty), Powders; Hair, Tooth, Nail, and other Toilet Brushes, per cent. ad val. 10
Playing Cards, per cent. ad val. 10
Peppermint, (See Brandy.) Perfumery. (See Brandy.)
Porter. (See Ale.)

Ribbons, not otherwise provided for, per cent. ad val. . . 10
Rice. The product of any country with which this Government has no existing treaty, cleaned, per lb. . . . 01½
  All other, per cent. ad val. 01

Silks, Satins, and Silk Velvet, and all articles of which silk shall form the principal material, per cent. ad val. . . 10
Sugar. The product of any country with which this Government has no existing treaty, per lb. 02
  All other, per cent. ad val. 10
Silverplate, Plated Ware or Gilt Ware, per cent. ad val. . 10
Soaps, per cent. ad val. 10
Tea, per cent. ad val. 10
Toys, per cent. ad val. 10
Tobacco (except China), and all manufactures thereof, per cent. ad val. 15
Watches and Clocks, in whole or in part, per cent. ad val. . 10
Whiskey. (See Brandy.)
Wines. Madeira, Sherry, Port, and all other Wines, Cordials and Bitters, and all other articles of merchandise containing alcohol, or preserved in alcohol or spirits, above eighteen per cent. and below thirty per cent. of alcoholic strength, unless otherwise provided for, per gallon 2 00
Wines. Champagne, Sparkling Moselle, and Sparkling Hock,
  per dozen quarts 3 00
  per dozen pints 1 50
Wines. Claret, Rhine Wine, and other light Wines, Bitters and Cordials of a higher quality than Wines of "Cargaison," when below eighteen per cent. of alcoholic strength, per
  dozen quarts 40
  per dozen pints 20
  per gallon in bulk 15

  Upon all other Goods, Wares, and Merchandise, of whatever description, imported into this Kingdom, there shall be levied, collected

21 *

and paid, a duty of ten per cent. ad valorem, including all charges as per original invoice, except the following :—

	$ c.
China Tobacco. per lb. .	0 50
Cigarettes and Paper Cigars, per cent. ad val. .	25
Candies, per cent. ad val. .	25
Camphor Trunks, each	50
China Matting, per roll .	1 00
Kid and Leather Gloves, per dozen pair .	3 00
Pipes and Pipe Fixtures, per cent. ad val. .	25
Peanut Oil. per cent. ad val. .	25
Fireworks and Fire Crackers, per cent. ad val. .	25

All Invoices of Merchandise, presented at any of the Custom Houses of this Kingdom for entry, must be accompanied by the certificate of the Hawaiian Consul at the port of shipment, otherwise 25 per cent. will be added to the original value, and the usual duties levied on the increased value thereof.

Arrival and Entry of Vessels.

MERCHANTMEN.—The commanding officer of any merchant vessel, immediately after her arrival at either of the legalised ports of entry, shall make known to the Collector of Customs the business upon which said vessel has come to the port, and deliver him, under oath, a full, true, and perfect manifest of the cargo with which said vessel is laden before allowing any parcels to be landed, except the *Mail Bags* delivered to the order of the Postmaster; which manifest shall contain an account of the packages, with their marks, numbers, contents, and quantities, also the names of the importers, or consignees, and shippers; and furnish him with a list of her passengers before allowing any baggage to be landed ; and deliver him, under oath, a list of all stores on board his vessel, under penalty of forfeiting all stores not mentioned in such list, and a fine of one hundred dollars.

When any such officer shall fail to perform any or all of the acts above mentioned within forty-eight hours after his arrival, he shall be subject to a fine not exceeding one thousand dollars.

All letters under the care of the captain, or within his power, except such as are directed to the owner or consignee of the vessel, must be delivered to the Postmaster of the port before entry can be made or report received.

All goods imported in any vessel, and which are not included in her inward manifest, shall be liable to seizure and confiscation, and the vessel and master shall be liable to a fine not exceeding one thousand dollars.

When all the goods included in the inward manifest are not pro-

NOTE.—There are no transit or export duties, or charges other than the cost of Entry forms, as required by law.

duced or accounted for to the Collector, the vessel and master shall be liable for the appraised value of such deficiency and the duties thereon, together with a fine not exceeding one thousand dollars.

No goods or articles of any description shall be landed at any of the ports of this Kingdom on any Sunday or national holiday, nor on other days except between sunrise and sunset, nor until the same shall have been duly entered at the Custom House, and landing permit issued, under penalty of seizure and confiscation.

WHALEMEN.—Masters of whaling vessels shall enter their vessels at the Custom House within forty-eight hours after their arrival at either of the ports of entry, and previous to discharging or shipping any seamen, or taking off any supplies or stores, under penalty of not less than ten, or more than one hundred dollars.

They shall also, within the time above stated, furnish under oath a list of all wines and spirits on board as stores, and a manifest of all cargo and freight, except the product of their fishery and the outfit, provisions, and furniture of their vessel, under penalty of forfeiting all such stores, cargo, and freight as are not on the list of stores or manifest, and a fine of one hundred dollars.

Every master of a whaling vessel, who shall have duly entered his vessel at the Custom House, shall be entitled to a permit from the Collector to trade or barter goods for refreshment and supplies to the amount of twelve hundred dollars, original invoice value, two hundred dollars of which shall be free of duties.

This privilege to trade or barter may be used at one or more ports of the Kingdom, but shall not be construed so as to permit any such vessel to trade or barter goods to a greater amount in all than twelve hundred dollars during one visit to the Kingdom.

Whalers' Permits do not include the trade, sale, landing, or disposal of spirituous liquors, and all such traffic on the part of whaling vessels shall subject them to all the charges of merchant vessels, and to all other legal liabilities.

The same duties shall be exacted of whaling vessels as are exacted of merchant vessels for any goods landed or disposed of by them exceeding the value of two hundred dollars ; and in case such excess amounts to more than one thousand dollars, they shall be deemed in law to have become merchantmen, and be subjected to all the charges of merchant vessels.

All articles to be landed on Whalers' Permit must be entered upon it with ink, and the value carried out, before leaving the vessel.

Every master of a whaling vessel who shall fail to produce his permit, when called for by any officer of Customs, shall be liable to a fine of not less than ten, nor more than fifty dollars, to be imposed by the Collector.

LIGHT DUES.—There shall be levied upon all vessels arriving from abroad at any port of this Kingdom where a lighthouse may be established, the sum of three dollars, which shall be paid before departure, to the Collector-General of Customs.

All vessels engaged in the coasting trade shall pay ten cents. per ton as light dues, in consideration of which they shall be entitled to visit all ports where lighthouses may be established, for the term of one year, without further charge.

CUSTOM HOUSE GUARDS.—The Collector shall provide an officer to be present on board any vessel during her discharge, or at any other time when he may deem it necessary, to superintend the landing of her cargo, and see that no other or greater amount of goods are landed than is set forth upon the permit to discharge.

It shall be the duty of the commanding officer of any vessel, when boarded by an officer of the Customs, to furnish him promptly with any and all information which he may require in regard to the vessel, her cargo, stores, passengers, &c., and exhibit for his inspection her manifest, register, or other papers relating to the same.

Every vessel of not more than five hundred tons shall be allowed six days, and every vessel of five hundred tons and upwards shall be allowed twelve days after entry in which to discharge, but for all days in excess, the compensation of the officer superintending the landing of the cargo shall be a charge against the vessel. Sundays and holidays shall not be counted in the number of days allowed for discharge at the expense of the Government.

PASSENGERS.—If the master of any vessel arriving at any port of entry of this Kingdom from a foreign port shall suffer the baggage of any passenger on board his vessel to be removed on shore from such vessel, unless a permit therefor has been obtained from the Collector of the port, such master shall be liable to a fine not exceeding fifty dollars, in the discretion of the Collector of Customs.

If any passenger arriving at a port of entry of this Kingdom on board of a vessel coming from a foreign port, shall remove his baggage on shore from such vessel without first obtaining a permit therefor from the Collector of the port, such passenger shall be liable to a fine not exceeding fifty dollars, in the discretion of the Court.

Any passenger arriving from a foreign port at any of the ports of this Kingdom shall be subject to a tax of two dollars, for the support of hospitals for the benefit of sick and disabled Hawaiian seamen, which shall be paid to the several Collectors of Customs before any permit is issued to such passenger to land his baggage.

If the master of any vessel shall allow any passenger to land his baggage or other effects at any port of this Kingdom without payment of the aforesaid tax, he shall be liable therefor, and also to a penalty of not less than ten nor more than fifty dollars, to be imposed by the Collector, in his discretion; such baggage or other effects shall also be subject to seizure and sale.

MARINE HOSPITAL TAX.—The master or owner of every ship or vessel under the Hawaiian flag, arriving from any foreign port, or from sea, at any port of the Hawaiian Kingdom, 'shall, before such ship or vessel is admitted to entry, render to the Collector of such port a true account of the number of seamen who have been employed on board since the last entry at any Hawaiian port, and pay to said Collector at the rate of twenty-five cents per month for each and every seaman so employed, for the benefit of the Marine Hospital Fund, which amount such master or owner is authorized to retain out of the wages of said seaman.

The master of every coasting vessel employed in the carrying trade between the different ports, roadsteads, or harbours of the Hawaiian Kingdom, shall render quarterly to the Collector-General of Customs, or to any Collector under his directions, a true list of all seamen employed by him during the preceding three months, and pay to said Collector-General, or Collector, at the rate of twenty-five cents per month for each and every seaman so employed, for the benefit of the Marine Hospital Fund, which sum said master is authorized to retain out of the wages of such seaman.

The returns required as above shall be made under oath, in such manner and form as the Collector-General may prescribe. If any owner or master shall make a false return, he shall be deemed guilty of perjury and punished accordingly. He shall also be subject to a penalty of one hundred dollars, for the benefit of the said Marine Hospital Fund, and his vessel shall be liable to seizure, condemnation and sale, to secure the payment of such penalty.

PASSPORTS.—Every adult who may have resided on these Islands for more than thirty days, wishing to leave the Kingdom, shall make application to the Collector of the port from which he intends to sail, for a passport.

It shall be lawful for the Collectors of Customs to grant passports to all applicants for the same except in the following cases :

First. In case of the indebtedness or obligation to pay money, of the applicant, to the Government or to any private individual, of which the Collector has received written notice, accompanied by a request not to grant a passport.

Second. In case the applicant is a party defendant in a suit, civil or criminal, pending before any court of this kingdom, of which the Collector shall have received written notice.

Third. In case a writ *ne exeat regno*, or any other process to arrest or stay the departure of the applicant, shall have been issued by any court of the kingdom, of which the Collector shall have received notice in writing.

Fourth. In case of a written complaint being made to the Collector that the applicant is about to depart the Kingdom, leaving his wife or family unprovided for.

Every Collector of Customs may, after granting a passport, cancel the same upon being satisfied that it was obtained by any deceit or misrepresentation, or that the permission to leave the Kingdom will work great wrong or injustice to the Government or to any individual.

Every master or commanding officer of a vessel who shall convey out of this Kingdom any person not having a passport, shall be subject to a fine of fifty dollars and be liable for all debts which such person may have left unpaid in this Kingdom. And if he shall fail to pay such fine and debts, such vessel shall be subject to seizure, condemnation and sale, for the payment thereof . provided always that these provisions shall not be construed as applicable to any seaman legally shipped on board of any vessel.

STORAGE REGULATIONS.—The expense of putting in, stowing and taking out of stores will be borne by the importers or owners. Any loss by leakage, breakage, or fire, shall be at the responsibility of the party or parties who place the goods in store.

SPIRITUOUS LIQUORS.—The importer is permitted to take out as a sample of each kind and quality one bottle for every one hundred gallons, and one bottle for every fifty cases, free of duty ; but for every succeeding sample there will be a charge of one dollar for each bottle.

Before taking a package out of the stores, the importer will present an order to the Collector, giving the marks, numbers, and contents thereof, and stating whether it is intended for exportation or consumption.

If the liquor to be withdrawn is intended for consumption, the duties must then be paid ; but if it is intended for exportation, an outward entry must be made in the usual form, stating by whom it is to be exported, date of inward entry, vessels' and masters' names by which imported and by which it is to be exported.

All liquors in casks will be gauged as they are taken out of the stores for consumption, and duties charged only upon the quantity delivered.

Liquors taken out of the stores for exportation or consumption, must not be in less quantities than a single and original package. (Exceptions are made where the package is a hogshead or pipe.)

OTHER GOODS.—Goods taken from the stores must be in original packages. If for consumption, not less than one hundred dollars in value will be delivered, or the remainder of an importation. Nothing less than a whole package will be delivered, except as samples, and then in the least quantity that will make a fair sample. In ordering goods out of the Bonded Stores for exportation or consumption, the same form must be observed as with spirits.

Rates of Storage.

For Liquors in casks and kegs, 1 cent per gallon per month.

For Liquors in cases, ½ cent per gallon per month.

For bags of Flour (200 lbs.), 4 cents each per month—other sizes in proportion.

For barrels of Flour, Meal, and Bread, 4 cents each per month.

For barrels or cases of bottled Ale, Beer, and Porter (4 dozen each), 4 cents each per month.

For barrels of Beef, Pork, and Fish, 5 cents each per month.

For barrels of Pitch and Tar, 7 cents each per month.

For bundles Shooks, and casks Heads and Hoops, 1 cent per barrel per month.

For Whaleboats, 1 dollar each per month.

Goods (except the above-named), 40 cents per ton per month.

Storage bills on liquors will be rendered every quarter; on other goods every six months, or as required.

QUANTITY OF GOODS TO COMPOSE A TON.—Forty feet (cubic measure); 2,000 lbs. pig and bar Iron, Sugar, Rice, Nails, and similar articles ; 200 gallons (wine measure), reckoning the full contents of the cask, of Oil, Vinegar, Lime Juice, Ale, Beer, and Porter, not bottled.

Not less than one month's storage to be charged, and (after the first month) if less than twelve days, nothing ; over twelve days, a full month.

From the date of each transfer the storage commences anew.

Registry of Hawaiian Vessels.

No vessel shall be entitled to a Hawaiian Register unless the same be wholly owned by a subject or subjects of this Kingdom ; Provided, however, that any vessel fitted out for the Whale or Seal Fishery may be registered in the name of any part owner of such vessel actually domiciled in this Kingdom, whether a subject or not.

Application for a Register must be made to the Collector-General of Customs, under oath, setting forth the name of vessel, where built, and a general description of the same ; and accompanied by evidence of the title of the party making the application. Either of several owners of a vessel may make application for her registry, but he shall set forth in his application the share of each owner respectively.

Upon being satisfied that no legal impediment exists (more particularly if the vessel be foreign built) to her registry, the Collector-General shall cause the said vessel to be examined by the Government Inspector of Vessels, and should she be found seaworthy, he shall cause her to be measured according to the rule fixed by law.

Before receiving a Certificate of Hawaiian Registry, the owner of said vessel shall file a bond with the Collector-General, in the penal sum of not less than two hundred, or more than two thousand dollars, conditioned that said certificate shall be used solely for the vessel for which it is granted, and shall not be sold, loaned, or otherwise disposed of ; and that in case said vessel (if the same be not a vessel employed in the whale or seal fishery) shall become either wholly or in part the property of any alien foreigner or foreigners ; or in case she shall be lost, taken by an enemy, burnt or broken up; said certificate of registry shall be returned to said Collector-General within six months, or satisfactory proof furnished him that said certificate could not be preserved.

Upon receipt of the surveyor and measurer's certificate and the owner's bond, and being satisfied that no legal impediment exists to the registry of said vessel, the Collector-General shall cause the same to be enrolled at his office as a Hawaiian vessel, and issue to the owner or owners a certificate of registry in the form required by law, and the certificate of registry of such vessel shall be *prima facie* evidence of the ownership and nationality thereof.

All transfers, by sale or otherwise, and all mortgages or hypothecation of Hawaiian registered vessels, must be deposited, together with the register, with the Collector-General for record; otherwise no such transfer or hypothecation shall be valid. And all mortgages or hypothecation, when cancelled, shall entitle the mortgagor or pledger to a written release or satisfaction, which must be deposited with the Collector-General for endorsement upon the original record and register, under penalty of a fine and a further liability to pay all damages occasioned thereby.

In case of any transfer or mortgage on any Hawaiian vessel, it shall be the duty of the owner or owners to produce the certificate of registry to the Collector-General (for noting said transfer or mortgage) within three days, if said vessel be within the kingdom, or, if absent, immediately after her return, under penalty of seizure, condemnation, and sale.

COASTERS.—The Collector-General of Customs, under the direction of the Minister of the Interior, shall grant a coasting license for one year to any Hawaiian registered vessel, the owner of which shall have applied to him in writing, setting forth the vessel's name with the date and number of her register, which license shall be in such form as may be approved by the Minister of the Interior.

Upon granting such license, the Collector-General of Customs shall exact of the owner a bond, with at least one approved surety, in the penal sum of five hundred dollars, in such form and upon such condition as may be approved by the Minister of the Interior.

Any vessel which shall engage in the coasting trade of this Kingdom without a license shall be liable to seizure, condemnation, and sale.

The Minister of the Interior shall have power to establish rules for the guidance and government of all vessels engaged in the coasting trade, and in case any such vessel shall violate any of the said rules, he shall have the power to annul its license. He may also at any time impress any licensed coaster into the public service, upon just compensation, to be afterwards assessed by the Court of Admiralty of this Kingdom.

All vessels engaged in the coasting trade shall carry the Inter-

Island mails free of charge, under such regulations as may from time to time be provided by law, or prescribed by the Minister of the Interior, upon pain of forfeiting their license.

It shall not be lawful for any vessel to carry passengers between the different islands of this Kingdom, except such vessels as shall be especially licensed for that purpose, under a penalty of twenty dollars for each passenger so carried, to be recovered before any Police or District Justice.

Before obtaining the said license, it shall be necessary that the vessel should be thoroughly inspected by the Harbour Master of Honolulu, one of the pilots of said port, and some shipwright, to be appointed for that purpose by the Collector-General of Customs; and if the said inspectors shall certify the vessel to be staunch and well equipped, and of sufficient capacity and accommodations to carry passengers, the owner of such vessel shall be entitled to receive a license from the Collector-General to carry passengers between the Islands for one year, subject to all the passport regulations for the carrying of females, as provided by law.

No vessel shall carry more than one passenger for every two tons registered burthen, excepting steam vessels, the same being allowed to carry two passengers for every three tons burthen; and in case of any violation thereof, the master of such vessel shall be liable to a fine of five dollars for each passenger so carried, the same to be recovered before any Police or District Justice.

Each vessel licensed to carry passengers between the Islands shall carry on all her passages, secured on deck, one spare extra cask of the capacity of at least two barrels, filled with water; and under her deck, easily accessible, as many barrels of good sound bread or rice and salt provisions and water as may from time to time be required by the Harbour Master of Honolulu; and for disobedience of the orders of the Harbour Master, by not carrying the amount of water and provisions required by him, the vessel shall be liable to have her license revoked by the Collector-General, and the master shall be further liable to a fine not exceeding one hundred dollars, to be recovered before any Police or District Justice.

Registry Fees and Coasting Charges.

	$	c.
Inspector's Fee	3	00
Measurement, per ton		05
Registry, per ton		25
Enrollment Fee	2	00
Bond, Stamp	1	00
Coasting License—to 25 tons, per ton	1	00
Each additional ton		50
License Blank, Stamp	1	00
License Bond, Stamp	1	00
Application for Register, Stamp	1	00

Departure of Vessels.

Any vessel having, through her master or agent, fully complied with the laws and regulations affecting foreign trade, and with all the laws regulating the shipment and discharge of Hawaiian seamen, shall be entitled to depart after receiving from the Collector of the port a clearance in the form provided by law.

In case any vessel does not sail within forty-eight hours after receiving a clearance, it shall be the duty of the master to report the same to the Collector of the port, under a penalty of not exceeding twenty-five dollars, to be imposed by said Collector.

No vessel shall be entitled to a clearance unless all proper charges at the Harbour Master's office shall have been settled, and the Collector may require the master or agent of the vessel to produce the Harbour Master's certificate to that effect.

To entitle any vessel to a clearance, it shall be incumbent on her commanding officer first to furnish the Collector of the port with a manifest of the cargo laden on board of such vessel, which manifest shall be given under oath; contain a full statement of all goods on board, expressing contents, quantities, and value, and distinguishing between domestic, foreign, and transhipped goods, and shall also contain a list of all stores taken from Bond. He shall also furnish in proper form, a list of all passengers intending to depart in said vessel.

When goods are exported from Bond, it is necessary that the person exporting the same shall make an outward entry at the Custom House, in the form required by law; which said entry must be made before the clearance of the vessel in which the same are to be exported.

If any vessel shall sail from any port in this Kingdom without first obtaining a clearance, the commanding officer thereof shall be subject to a fine not exceeding one thousand dollars, in the discretion of the court, for the payment of which fine the vessel shall be liable to seizure, condemnation, and sale.

PORTS OF ENTRY.—No goods of foreign growth or production shall be landed or unladen from a foreign vessel, or Hawaiian vessel from a foreign port, at any other port of the Hawaiian Islands than a port of entry for foreign vessels as created by law, under a penalty of seizure and forfeiture of the vessel in which such goods shall be brought, and of the goods imported therein, and so landed or unladen. And in passing from port to port no foreign vessel shall engage in the coasting trade of this Kingdom.

The following are the legal ports of entry: Honolulu, Island of Oahu; Lahaina and Kahului, Island of Maui; Hilo, Kawaihae and Kealakekua, Island of Hawaii; Koloa, Island of Kauai. In addition to the above, foreign vessels engaged in the whale fishery shall have access to the port of Hanalei, Island of Kauai, for the purpose of recruiting and refreshment.

It shall be lawful for any vessel from abroad, with the written permit of the Collector-General of Customs, to proceed to any other port or place in the Kingdom not a port of entry, for the purpose of debarking cargo, the duties upon which have been paid, or of embarking cargo, or of obtaining refreshment.

The Collectors of Customs at other ports in the Kingdom than Honolulu, may grant such permits for their respective collection districts.

REGULATION CONCERNING STAMPS AND BLANKS ON INWARD ENTRIES.— On and after March 11, 1864, the charges for stamps and blanks on invoices valued at ten dollars and under, will be one dollar; on invoices valued over ten dollars, and not exceeding twenty dollars, one dollar and a half ; on invoices valued over twenty dollars, the usual charge of two dollars and a half.

REGULATION CONCERNING RETURN GOODS, EMPTY BAGS, CONTAINERS, &c.—From and after the 1st of June 1867, it will be required that all invoices of " Return Goods, Empty Bags, &c.," intended to be entered free, must be accompanied by the Hawaiian Consul's (of port of shipment) Certificate, that they are the same goods and in original packages as shipped from this port.

Custom House Charges.

	$	c.
For visit of Health Officer when required	5	00
When necessarily detained on board, per day	10	00
Health fee, vessel not anchored by the pilot	5	00
For Bill of Health on departure	1	00
Pilot's and Boarding Officer's Fees. (See Pilotage.)		
Buoys	2	00
Lights—Vessels from abroad	3	00
Coasters, each year, per ton		10
Inward or Outward Manifests	2	00
Mail Oath	1	00
Inward Entry, Goods paying Duties	2	50
„ Goods free under Reciprocity Treaty	2	50
„ Goods Bonded	4	50
Outward Entry, Goods Bonded	1	50
Transit Entry	2	50
Bond to secure payment of Duties	2	00
Passports	1	00
Passport Protest	3	00
Every Stamped Certificate or Blank furnished by the Collector	1	00
Recording Bill of Sale, Mortgage or Hypothecation of a vessel, or copying the same, or copying Certificate of Registry, per one hundred words		50
Acknowledgments, each	1	00

The Custom House charges for all other acts and duties not expressly provided for by law, as also the rates of storage, shall be such as may from time to time be prescribed by the Minister of Finance.

Port Regulations—Pilotage.

Upon the arrival of any vessel making the usual marine signal for a pilot, it shall be the duty of the pilot at the port to immediately put off to such vessel, taking with him a white and a yellow flag ; to inquire into the sanitary condition of the ship and the health of those on board ; and upon being assured to his satisfaction that there is no danger to be apprehended from any contagious disease, be shall board such vessel, but not otherwise.

Upon boarding the vessel, the pilot shall present the commanding officer with a Health Certificate to be signed by him, and in case the same shall be signed, the white flag shall be immediately hoisted at the main, and the pilot shall be at liberty to bring the vessel into port ; but in case the commanding officer shall decline to sign the certificate of health, the pilot shall deliver him a yellow flag, which the master shall hoist at the main, and the vessel shall be placed in quarantine, outside of the harbour, and anchored where the pilot may direct.

Any pilot who shall conduct a vessel into any port in this Kingdom, in violation of the provisions of this law, or any of the Regulations of the Board of Health, or knowing that there is just ground to suspect the existence of contagion on board, shall be liable to a fine not exceeding five hundred dollars.

Every vessel, the master of which shall have declined to sign a certificate of health as above prescribed, shall, upon entering port, be liable to seizure, confiscation and sale.

If the pilot, after boarding any vessel, shall discover the existence of a contagious disease, he shall not return on shore ; neither shall it be lawful for any of the ship's company or passengers to land or communicate with the shore, or board any other vessel, without permission of the Board of Health, or the Collector, under penalty of a fine not exceeding five hundred dollars.

The pilots of Honolulu shall bring the vessel which they may take charge of, fully within the harbour (within the inner buoy unless otherwise directed by the Harbour Master), and anchor her in a suitable and convenient place, under penalty of forfeiting their commission.

No pilot shall take out any vessel that may be under attachment or arrest by virtue of any process, nor before she has obtained her clearance, under penalty of forfeiting his commission and paying a fine not exceeding one thousand dollars.

If any foreign vessel, or Hawaiian vessel engaged in foreign trade, shall enter or depart from any of the ports for which pilots may be appointed, without a pilot, such vessel shall be liable to one half pilotage.

All vessels anchoring outside the reef at Honolulu shall, when so requested by the Habour Master or any pilot, change their anchorage and anchor in such place as he may direct, under penalty of a fine not exceeding one hundred dollars.

At ports where there are no pilots, the regularly appointed boarding officers shall do and perform all the duties prescribed for pilots.

The pilot's fees, boarding officer's fees and health fees shall form a part of the port charges, which shall be paid by every vessel to the Collector of the port before a clearance is granted.

Pilot's Fees.

	$ c.
On all War Vessels, Mail Steamers, and vessels under 200 tons, per foot	1 50
On all other vessels over 200 tons, per ton	05
No vessel to be charged more than $50, in or out.	
For anchoring a vessel outside	15 00
In case such vessel comes into the harbour	10 00
If detaining pilot over 24 hours, additional pay per day . .	5 00
Boarding Officer, at ports where and when no pilotage is charged	5 00

Towage Rates—Port of Honolulu.

	$ c.			$ c.
Vessels under 500 tons .	40 00	Whalemen . . .		40 00
Vessels over 500 tons .	45 00	Vessels under 200 tons	.	30 00
Vessels over 1,000 tons .	50 00	Vessels over 200 tons	.	35 00

Harbour Regulations.

The Harbour Masters of Honolulu and Hilo shall have authority over the anchoring, mooring, and making fast of all hulks, coasters, boats, and other craft in their respective harbours, and are charged in general with the enforcement of all harbour regulations. They shall also be wharfingers at the ports for which they are appointed. They shall be entitled to receive, in addition to their usual fees, all amounts disbursed by them for the use of boats, warps, and labour in mooring and making fast any vessel, and if necessarily detained on board more than two hours at any one time, they shall be paid at the rate of one dollar per hour for such extra detention.

All vessels that may enter any port shall be anchored in the place designated by the Harbour Master, and moved from one anchorage to another as he may direct ; and no vessel, except coasting vessels under fifty tons burthen and vessels about to leave the harbour, shall quit her anchorage or moorings until the commanding officer shall have received the written permission of the Harbour Master, under penalty of a fine not exceeding one hundred dollars.

The Harbour Master or any pilot, while removing a vessel from one anchorage or mooring to another, may make fast to any other vessel, or to any warp or wharf; and any person resisting the same, cutting away or casting off the warp or fastening, shall be subject to a fine not exceeding one hundred dollars; and if such person belong to any vessel, the master of such vessel shall be responsible for any damage resulting from such resistance, cutting away, or casting off, as well as for the fine imposed upon the offender.

In order to facilitate the removing and placing of vessels in their proper berths, all vessels in the harbour shall, when requested by the Harbour Master or any pilot, slack down their stream cables and other fastenings, and also their bower chains, under penalty of a fine not exceeding one hundred dollars.

Any vessel entering port shall, if so requested by the Harbour Master or any pilot, rig in her jib, flying jib, and spanker booms and spritsail yards, and top the lower and topsail yards, within twenty-four hours after anchoring in such port; and in all cases before attempting to come alongside of, or make fast to, either of the docks or wharves, and keep them so rigged in and topped until within twenty-four hours before leaving the harbour, and until after removing from any wharf or dock, under penalty of a fine not exceeding one hundred dollars.

No combustible materials such as pitch, tar, resin, or oil, shall be heated on board any vessel within the harbour of Honolulu; but all such combustible articles shall be heated either on shore, or in a boat, or on a raft, at a reasonable distance from the vessel, of which distance the Harbour Master shall be the judge. Every person violating the provisions of this Section shall be liable to a fine not exceeding one hundred dollars.

No stones or other rubbish shall be thrown from any vessel into the harbour of Honolulu or Hilo, under penalty of a fine not exceeding one hundred dollars; and the master of the vessel from which the same are thrown shall be subject to a like fine.

Any person who shall leave, or cause to be left, for the space of six hours, upon the shores or reefs of any harbour in this kingdom, any dead animal, shall be subject to a fine not exceeding one hundred dollars, and shall cause the same to be removed without delay.

Every vessel taking on board or discharging any ballast or coals within the harbour of Honolulu, shall have a tarpaulin properly stretched and spread, so as to prevent any from falling into the water, under penalty of a fine not exceeding one hundred dollars.

No vessel having Gunpowder on board will be permitted to remain at the wharf more than twelve hours; and if the vessel shall be at the wharf over night, a policeman or watchman shall be kept on duty on board all night. All gunpowder deposited on the wharf for shipment shall be immediately passed on board the vessel to receive the same.

Harbour Master's Charges.

WHARFAGE.—Per registered ton (Sundays and Government holidays not counted), 2 cents per day.

STORAGE.—Bricks, Coal, Coolers, Kettles, Stone Ballast, Sand, (space of 32 square feet measurement), 1 cent per day; Oil, on wharves, for every 10 barrels, 1 cent per day; Lumber, Firewood (space of 32 square feet measurement), 1 cent per day; Anchors, Chains, Pig Ballast, and Old Iron, per ton of 2,000 lbs., ¼ cent per day.

Harbour Master's Fees.

	$ c.
Boarding vessel on arrival	3 00
Boarding vessel on departure	3 00
Moving vessel, each time	3 00

Shipping and Discharging Native Seamen.

Shipping, each man	0 50
Discharging, each man	0 50
Government Tax, each man	6 00
Shipping Articles, Stamp	1 00
Master's Bond, Stamp	1 00
Application to Governor	1 00

[All the above charges must be paid by the ship.]

Discharging Foreign Seamen.

Seaman's Permit	0 50
Seaman's Bond	1 00
Permit for deserter to ship	0 50

Boat Regulations—Port of Honolulu.

The owner of any boat duly licensed for the harbour of Honolulu, shall be entitled, if hired on time, to charge one dollar for each passenger for the first hour, and fifty cents for each succeeding hour, if the boat have four or more oars, and only half these fares if the boat have less than four oars. If hired by distance, twenty-five cents for each passenger to and from any ship or point within the inner buoy; fifty cents to and from any point between the inner and outer buoys; and two dollars to and from any ship or point in the anchorage outside of the buoys, if the boat have four oars, and only half of said fares if the boat have less than four oars : Provided always, that if the boat shall be detained by any passenger alongside of any ship, or at any point, over fifteen minutes, the owner shall be entitled to charge 50 cents additional for every half hour of such detention.

Any person plying a licensed boat, who shall refuse to take a passenger at the rates prescribed in the preceding sections, or who shall charge any person more than the said rates, shall be fined five dollars.

Every person hiring any such boat shall be entitled to carry with him, free of charge; one hundred pounds of luggage or goods, and no more ; and for all extra luggage or goods he shall pay according to agreement with the person plying the boat.

Lighthouses.

HONOLULU.—A lighthouse has been erected on the inner edge of the western reef, bounding the entrance of the channel into Honolulu harbour. The light is a Fresnal of the fourth order, at an elevation of twenty-six feet above the sea level, and can be seen from the deck of an ordinary sized vessel at the distance of nine nautical miles, in a radius from S.E. by E. to W. from the lighthouse.

From the lighthouse the Spar or Fairway Buoy bears (magnetic) S. 11° W. 6¼ cables ; the eastern end of the new wharf, N. 85° E. 1½ cables ; Diamond Point, S. 56° E. ; Barber's Point, S. 88° W., and the eastern corner of the Custom House, N. 15° E., near to which corner another light-tower has been erected, at an elevation of twenty-eight feet above the sea level, and can be seen about five miles out at sea. The light in this tower is green.

To enter the harbour by night, bring these two lights in one,. bearing N. 15° E. (magnetic), and keep them in one till within a cable's length of the lighthouse on the reef, when by hauling a point to the eastward you will avoid the end of the spit on which the lighthouse is built, extending off from it about twenty-five feet to the eastward. Steer for the east end of the new wharf, and when half-way between the light on the reef and the new wharf, keep away N.W. and along the Esplanade to an anchorage inside. All bearings magnetic.

HILO, HAWAII.—A lighthouse has been erected at Paukaa Point, entrance to Hilo Harbour, Hawaii. The light is at an elevation of fifty feet above the sea level, a plain fixed light, and can be seen easily ten miles out at sea. From the lighthouse the outer point of the reef bears S. 58° E., inner point of the reef, S. 39° E. ; Governess' flagstaff (about the centre of the harbour), S. 22° E. ; Leleiwi Point, S. 79° E., and Makahanaloa Point, N. 2° W. Bearings magnetic.

KAWAIHAE, HAWAII.—For the anchorage at Kawaihae a white light, about fifty feet above the sea level, has been erected, at a point bearing from the N.E. corner of the reef N.E. by N. ¼ N. The light can be seen at a distance of ten miles out at sea. With this light bearing E.N.E. there is a good anchorage in eight fathoms of water, about a quarter of a mile from the shore. All bearings magnetic.

LAHAINA, MAUI.—A lighthouse has been erected at the landing, Port of Lahaina. The window on the sea side of the light-room is of 20 by 24 inch glass, with red glass at the N.W. and S.E. ends. The

coloured glass stands at equal angles, side and front, and a vessel in
ten fathoms of water will have two bright lights for about half a
mile each way from directly in front of the lighthouse. At a greater
distance, it will show a coloured light until the lights almost appear
like one, or the red light like a reflection from the other light. The
light towards Molokai is the brightest, so that the lights now have
the appearance of a large and small light close together. The lights
stand about twenty-six feet above the water, and can be seen across
the Lanai channel.

Consular.

Every Minister, Commissioner, Consul, or Vice-Consul of the
Hawaiian Islands, in any foreign country, may take and certify
under his official seal, all acknowledgments of any deed, mortgage,
lease, release, or any other instrument affecting the conveyance of
real or personal estate in this Kingdom, and such acknowledgment
shall entitle such instrument to be recorded. They shall also have
power to take acknowledgments of powers of attorney, to administer
oaths, and to take depositions and affidavits, to be used in this
Kingdom.

CONSULAR FEES.

For shipping or discharging Sailors, each $1 00
For signature of Ship's Manifest, when required . . . 2 00
For signature of Muster-roll, when required . . . 2 00
For certificate of Invoice of Goods to be landed in Hawaiian
  ports—On Invoices of less than $500 . . . . 1 00
          On Invoices of $500 and upwards 2 00
For certificate of the landing of Goods exported from Hawaiian
  ports 3 00
For certificate of origin of Goods shipped for Hawaiian ports,
  or of ship 2 00
For attestation of a Signature, when required . . . 1 00
For administering an Oath, when required 50
For Seal of Office and signature to any other document, when
  required 1 00
For noting a Protest, or for extending a Protest or Survey . 1 00
For Bottomry or Arbitration Bond 2 00
For Order of Survey 2 00
For Registrations in Book of Consular Record . . . 1 00
For every Passport to parties bound to Hawaiian ports . . 2 00
For Visa of every Passport 50
For valuations of Ships, Goods, &c. . . . . 1 per cent.
For sale of Ships, Goods, &c. when employed to do so 2½ per cent.
For attending such sales, in cases where there has been
  no charge for valuation . . . . . . 1 per cent.

22 *

For attendance at place of shipwreck, or where the
wrecked ship and property may be, over and above
travelling expenses . . . . 5 per cent.
For attendance on opening a Will $5 00
For extending a Will, where the value exceeds $100 . . . 2 00
For attesting ditto 1 00
For administering to Estate of Hawaiian subjects, when
required, or when dying intestate . . . . . 2½ per cent.
On amount of disbursements on account of the Hawaiian
Government, when not in funds, besides interest
thereon at the rate current in the place of the Con-
sul's residence . . . . 2½ per cent.
On receiving and paying away money by order of the
Hawaiian Government . , ... 2½ per cent.

COLLECTOR-GENERAL'S OFFICE, Nov. 19, 1879.

By order of His Excellency the Minister of Finance, from and after
this date all cotton goods, when manufactured into clothing, the same
being the growth, manufacture, or produce of the United States, will
be admitted free under the provisions of the Reciprocity Treaty.

W. F. ALLEN, Collector General.

COLLECTOR-GENERAL'S OFFICE, Nov. 20, 1879.

By order of His Excellency the Minister of Finance, from and after
this date all invoices of rice, claiming to be the growth and produce
of any country with which this Government has treaty relations, must
be accompanied with certificates from country where originally grown.

W. F. ALLEN, Collector-General.

*Table of Foreign Coins adopted as the Current Rates in Hono-
lulu, H. I.*

By resolution of His Majesty the King in Privy Council, and published by the Finance Department, the values of the following coins
have been fixed and determined at the rates set opposite to them, respectively, viz. :

GOLD.	U. S. HLF. DOLS.	GOLD.	U. S. HLF. DOLS.
U. S. Double Eagle, at . . .	40	Italian 20 Lire, at	8
U. S. Eagle, at	20	Italian 10 Lire, at	4
U. S. Half Eagle, at . . .	10	Russian 5 Roubles, at . . .	8
U. S. Quarter Eagle	5		
English and Australian Sove-			
reigns, at	10	SILVER.	
English and Australian Half			
Sovereigns, at	5	French 5 Francs, at	2
French 50 Francs, at . . .	20	Mexican Dollar, old die. . .	2
French 20 Francs, at . . .	8	Belgian 5 Francs, at	2
French 10 Francs, at . . .	4	Italian 5 Lire, at	2

English Shilling, Spanish, Mexican and Peruvian Quarter-Dollars at 25 cents each.

Other coins than the above are not current, or legal tender, in the Hawaiian Islands.

The following are the values at which the several respective named coins pass, viz. :—

Mexican Dollar, new die	70 cents	Half Dollar, new die.	. 35 cents
Chilian Dollar, un Peso.	70 cents	Half Dollar	. 35 cents
Peruvian Dollar, So .	. 70 cents	Half Dollar	. 35 cents
Half Crown, English	. 50 cents	Florin, English	. . . 35 cents
Rupee, India	. 35 cents		

For the benefit of strangers and enquirers it must be understood that they are uncurrent, and persons are not obliged to take them.

The Currency Act of 1876 makes U. S. gold coin the standard, and payable with silver in the following proportions :—

Debts not exceeding fifty dollars payable in silver.

Debts from fifty to one hundred dollars, all over fifty payable in gold.

From one hundred to one thousand dollars, seventy-five per cent. payable in gold.

Amounts exceeding one thousand dollars, above the first thousand, eighty-five per cent. payable in gold.

All import duties and interest on Government Bonds shall be paid in U. S. gold coin or its equivalent.

Hawaiian stamps being in much request, we find that in searching for the time of the first issues, which Lallier's Album and Gray's Illustrated Catalogue of Stamps set down as in 1852, we have naturally been led to the History of the Post Office itself.

This important branch of the public service was not established until 1850, when, by Act of the Privy Council, it was established December 21st, with H. M. Whitney as Postmaster. The same Act defined the postage rates at five cents per one-half ounce or part, on letters, and two cents on each paper. The Legislature of 1851 ratified this Act of the Privy Council, and authorized the Postmaster to issue stamps of such denominations as were necessary. The *Polynesian*, of September 13th, 1851, published this law, and makes the following mention : " We publish in to-day's paper the Post Office Law as amended and passed by the Legislature, which reduces it to five cents on all letters weighing less than one-half ounce, and requires that the Hawaiian Postage on all letters sent foreign be prepaid . . . Postage to Oregon and California twelve cents, east of the Rocky Mountains thirteen cents if prepaid, or nineteen cents if the United States Postage is not prepaid. The above rates include the entire Hawaiian and United States Postage on single letters, and are an important reduction from the former rate of fifty cents. Postage on papers under the new United States Law is higher than formerly, being five cents, which, with the Hawaiian two cents, makes seven cents on a paper. . . . " The reduction of Postage here mentioned had reference to the change in the United States, and not the Hawaiian.

With the publication of the Law it went into effect, and on the 1st of October following, the first Hawaiian Stamps were printed. In the *Polynesian* of October 4th, we find this first allusion or notice of them : " Postage Stamps of two, five, and thirteen have been prepared and can now be had at the Post Office." These are the first numeral Stamps which were set up from types, with the figured or pattern border around the numerals, and plain double-line border around the whole, as the denominations mentioned agree with the numerals issued, whereas the engraved "bust " Stamps of Kamehameha III. were only of five and thirteen cents. It is a matter of regret that no record was kept in the office, or can be found there, to throw light on any of the early emissions.

The history of the thirteen-cent Stamp has been sought for with interest, as there is nothing in the rates that ever ruled at these Islands that called for such a denomination. From the above quotation from the *Polynesian*, it must have been through a courteous arrangement with the San Francisco Post Office, which included also the prepaid United States and Sea Postage rates, for the second issued thirteen-cent numeral, and the engraved "bust " thirteen-cent Stamp shows the joint interest. Such views on this matter we learn are fully corroborated by Mr. Whitney, who states that much credit is due to the late J. B. Moore, who was Postmaster of San Francisco from 1850–52, for his many courteous acts and great assistance in the establishment of the Postal Department of these Islands. The Postage under this mutual arrangement was settled for at the end of each quarter. The numeral Stamps—of this and subsequent issues—were struck off in the Government Printing Office in this city as they were required from time to time, and upon thin plain letter-paper such as was to be had at the time in the market, which accounts, in a measure, for the great variety of kinds. The first three engraved Stamps, viz.: Kamehameha III. five and thirteen, and the Kamehameha IV. two cent, were engraved in Boston, the two first arriving here in April 1853 ; the latter was gotten up subsequent, which has generally been conceded to follow the establishment of inter-island Postage, appearing here in 1862, but Mr. Whitney places its date of issue for 1855. The latter two-cent Kamehameha was issued in 1864. and is our first perforated Stamp. This, and all subsequent issues of engraved Stamps have been gotten up by the National Bank Note Company of New York.

The emission of the plain-bordered numeral Stamps followed close upon the establishment of inter-island Postage, which we find to be by Act of the Legislature of 1859 ; prior to this all inter-island mail matter passed through the office free, or by the hands of masters of coasters and others. The interest of Philatelists all over the world have been drawn to these emissions of numeral Stamps, and various are the designs and uses assigned for them. For the benefit of all such we would state that these were issued to meet the requirements under the new inter-island Postage Law, which was the first necessity for a one-cent Stamp. As before stated, these were gotten up in the Government Printing Office, and were set up in forms of ten for printing. It has been impossible to ascertain the dates of the various issues, but we have every reason to believe that the pale blue on white, or the dark blue on blue tinted paper were the first. The last were black on blue. The five-cent numeral Stamp was issued in 1865. In 1866 an effort was made here, by a Mr. J. Costa, to produce an engraved one-cent Stamp with bust of Kamehameha I., to the order of the Post Office, but it failed.

In order to avoid confusion, we will proceed to describe them in their order, making such notes as belongs thereto, with cuts of all obtainable.

1. Type-printed; numerals of value in fancy border around the figures, with inscription above and value at foot; in plain rule or linear frame. HAWAIIAN POSTAGE at top. Col. imp., rect.
Two cents, pale blue; five cents, pale blue; thirteen cents, pale blue. Time of issue, 1851.

2. Type-printed; similar in its general style to No. 1, though differing in the pattern of the fancy border, and in the foot line. H. I. & U. S. POSTAGE at top. Col. imp., rect.
Thirteen cents, pale blue. Time of issue, 1852.

NOTE.—These four described Stamps are on uniform thin white French (overland) letter paper, in pale blue, and are uniform in colour. In a full set before us we note no difference, though Gray's Catalogue mentions the two as darker. We attribute this to the body of the figure. This series have been exceedingly rare here, from the fact that their use was altogether for foreign mails, and so went out of the country. The type have long since been shipped away among old type metal.

3. Engraved portrait of Kamehameha III., in military uniform in rectangular disc, having inscribed arched label above; inscription at sides and value below on plain ground; figures of value in upper corners. HONOLULU at left side, POSTAGE in arch and HAWAIIAN Is. at right side. Col. imp., rect.

    a. On white paper. *Five cents*, blue.
    b. On bluish paper. *Five cents*, blue.
    Time of issue, 1859.

4. Similar in design to No. 8, but with figures of value in three corners, and differently disposed inscription. HAWAIIAN—5 cts. at left side, POSTAGE in arch at top, UNITED STATES —8 cts. at right side, HONOLULU HAWAIIAN Is. at foot, Cts. in right lower corner. Col. imp., rect.

Thirteen cents, vermillion on white paper.
Time of issue, 1853.

NOTE.—Gray's Catalogue mentions that a specimen of this stamp exists authentically surcharged with a large written figure 5, showing that it had been sold as a 5-cent stamp. All of Type 4 and many of Type 5 (the first Kamehameha IV. 2-cent stamp) have been surcharged *specimen*, while the 5-cent stamp, Type 3, have been surcharged *cancelled.* This has been done here by the Post Office authorities, and are only sold as specimen stamps at their full face value. The plates of Type 3 and 4 were received here in 1867, and—we regret to say—have been destroyed.

5. Portrait of King Kamehameha IV. to left in military uniform, on arched disc, with inscription UKU LETA above, and value in words at foot, on plain ground; numerals in upper corners and foliated border at the sides. Col. imp., rect.

Two Cents, vermillion on white.
Time of issue, 1855.

NOTE.—Various albums and Gray's Catalogue calls for two distinct stamps on account of colour, but a careful examination of many sheets leads us to the conclusion that it is not so much a separate colour with which they have been printed, as it is the quantity of ink in the printing. Gray's Catalogue gives the issues of 1862 as a pale rose, and of 1863 a carmine, and, what is an entire new idea, that these are lithographs. He gives an engraved stamp of a vermillion colour, but makes this note: "There is no proof that the engraved stamp was ever used. It is known only by reprints or remainders. It may have been prepared for use." This plate is now in the Honolulu Post Office, but their stock of the stamps are entirely exhausted, having been sold with equal quantities of Type 3 and 4 to dealers in this city.

6. Large numeral of value on rectangular disc, in plain rule or linear inscribed frame ; on plain ground. HAWAIIAN POSTAGE at left side, INTER ISLAND at top, UKA LETA at right side, value at bottom. Rect.

(1) Col. imp. (*a*) on blue tinted paper, *one cent*, pale blue; *two cents*, pale blue.

(*b*) *two cents*, dark blue.

(2) Blk. imp. (*a*) on bluish paper, *two cents*, black.

(*b*) on white paper, *one cent*, black ; *two cents*, black.

7. Same design as No. 6, but with INTERISLAND in one word at the left side, UKA LETA at top, and HAWAIIAN POSTAGE at the right side. Col. imp., rect., on white paper.

One cent, dark blue ; *two cents*, dark blue.

Time of issue, 1859-65 ; or perhaps 1866 ; none later.

NOTE.—The plain-bordered numerals are the only ones having inter-island on them, as they were gotten up here to supply the requirements of the law of 1859, establishing inter-island postage. UKA LETA signifies *postage,* and not *paid letter,* or *local tax,* as has been assigned to it abroad. Many of these stamps are met with obliterated with pen strokes, which was the method of cancellation by captains of coasters and others when letters were conveyed outside of the Post Office, in accordance with the law. Like Types 1 and 2 these have long since been shipped away among old type metal.

8. Portrait of King Kamehameha IV. to left on oval disc, in plain dress, in a very neat scrolled inscribed frame, having numerals in the upper corners, with HAWAII at the top and ELUA KENETA —signifying *two cents*—in the foot scroll. Col. imp., rect., perf.

Two cents (elua keneta), vermillion.

Time of issue, 1864.

NOTE.—We regret being unable to procure the cut for the above, which was the first perforated stamp, and in design and execution was a remarkably fine engraving.

9. Same design as No. 6, but with different inscription. UKU LETA at top, HAWAIIAN POSTAGE on each side, 5 cents at foot. Col. imp., rect.
Five cents, dark blue on blue paper.
Time of issue, 1865.

10. Same design as No. 7, viz.: with INTERISLAND in one word at the left side, UKA LETA at top and HAWAIIAN POSTAGE at the right, 5 cents at foot. Col. imp., rect.
Five cents, dark blue on blue paper.
Time of issue, 1865.

NOTE.—No. 10 might properly be called an "error stamp," from the fact that inter-island rates require no such denomination as a 5-cent stamp, and must have occurred by the printers substituting the figure 5 for that of the 1 or 2 in the form that happened to be standing in the office. The idea abroad that some of these issues were in blue on white paper is an error, or that any of these numerals were issued as late as 1867. If so, it was not for or from the Post Office.

11. Similar design to No. 8, but with portrait of King Kamehameha V., full face, in military uniform; numerals in the upper corners, HAWAII in top and ELIMA KENETA in foot scroll. Col. imp., rect., perf.
Five cents (elima keneta) deep blue on white.
Time of issue, 1866.

NOTE.—This cut gives but a very poor idea of the stamp described, and shows no perforations.

12. Full-face portrait of Princess Victoria Kamamalu on oval disc; inscription and value in curved labels above and below, and numerals in circular discs, occupying each corner. HAWAII at top, AKAHI KENETA at foot. Col. imp., rect., perf.
One cent (akahi keneta), violet on white.
Time of issue, 1871.

13. Portrait of King Kamehameha V. to right on shaded oval disc; inscription Hawaii at top in curved label and value in words, Eono Keneta at foot; numerals in circular discs at the upper corners. Col. imp., rect., perf.
Six cents (eono keneta), green on white.
Time of issue, 1871.

14. Full-face portrait of His Highness M. Kekuanaoa in similar frame to No. 13. Hawaii at top in curved label between the numerals of value in corners, and Keneta at foot on a scroll between numerals of value repeated. Col. imp., rect., perf.
Eighteen cents (keneta), brick red on white.
Time of issue, 1871.
Note.—The above *six cent* stamp, as also the *eighteen*, were gotten up to meet the requirements of the Postal Convention with the United States, of May 1870.

15. Portrait of King Kalakaua to left on oval disc, in plain dress, with elaborate scroll design borders ; numerals in each corner with inscriptions, H. I. Postage curved at the top, and Elua Keneta in curve at the foot. Col. imp., rect., perf.
Two cents (elua keneta), dark brown on white.
Time of issue, 1875.

16. Portrait of H.R.H. Prince Leleiohoku, to left, in uniform, on oval medallion disc, with numerals of value in designed angles at each corner; inscription H. I. Postage in the top curve, and Keneta with two stars at each end in the lower curve. Col. imp., rect., perf.
Twelve cents, black on white.
Time of issue, 1875.
Note.—This 12-cent stamp was gotten up to meet the requirements of the Postal Convention with New South Wales, of 1874.

SAMPLES OF CORRESPONDENCE.

LETTER.

"Honolulu, Oahu.

"DEAR SIR,

"I am expecting to leave with a friend for Hilo, in the next Steamer, 'Likelike,' and wish you to hire for me two good saddle-horses, both well shod, for a trip to the Volcano and back. The horses must be well found with saddles and bridles, and be ready immediately on the arrival of the steamer. If you cannot accompany us yourself, please obtain a good guide.

"Yours truly,
"P. R. O."

NA PALAPALA.

"Honolulu, Oahu.

"ALOHA OE,

"Ke makemake nei au e holo aku i Hilo, me kekahi aikane a'u ma keia holo ana aku aka mokuahi 'Likelike,' a ke makemake nei au ia oe e imi iho i elua mau lio maikai i paa i kapuai no ka pii ana i Kalua-o-Pele a hoi mai. O na lio, e hoolako pono ia me na noho lio maikai a me na kaulawaha, a e ku makaukau no ka wa e ku aku ai ka mokuahi. Ina aole e hiki ia oe ke alakai kino ia maua, e imi aku oe i alakai kupono.

"Me ka oiaio,
"P. R. O."

(REPLY TO THE FOREGOING.)

"Hilo, Hawaii.

"DEAR SIR,

"I have just received your letter, and hasten to reply by the same conveyance. I will have two good horses ready on your arrival. The charge for each horse will be twenty-five dollars, to the Volcano and back. I will be ready also to accompany you myself. The charge for a guide is two dollars a day.

"Your obedient servant,
"C. O. N."

(HE PANE I KA LETA MUA.)

"Hilo, Hawaii.

"ALOHA OE,

"Ano no ka loaa ana mai la o kau leta, a ke wikiwiki nei au e pane aku ma ka moku hookahi nana i lawe mai. E makaukau ana au me na lio elua ma kou wa e ku mai ai. O ka uku no ka lio hookahi he Iwakaluakumamalima dala no ka pii ana a me ka hoi ana mai. E pii pu ana no hoi au me olua. O ka uka no ke alakai, hehoolua dala no ka la.

"Kau kauwa hoolohe,
"C. O. N."

London: Printed by W. H. Allen & Co 13 Waterloo Place S.W

www.ingramcontent.com/pod-product-compliance
Lightning Source LLC
Chambersburg PA
CBHW030909270326
41929CB00008B/622